Taking Stock of Shock

Taking Stock of Shock

Social Consequences of the 1989 Revolutions

KRISTEN GHODSEE AND
MITCHELL A. ORENSTEIN

OXFORD
UNIVERSITY PRESS

OXFORD
UNIVERSITY PRESS

Oxford University Press is a department of the University of Oxford. It furthers
the University's objective of excellence in research, scholarship, and education
by publishing worldwide. Oxford is a registered trade mark of Oxford University
Press in the UK and certain other countries.

Published in the United States of America by Oxford University Press
198 Madison Avenue, New York, NY 10016, United States of America.

Library of Congress Cataloging-in-Publication Data
Names: Ghodsee, Kristen Rogheh, 1970– author. |
Orenstein, Mitchell A. (Mitchell Alexander), author.
Title: Taking stock of shock : social consequences of the 1989 revolutions /
Kristen Ghodsee and Mitchell A. Orenstein.
Description: New York, NY : Oxford University Press, [2021] |
Includes bibliographical references and index. |
Identifiers: LCCN 2021000852 (print) | LCCN 2021000853 (ebook) |
ISBN 9780197549230 (hardback) | ISBN 9780197549247 (paperback) |
ISBN 9780197549261 (epub) | ISBN 9780197549278 (digital online)
Subjects: LCSH: Europe, Central—Economic conditions—1989– |
Europe, Eastern—Economic conditions—1989– |
Asia, Central—Economic conditions—1991– |
Former communist countries—Economic conditions.
Classification: LCC HC244 .G495 2021 (print) |
LCC HC244 (ebook) | DDC 330.943/0009049—dc23
LC record available at https://lccn.loc.gov/2021000852
LC ebook record available at https://lccn.loc.gov/2021000853

DOI: 10.1093/oso/9780197549230.001.0001

1 3 5 7 9 8 6 4 2

Paperback printed by Marquis, Canada
Hardback printed by Bridgeport National Bindery, Inc., United States of America

For our children and other members of Generation Z who started university in the midst of a pandemic. May the shocks to come not limit your horizons.

Contents

Contents

Figures

Tables

Acknowledgments

THIS BOOK BEGAN as a discussion between Kristen Ghodsee and Mitchell Orenstein on whether the economic transition from state socialism to capitalism had been an economic success. We debated these issues, responding to economist Branko Milanovic's short 2014 blog post, "For Whom the Wall Fell," and came to realize that our disciplinary understandings and regional experiences diverged sharply. We began to collect data from a wide variety of sources and to reach out to scholars from different disciplines to discuss and present our preliminary findings. We deeply appreciate the feedback we received from presentations at Penn's Population Studies Center, the Philadelphia Europeanists Workshop at Temple University, the International Conference on Global Dynamics of Social Policy at the University of Bremen, the Polish Sociological Congress in Wrocław, and Berlin's Center for East European and International Studies (ZOiS). We also drew insights from participants from the conference that we organized on the Social Impacts of Transition at the University of Pennsylvania and from the World Bank's Europe-Central Asia Chief Economist's Office, including Maurizio Bussolo, who co-sponsored the conference. We would like to thank all sponsors of that conference, including Penn's University Research Fund, School of Arts and Sciences Dean's Office, Population Studies Center, and Perry World House, whose workshop grant provided core funding and research assistance.

Our greatest appreciation goes to Nicholas Emery, a graduate of the University of Pennsylvania who is now a PhD student in political science at UCLA. Nicholas served as our research assistant on the project, gathering, displaying, and analyzing a large quantity of data that was the lifeblood of the project. His assistance was indispensable. He is the lead author of the Social Impact of Transition dataset that came out of this project and is published online at www.takingstockofshock.com for others to use. We also appreciate the contributions of Phil Zanfagna, Louis Galarowicz, Cole McCann-Phillips, and other undergraduate research assistants at the University of Pennsylvania who helped at various stages of this project. We also thank Foreign Policy Research Institute for providing a home for some of our researchers.

We deeply appreciate the support of Oxford University Press editor David McBride, his assistant Holly Mitchell, and others at the press for encouraging, designing, and organizing the publication of this manuscript, and we are grateful to the two anonymous peer reviewers, who gave us excellent suggestions for revisions. We retain responsibility for any errors or misinterpretations.

We are further grateful for the support of our wonderful colleagues in Russian and East European Studies at the University of Pennsylvania, and especially Alina Yakubova, who organized and dealt with many logistics regarding the conference. Working as we do in an interdisciplinary area studies department helped to generate this project, gave us the freedom to engage in it, and provided many valuable insights.

Authors' Note on Terminology

ANYONE WRITING AN interdisciplinary book that includes perspectives and data from economics, political science, sociology, demography, and cultural anthropology will inevitably encounter disagreements about terminology. Different disciplinary traditions have specific vocabularies, and the same term can acquire vastly different meanings across scholarly contexts. In this prefatory note, we try to address a few of the most contested terms and concepts as they are used in this book.

In the discipline of political science, it is common to refer to the countries of Eastern Europe that once had planned economies and authoritarian rule as "communist" countries, because these countries were led by communist parties (the Bulgarian Communist Party, the Romanian Communist Party, etc.) that often referred to themselves as "communists." These communists, however, called the political and economic system of their countries "socialism" or "real-existing socialism" because in Marx's historical materialist view, socialism was a stage on the way to communism (when the state would eventually wither away). Communism was their ultimate goal, but they recognized that they were stuck in the "dictatorship of the proletariat" stage of socialism. In anthropology and history, therefore, these countries tend to be referred to as "socialist" or "state socialist" (to differentiate them from the "democratic socialist" or "social democratic" countries of Scandinavia). When referring to the period after 1989 or 1991, different disciplines call these countries "postcommunist" and "postsocialist," and scholars and citizens in the region use these terms interchangeably. Some scholars, activists, and policymakers prefer to use the terms "communism" and "postcommunism" to refer to the twentieth-century experiments with Marxist ideology so they can differentiate those experiences from the contemporary salience or potential future for something called "socialism" or "democratic socialism." Others prefer to call these societies "socialist," because that is what they called themselves. In this book, we use these terms interchangeably, particularly when quoting from different scholarly sources that use the terms in different ways. This will inevitably cause some confusion for the reader, but we want to make it clear that as authors we are trying to respect the terminologies of different disciplines without making political judgments.

Similarly, anthropologists have critiqued the term "transition" to refer to the changes in Central and Eastern Europe and Central Asia following 1989–91 because it implies the inevitability of an endpoint of multi-party democracy and capitalism. Some scholars preferred the term "transformation" because it kept open the possibility that these countries might transform into different forms of authoritarianism or even return to some kind of feudalism before they embraced parliamentary democracy. Moreover, the term "transformation" recognizes that the transition to a functioning market economy might not happen at all, and instead these countries might transform into oligarchies or dysfunctional state kleptocracies. Despite these nuances, we favor the term "transition" because it is the term used most frequently by international financial institutions, Western politicians, and policymakers as well as by politicians and policymakers in the region.

We are also well aware of the ongoing debates about whether we should still be using the "transition" paradigm and whether these countries should be pigeonholed as postsocialist or postcommunist, since the socialist era only represented a small fraction of their histories. Chari and Verdery argue that we should be talking of a shared global "post–Cold War" history, since the term "postsocialist" ghettoizes Eastern Europe and prevents a shared analysis with those working in the post-colonial context.[1] While acknowledging problems of continuing to use the "post-" prefix for a political and economic reality that ended over three decades ago, we believe that the postsocialist framework remains relevant because of the unique shared experience of dismantling centrally planned state-owned economies and their sudden insertion into a global capitalist economy that produced distinct classes of winners and losers.

Finally, many scholars have resisted the formulation of "Eastern Europe and Central Asia" as a coherent region, insisting that these countries have centuries of history, and charge that it is intellectually imperialist of Western scholars and policymakers to define them by a mere four to seven decades of their recent history. While we are both sensitive to and cognizant of this critique, we persist with this framework because we are specifically interested in examining the social impacts of the transition/transformation of these societies after 1989–91 when they entered (or were forced to enter) the global capitalist economy. More important, economists and policymakers still consider this region as some kind of coherent whole and are deeply invested in ensuring that the transition from communism to capitalism is perceived to be a historical success, thanks to the advice of Western experts working in concert with local elites. Anthropologists, architects, and urban planners also tend to see important similarities in the post-socialist cultures, physical structures, and built environments of the region, examining the affective and material legacies of the shared socialist past. We therefore adopt this conception of the region in part to engage with these claims on their own terms.

The attempt to write a book across so many disciplinary boundaries and engage with the frameworks proposed and propagated by international financial institutions requires that we adopt some terminologies that we ourselves might find problematic. We accept that scholars and policymakers from different backgrounds might find issues with the way we label different concepts, or question the relevance of the concepts themselves, but we sincerely hope that these largely semantic differences can be overcome for the sake of creating a robust interdisciplinary conversation about the social impacts of the events of the last three decades in Eastern Europe and Central Asia.

Introduction

IF YOU HAD traveled to Prague, Sofia, Warsaw, Dushanbe, Kiev, Baku, or Bucharest in 2019, you would have found glittering new shopping malls filled with imported consumer goods: perfumes from France, fashion from Italy, and wristwatches from Switzerland. At the local Cineplex, urbane young citizens queued for the latest Marvel blockbuster movie wearing the trendiest Western footwear. They stared intently at their smart phones, perhaps planning their next holiday to Paris, Goa, or Buenos Aires. Outside or below ground, their polished Audis, Renaults, or Suzukis were parked in neat rows, guarded by vigilant attendants. The center of the city was crammed with hotels, cafes, and bars catering to foreigners and local elites who bought their groceries at massive German and French hypermarkets selling over fifty types of cheese. Compared to the scarcity and insularity of the bleak communist past, life in Central and Eastern Europe and Central Asia had improved remarkably. Gone were the black markets for a pair of Levi's jeans, a skateboard, or a pack of Kent cigarettes. Banished were the long lines for toilet paper. People could leave the country if they pleased, assuming they had the money.

In these same capital cities, often not too far from the fashionable center or in their rural and industrial hinterlands, pensioners and the poor struggled to afford even the most basic amenities. Older citizens chose between heat, medicine, and food. Unemployed youth dreamed of consumer goods and foreign vacations they could never afford. Homeless men slept haphazardly on park benches, and frail grandmothers sold handpicked flowers or homemade pickles to busy passersby. In rural areas around the country, whole families had returned to subsistence agriculture, withdrawing from the market altogether and farming their small plots much as their ancestors did in the nineteenth century. Young people without resources fled the countryside in droves, seeking better opportunities in metropoles such as Warsaw, Moscow, and St. Petersburg or in Western Europe. Even those with resources were desperate to live in a "normal" country and often sought to further their education and employment opportunities abroad. No country was too far if the wages were higher than those at home. Faced with ongoing struggle, many women delayed childbearing, giving up hope that their countries could reform. Economic suffering and political nihilism fueled social distrust as nostalgia for the security and stability of the authoritarian past grew. New populist leaders seized this discontent to dismantle democratic institutions and undermine fair market competition.

These two worlds existed side by side. Both were born in the wake of the dramatic fall of the Berlin Wall in November 1989. After a decades-long ideological conflict that defined much of the twentieth century and brought the world to the brink of total nuclear annihilation, the Cold War just ended. Almost overnight, more than 400 million people found themselves in nations transitioning from state socialism and central planning to liberal democracy (in most cases) and free markets. With remarkable speed and relatively little bloodshed, the once communist countries of Central and Eastern Europe and Central Asia threw off the chains of authoritarianism and decided that if they couldn't beat the West, they might as well join it.

For the most part, the world celebrated the peaceful ending of superpower rivalry. Leaders and citizens of the prosperous, colorful West imagined themselves as welcoming saviors to the tired and downtrodden masses of the poor, gray East. Celebrating access to previously inaccessible bananas and oranges, color TVs and erotic toys, leaders of the triumphant West promised prosperity and liberty. For the prize of political freedom and economic abundance, no cost seemed too high, and the initial postsocialist years were a mixture of euphoria and heightened expectations. But like the promised land of the once bright communist future, the new utopia could only be achieved by suffering through a time of great sacrifice. Privatization, price liberalization, and labor market rationalization upended a decades-long way of life behind the former Iron Curtain. Politicians and policymakers understood that there would be social costs associated with the transition to market economies, but no one knew how high they would be. And like the communist leaders before them who hoped to build a new world, no one stopped to ask how high a cost was too high a cost to pay. The social, political, and economic transformation proceeded with limited attention to the human lives that might be devastated by the process. More than three decades later—and with the benefit of hindsight—scholars are beginning to wonder about the people whose lives were upended by the process popularly known in some Eastern European countries as "the Changes." This book offers an interdisciplinary examination of one key question: What were the social impacts of the transition that started in 1989 in Central and Eastern Europe and in 1991 in the Soviet Union?

Without a doubt, the collapse of communism had an immense impact on both theory and practice. Communism or state socialism[1] represented the most powerful alternative political-economic system to global capitalism and had a direct impact on hundreds of millions of people spread over 10,000 kilometers from Budapest in the West to Vladivostok in the Far East. Despite the massive scale of its world-historic implosion, evaluations of the transition have been sharply divided. On the one hand, some argue that the transition has been largely a success.[2] Economic reforms led to a recession that lasted a few years in some countries and was more prolonged in others but eventually generated improved rates of economic growth and gains in wealth, per capita income, and life satisfaction. Advocates of this J-curve perspective—so called since the trajectory of economic production and consumption were supposed to follow a J-curve (imagine a Nike swoosh: an initial dip in GDP followed by a gradual but steady increase in the long run)—acknowledge that the transition produced some losers and even aggregate declines at the start. But the belief is that these initial losses (although severe) were more than made up for by improved economic prospects for people over the longer term. Embracing radical change was justified, despite the costs, since the speed of reform largely dictated whether gains were realized more quickly or slowly.

From the opposite point of view, some scholars and politicians portray the transition as a socioeconomic catastrophe of enormous proportions.[3] Its effects have been tantamount to the Great Depression of the 1930s. People thrown out of work during the transition never recovered. Social ills grew exponentially. Prostitution and human trafficking thrived. Substance abuse exploded. Poverty deepened. Fertility and family formation plummeted. Life expectancy dropped, catastrophically in some cases. Millions of people abandoned failing states and moved abroad in search of a better life. Governance also suffered: communist institutions collapsed and were replaced not by well-governed Western ones but by corruption, criminality, and chaos. Rather than bringing long-term benefits, the transition produced gains that disproportionately went to a narrow group of people at the top of the income distribution—especially scheming oligarchs with links to organized criminal syndicates and/or former communist state security services. The rest of the population suffered serious long-term damage from which many never recovered. The transition process created a form of insidious klepto-capitalism that reduced hundreds of millions of people to relative poverty and social dislocation, especially when compared to their previous standard of living before 1989/1991.

Which of these two portraits of transition more accurately reflects reality and for whom? These questions have taken on greater salience since the global financial crisis that began in 2008, which some have dubbed the Great Recession. The fallout from Wall Street's collapse emboldened and empowered far-right and far-left populists, who represent a public that seems disenchanted with both markets and liberal democracy. The 2020 coronavirus pandemic and planet-wide economic shutdowns have further shaken faith in the ability of democratically elected leaders to protect their citizens from public health crises and financial ruin. Opinion polls show that people want a better life and are willing to accept authoritarian governance and crony capitalism to produce jobs and economic growth at home. Since many of these politicians and parties in Eastern Europe support a negative image of the transition period, it is an important time to ask: what exactly were the social impacts of transition? Why did perceptions of it become so bifurcated? Why is there no consensus among social scientists about its results? Answering these questions will help to address the most important one of all: Can the negative aspects of transition be addressed without the complete unraveling of the system of markets and democracy that was launched in 1989/1991? And with what repercussions for the West?

It should perhaps come as no surprise that the "winners" of these processes are those most invested in promoting the idea that the shift to liberal democracy and market economy were a qualified success. All questions about the legality or fairness of transition challenge the legitimacy of their newfound wealth. On the other hand, opponents of the Western international order and "losers" of transition point to the many deficiencies of the process, including the violence and theft that characterized the 1990s. A narrative of victimization and belief in conspiracy theories allows those left behind—and those who seek to lead them in a different direction—to blame corrupt elites and foreign powers for their ongoing postsocialist woes. In her book, *Second-Hand Time*, Belarusian Nobel Prize–winning author Svetlana Alexievich gives eloquent voice to the *Sovoks*, the last of the Soviets, for those willing to listen.[4] These populations cling to their nostalgia for the past, spinning tales about the good old days of state socialist stability and security. As a result, just asking the question—what were the social impacts of transition?—is a deeply political and contested question in the region and the West because different parties have conflicting vested interests in the answer.

An Interdisciplinary Perspective

Ever mindful of this larger context, our initial conversations blossomed into an interdisciplinary perspective where we combine both quantitative and qualitative data to produce a more robust picture of how transition worked in practice and who were the main winners and losers. The reasons for this approach are simple: different social science disciplines have arrived at contradictory images of the transition process. This is largely because each discipline has employed different methods, different metrics, and different theoretical perspectives. In short, different ways of looking at the transition have produced sometimes incompatible narratives of what happened. While it may be too much to hope that one could reconcile these opposing viewpoints, we believe that we are well placed to present a more holistic view informed by the disciplines of economics, demography, political science, sociology, and anthropology.

Kristen Ghodsee is an ethnographer who has been conducting fieldwork and research in Eastern Europe for almost twenty-five years, and Mitchell Orenstein is a political scientist who has specialized in the political economy of Eastern Europe since 1990. Although our training is in different fields, we have always worked at the intersections of a number of disciplines to examine gender issues or social policy. We have collectively published fifteen books and over ninety journal articles and essays about Eastern Europe and the transition process. In addition to our academic work, we have both written for policymakers and general audiences, trying to engage the wider public in discussions about East European politics, history, and culture. In this book, we hope to provide a general overview of the state of scholarship in several key fields and synthesize it in a new way to make sense of a transition whose bifurcated understandings undermine clarity. We believe that Manichean views are the enemy of true understanding, and that a more nuanced view of the transition process will help us to see what is going on today with the hope of reaching a better tomorrow.

The J-Curve Perspective

One of the two mainstream perspectives on transition is what we call the "J-curve" perspective.[5] This perspective is popular in economics and political science and bears a close relation to early theories of transition. It is represented in journals such as *Economics of Transition* and embedded in international organizations such as the European Bank for Reconstruction and Development (EBRD) and the World Bank. In many ways, the "J-curve" perspective is the official narrative on transition, pronounced by Western governments, international organizations, think tanks, thought leaders, and their Central and East European partners. It is also the perspective most often championed by the so-called winners of the transition process and embraced by some of the economists responsible for designing transition programs. For instance, Andrei Schleifer and Daniel Treisman argued in 2014 that transition had been an undoubted success.[6] World Bank economist Marcin Piatkowski claimed that "Poland, the largest economy among post-socialist EU member states and the sixth largest economy in the European Union on the purchasing power parity basis, has just had probably the best 20 years in more than one thousand years of its history."[7]

In this perspective, transition to markets and democracy in postcommunist countries was bound to be difficult. The move from communism to capitalism would entail a process of what Joseph Schumpeter called "creative destruction."[8] The old institutions and practices of communism had to be thoroughly destroyed before new capitalist enterprises and practices could be adopted. This destruction initially would create a deep transitional recession. However, the great creativity unleashed by capitalism would soon wipe out the losses and produce substantial gains. Economic growth and household consumption would dip at first, followed by long-term gains in the shape of a J-curve.

Proponents of a J-curve transition expected that economic growth and household consumption would decline and poverty would grow—for a time. How long? That was never specified exactly, but it was assumed that a few years would be an appropriate length of time. Moreover, reformers expected that the more *radical* and thorough the economic reforms, the *faster* the return to growth would be. Therefore, advocates of the J-curve did not worry too much about severe dips in household consumption. These were expected to be temporary, despite the possibility that if they lasted too long, countries could get caught in a poverty trap.[9] Reformers advocated safety-net measures and unemployment insurance to prevent the worst suffering, but they also believed that transition had to happen quickly to prevent more severe long-term agony and/or a return to the planned economy. And indeed, advocates of the J-curve hypothesis still insist that this is exactly what happened.[10] Countries that reformed faster and more thoroughly returned to growth quicker. Measures to slow or ameliorate this process only prolonged and magnified the pain—by making the transition recession last longer.

In terms of real-world examples, the Visegrad countries of Poland, Hungary, Czechia, and Slovakia best illustrate the workings of the J-curve transition. These countries experienced anti-communist revolutions in 1989 and began to reform their economies in 1990. Neoliberal economic reforms brought on a deep transitional recession, with per capita GDP declining by between 10 to 23 percent. But these economies bottomed out in 1992 or 1993 and soon began to grow again. By 1998–2000, the Visegrad countries had surpassed their 1989 levels of per capita gross domestic product (GDP). They grew strongly in the 2000s and by 2007 produced per capita GDP levels 40 to 66 percent higher than in 1989. From a strictly economic point of view, these countries achieved a model transition, avoiding the longer and more severe recessions of less avid reformers.

Growth picked up again in the mid-2010s following the global financial crisis. Mercedes, for instance, broke ground in 2018 on a new €1 billion car plant in Kecskemét, Hungary, beside an existing plant where it already employed 4,000 people and produced 190,000 compact cars in 2017. In 2019, Mercedes reached a wage agreement with Hungarian trade unions to increase pay by 35 percent over a two-year period as well as other benefits, including retention incentives.[11] Hungary had become one of the leading automotive producers in Europe, accounting for 29 percent of Hungarian industrial production, approximately 9 percent of its total economy, 17 percent of its exports, and 4 percent of total employment.[12] Based on this and successes in many other industries from fashion to furniture, one 2019 report concluded that the Visegrad countries (plus Slovenia and the Baltics) "managed to make a transition from a socialist past to modern economies that started to reindustrialize after 1996 and subsequently made substantial progress in catching up to Western Europe in terms of GDP per capita, labour productivity and living standards."[13]

For some citizens, the transition away from planned economies created a new world of exciting opportunities. The journalist John Feffer, who traveled across Eastern Europe in 1989/1990 and then returned again in 2016 to observe the changes, recounts the story of Bogdan, a man who had been a psychologist at the Polish Academy of Sciences when Feffer first met him. After 1989, Bogdan left academia, divorced his wife, and applied for a managerial position at the Swedish home-furnishing company, IKEA. Bogdan tells Feffer, "At that time, you opened a newspaper and you saw: financial director for Procter & Gamble, marketing direction for Colgate Palmolive. . . . All those companies were looking [to fill] top positions."[14] Bogdan shot up to become a member of the board of directors within a week and almost overnight became a high-level executive with a new car, a new wardrobe, and an entirely new life. He helped establish IKEA in Poland and then moved on to a lucrative career as a management consultant to other Western multinational companies hoping to do business in his country.

Bogdan is a member of what Feffer calls the "fortunate fifth," the portion of the East European population that used the events of 1989 to reinvent their lives and seize new economic and political opportunities made possible by the coming of democracy. There is Vera, a woman who became the first Roma-Bulgarian news anchor, something that would probably have been impossible under the old regime. A new generation of dissident voices used their guaranteed free speech to attempt to keep governments accountable to the people. Newspapers and television stations proliferated. Gays and lesbians came out of the closet and enjoyed free self-expression in newly open societies with the support of the international lesbian, gay, bisexual, transgender, and queer (LGBTQ) community. Consumer shortages disappeared and a cornucopia of new goods rushed in to meet decades of pent-up demand. Young people won scholarships to study at foreign universities, and professionals enjoyed new avenues for retraining in Western Europe and the United States. Feffer writes:

Some of the activists, scholars, and politicians I met in 1989/90 went on to fame, fortune, or both. The Czech economist Milos Zeman became the Czech president in 2013. The representative of the Young Liberal Party in Romania, Dinu Patriciu, invested in the oil industry and became one of the country's richest men. Civil society activist Jan Kavan rose through the political ranks to become the Czech foreign minister and then president of the UN General Assembly. Like Bogdan, they were presented with once-in-a-lifetime opportunities to become born again: as new people in a new world.[15]

Perhaps most important, with communism's cruel travel restrictions lifted, hundreds of thousands of East European citizens were now free to leave their countries and make new lives for themselves in the West. A tidal wave of former socialist citizens set out for Western Europe, the United Kingdom, Canada, the United States, and Australia. Britain (before Brexit) became one of the first European Union (EU) countries to officially open its labor market to immigrants from the new member states. Within two years of accession in May 2004, "560,000 accession migrants joined the UK labour market . . . roughly equivalent to 2 percent of total employment," one of the largest inflows in British history.[16] By 2017, 1.4 million immigrants from the Central European and Baltic states lived in the United Kingdom (UK), including nearly 1 million Poles.[17] Despite initial hardships and periods of culture shock, East European immigrants forged their own communities, found jobs, bought houses, and started families, achieving standards of living much higher than those in their home countries. In 2013, Polish became the most popular language after English in the United Kingdom.[18] Many Polish children born in the 1990s grew up as Britons, enjoying freedoms and material privileges unknown to their parents. Hundreds of thousands of new EU citizens emigrated to Ireland to work in factories, to Portugal to work in construction, or to Germany to study. Young people with talents and skills undervalued at home could strike out and build lives for themselves anywhere in Western Europe. For the fortunate minority, the transition created a bonanza of opportunities, which they seized with both hands.

The Disaster Capitalism Perspective

The second view on the social impact of transition is the disaster capitalism perspective,[19] which uses equally strong evidence to suggest that the post-1989 transition produced a socioeconomic catastrophe of unforeseen and massive proportions. Mortality rates soared. Fertility rates collapsed. Governance indicators dropped. Corruption prevailed. Much of Central and Eastern Europe became unlivable and people left in droves. The average Central and East European country lost a little more than 8 percent of its population between 1989 and 2017. Social ills that had been suppressed before became prevalent: crime and delinquency, homelessness and hunger. Health systems deteriorated. Pensioners turned off their heat because they couldn't afford the cost of newly privatized utility bills. Millions suffered. Demographic data showed a level of social collapse rarely, if ever, before experienced during peacetime. Unfortunately, we cannot find fault in the data underlying this perspective either and this is the view clung to by the so-called losers of the transition process, as well as anti-Western elites who wish to steer their countries in a different direction. Arguing that the social costs were too high, they believe that Western advisors and East European elites cruelly subjected millions of people to economic and social pain in pursuit of an ideal that has never materialized. Populations put through the ringer of communism were once again promised a radiant future that never came. The realities of democracy and free markets proved just as disappointing. Now many are keen to go back to the system they were once desperate to abandon.

Moldova exemplifies the socioeconomic disaster perspective. Like many former Soviet states, Moldova suffered from an enduring and U-shaped transition. GDP per capita in Moldova did not bottom out until 1999, when it had lost 66 percent of its 1989 level, fully two-thirds of its economy, a "biblical collapse of output," according to one report from the United Nations Children's Fund (UNICEF).[20] By contrast, US GDP per capita declined by 39 percent during the Great Depression of the 1930s and growth resumed after four years, not ten.[21] In 2007, GDP per capita in Moldova was still 42 percent lower than in 1989. Because jobs disappeared, people left en masse. In 2002, a World Bank study found that nearly half the children in village schools in Moldova had one—or less frequently both—parents working abroad.[22] Although Moldova grew substantially after the global financial crisis, its 2016 level of GDP per capita remained 12 percent lower than in 1989. It would be very hard to characterize Moldova's transition as a success. And Moldova was not alone. We find five other postcommunist countries with GDPs per capita below 1989 levels in 2016: Georgia, Kosovo, Serbia, Tajikistan, and Ukraine. For these countries, transition brought unprecedented levels of economic pain and little gain, except for an elite few, for decades.

What is truly remarkable about the study of the social impacts of transition is that the data we have collected support *both* the J-curve and disaster capitalism perspectives, however divergent they are. As one former World Bank vice president for Europe and Central Asia put it, "The transition in Central Europe and the former Soviet Union can alternatively be viewed as a great success or a dismal failure."[23] Transition was both a path to faster growth, convergence with EU incomes, and happiness for a substantial proportion of the population,

concentrated in some countries, cities, and regions, *and* a socioeconomic catastrophe of historic proportions responsible for millions of excess deaths, mass out-
migration, and a variety of social ills mostly unknown under communism. The
problem we face in this book is to sew together these two divergent images of reality, the Janus faces of transition. Is it possible to create a comprehensive and realis-
tic narrative that will allow a policy approach to emerge that is neither rosy about
unbridled capitalism nor accepting of anti-Western nativist authoritarianism?

Broadening the Data

We believe that such an approach can be rooted in social science. However, a
central problem of this endeavor is that different academic disciplines collect and
analyze different sorts of data. Moreover, they generally regard the data collected
by other disciplines as irrelevant or problematic. Economists prioritize aggregate
statistics on economic growth, with a lesser emphasis on inequality. Growth is
prized above all, although other disciplines rely on different definitions of development. But economic data on transition is deeply flawed, as leading transition
economists have been the first to point out.[24] First of all, the 1989 baseline is hard
to calculate. Communist countries did not measure output in terms of GDP, as in
the rest of the world, but calculated instead an alternative measure, Net Material
Product.[25] Comparisons with the communist era thus rely on correcting and estimating earlier statistics, which was done imperfectly. Furthermore, many data are
missing or unreliable for the early transition years, in part because of the explosion of informal economies and the difficulties statistical offices had recording
production in new private enterprises. Finally, the German Democratic Republic
ceased to exist as did the USSR, Czechoslovakia, and Yugoslavia, each of which
broke into smaller republics, creating problems for data continuity.

But if economic data provide an imperfect guide to transition despair, where
should one turn? We look at demographic, public opinion, and ethnographic
studies in an attempt to triangulate a more accurate picture with the flawed and
incomplete economic data. Demographic data provide another avenue for measuring household well-being (we can take measures of life expectancy as evidence
of well-being, on the assumption that most people do not want to die). In most
advanced capitalist countries, life expectancy steadily increased in the post–
Second World War period (though in recent years, that long record has been
broken in the United States due to the opioid epidemic and other factors).[26] The
same can be done with mortality and fertility as well as out-migration because, all
things being equal, most people would prefer to live in their own countries. This
seems obvious, but few studies have sought to connect economic growth in transition countries with the most important demographic measures of well-being.

Relatedly, until recently, few studies addressed population growth or decline, which are important economic and political issues for the nations of Central and Eastern Europe. Only in 2016 did the International Monetary Fund (IMF) produce a major report, finding that out-migration has hurt growth in transition countries.[27] Sustained or declining fertility rates and massive out-migration of the young and educated have been mostly overlooked by disciplines outside of anthropology, sociology, and demography, but they need to be part of a composite picture of the social impacts of transition.

In addition, public opinion data from comparative international surveys and domestic polling have produced a different sort of knowledge, a perspective that is, in some cases, difficult to reconcile with data from other fields. Among some economists and political scientists, public opinion data are regarded as "subjective" and biased. But public opinion polls provide an important lens into what people are thinking and feeling about larger political and economic transformations. Surveys provide insights about the extent to which political and economic institutions rely on public consent. They allow scholars to study the linkage between happiness (and other subjective indicators) and economic well-being. Many studies have found that money does not always buy happiness and that people often prefer stability and security to economic growth—a result that questions many basic assumptions of Western economics. Some have suggested that gross domestic happiness, for instance, is more important than GDP.[28]

For the quantitative portions of this project, we collected data on twenty-nine transition countries (see the appendix and the full Social Impact of Transition database online).[29] A majority of the economic and demographic data came from the World Bank and United Nations, although for GDP and GDP per capita we chose to use data from the US Department of Agriculture's (USDA) Economic Research Service because it interpolates missing values in 1989 for a number of countries that are lacking in World Bank and United Nations (UN) data. Public opinion data were more limited, but we collected it from a variety of sources, including various Eurobarometer surveys, the Russian Longitudinal Monitoring Survey (RMLS), the World Happiness Report, the three EBRD Life in Transition surveys in 2006, 2010, and 2016, surveys conducted by Gallup and the Pew Charitable Trust, and selected domestic polling agencies. Although each of these surveys have their limitations, together they provide a fairly clear picture of public attitudes in the transition region, with the possible exception of Central Asia, where fewer surveys were conducted, and Eastern Germany, which was reunited with the West and generally not considered a transition country.

Finally, ethnographic research on postcommunist transition has been, in many ways, orthogonal to research from most other fields. Unlike scholars who look at macro-level aggregate data or those who conduct short-term in-country interviews or focus groups with the help of translators and local fixers, cultural anthropologists, qualitative sociologists, and other researchers using ethnographic methods are required to learn the language and spend an extended period of time living and working in the host nation (often eighteen months or more).[30] This fully immersed method of participant-observation tends to focus on the micro level of everyday life, which provides specific case studies of local places and populations that are not always easy to generalize. Because ethnographers submerge themselves in local cultures for long periods of time, they are far more attuned to the dynamics of personal suffering and social displacement that more macro studies tend to miss. Furthermore, where economists might focus on institutions and spend time trying to understand the perspectives of political and economic elites, ethnographers tend to concentrate on the ordinary men and women who have no particular power in their everyday lives. Some ethnographers also deliberately choose to study marginalized populations—for example, ethnic minorities, homeless people, alcoholics—in an effort to uncover the structural violence perpetuated by abstract ideals such as communism, liberal democracy, or free markets.

In the former socialist world, therefore, ethnographic research has largely focused on the stories of the losers of the transition process. These stories paint an entirely different and challenging picture of what happened during the transition to democracy and capitalism in Central and Eastern Europe and the former Soviet Union. Economists and political scientists are inclined to dismiss ethnographic studies as mere anecdotes, but in the long term, anthropologists have often been the first to discover emerging social phenomena before they bubble up into the national surveys or economic data. Furthermore, whereas other social science disciplines may focus on the big "what" questions, it is cultural anthropologists that often provide answers to the "why" questions—explaining why different social phenomena appear within certain cultures or subcultures but not others.

In this book, our approach is to broaden out and analyze a wider scope of data from different fields, both quantitative and qualitative. We start with questions about *what* happened during the transition period, looking at economic and demographic data collected by international institutions and government agencies. We then move on to examining opinion polls and a wide sampling of ethnographic studies to try to tease out the underlying reasons for the variety of transition experiences for different populations in the region. This interdisciplinary combination of both quantitative and qualitative data allows us to paint a far more nuanced portrait of the transition process than can be found in the knowledge production of one discipline alone. We understand that political scientists and economists may balk at our inclusion of subjective survey research and ethnographic case studies, just as we are aware that cultural anthropologists and qualitative sociologists may disagree with the reduction of the variegated social impacts of the complicated transition process to a series of numbers, but we believe that only the combination of these disciplinary perspectives can help to expose the Janus-faced nature of the transition. Rather than simply telling one story from one perspective, our interdisciplinary approach allows us to show that the transition produced both good and bad results at the same time, with lots of temporal and regional variation.

In addition to broadening the data we employ in this interdisciplinary analysis, we also broaden the criteria by which we analyze success or failure of transition. We believe that success is not only a matter of whether aggregate economic statistics improve but also an indicator of positive change in life expectancy, life satisfaction, and other indicators, such as democracy and governance indicators, faith in public institutions, perceptions of corruption, reduction of poverty, and the well-being of the bottom fifth of society. Population growth is also an important indicator, as it provides compelling evidence of suitability of a country for human life. The field of economics is primarily concerned with indicators like gross domestic product per capita, which are not sensitive to income inequality, household consumption, or poverty rates. Two different countries with a GDP of $10 billion could have the same GDP per capita even if in the first country the top 1 percent of the population earns most of the income while the rest live in poverty and, in the second, income is distributed more equitably to all citizens. High levels of growth can coincide with increasing human misery if most of the wealth generated by the growth goes to a handful at the top of any given society. For instance, the United States enjoyed positive GDP growth for three years between 2016 and 2018 despite an unprecedented three-year decline in life expectancy, mostly due to the opioid crisis and other "deaths of despair."[31]

Poverty shot up in the postcommunist countries after 1989. Using an absolute poverty line of $5.50 per day, we find that poverty increased by 23 percentage points (or 94 percent) between 1990 and 1999 in the postcommunist countries and only started to decrease in the median country after the first decade. In ten countries, including Poland, poverty rates increased by 49 percent or more before starting to decline. We find that at peak misery in 1999, 45 percent of all people in postcommunist countries—approximately 191 million people—lived below the absolute poverty line of $5.50/day. In 2010, this number had fallen to 66 million. Yet, we found eight countries where absolute poverty remained higher in 2015 than in 1989, more than twenty-five years later: Georgia, Tajikistan, Kyrgyzstan, Romania, Bulgaria, Latvia, Croatia, and Uzbekistan. Transition impoverished millions for decades.

How can growth and GDP per capita increase dramatically while absolute poverty remains as high as in 1989—or even higher? Inequality. While some

households increased incomes and life satisfaction, others were plunged into destitution. Communist countries had some of the lowest levels of inequality in the
world, equal to or lower than egalitarian West European societies such as Sweden.
Average levels of inequality in the postcommunist countries, as measured by the
Gini coefficient, increased by nearly 50 percent between 1988 and 2012. The share
of national income going to the top 1 percent of the population increased dramatically and the number of billionaires surged, while others experienced a level
of destitution unknown in communist societies. It is easy to see how some could
benefit enormously while others could be left in the dust. Communism, for all
its many faults and repressions, had provided nearly everybody with the basics
of modern life: housing, food, electricity, educational opportunities, social services, and transport. After communism, access to these basic goods and services
could no longer be taken for granted. Of course, some will argue that the very
lack of inequality in communist societies stifled innovation and ultimately led
to economic stagnation and that any transition from communism was bound
to increase inequality in absolute terms. Nonetheless, these were once societies
based on an ideal of egalitarianism that kept relative levels of inequality low compared to non-socialist countries. The sudden reversal after 1989 was bound to be a
shock even if it was a necessary result of the introduction of free markets.

Different Transitions, Multiple Disasters

Based on an analysis of a wide range of indicators, it seems clear that different sub-
regions experienced different transitions. The countries of Central Europe conformed most closely to the J-curve model, with a smaller and shorter transitional
recession followed by significant growth and improvement in life indicators, such
as population and life expectancy. Most other postcommunist countries experienced a U-curve transition, with a prolonged and deeper transitional recession,
bottoming out in 1999 and only attaining 1989 levels of GDP and life expectancy
after twenty years or more of transition. Some countries did worse, never returning to pre-1989 levels (see Figure 2.2).

Demographic indicators show that the former socialist countries were beset
by a number of crises during the transition period, but interestingly, these problems were often (but not always) geographically bounded. In many countries,
but particularly in European former Soviet republics, a mortality crisis occurred,
fueled by high alcohol consumption, unhealthy lifestyles, micronutrient deficiencies, and psychosocial stress. In Russia, life expectancy for males plunged.
Interestingly, however, this mortality crisis was much less severe in Muslim
Central Asia, where healthier lifestyle practices—in particular lower alcohol
consumption—led to longer life expectancies, despite similar or worse economic

conditions. At the same time, the Baltic countries and the Balkans have experienced an out-migration crisis, in which living conditions recovered slowly, but people did not wait around. They left in a process that was encouraged by European Union membership or proximity to the EU, sending these countries into a downward (and perhaps irreversible) spiral of demographic decline and lower growth (since a loss of productive population may translate into lower GDP). Central Asia's transition has been exceptional, with widespread poverty accompanied by high population growth and significant increases in life expectancy. Central Europe's transition conformed to the J-curve model, but this was the only group of countries to do so. While Central Asia and Central Europe enjoyed relatively favorable demographic indicators of well-being, the rest of the former socialist countries suffered terribly. Some experienced a drastic mortality crisis and others, particularly the Balkans and Baltics, hemorrhaged population.

Public opinion polls reflect the effects of these crises, leaving majorities in the former socialist countries with low trust in public (and international) institutions that they had counted on to manage the problems of transition. At the same time, we should not lose sight of the fact that significant minorities in all countries benefited from transition. Their experience challenges a sole focus on disaster capitalism. In fact, substantial proportions of the population report significant improvements in life satisfaction. The problem for most the former socialist countries, including many of the success cases in Central Europe, is that the benefits of transition were divided so unequally that majorities of the population no longer support the transition paradigm.

An Inequality Perspective

Our goal is to move beyond the J-curve and disaster capitalism perspectives on transition, that are deeply politicized in both the East and West. We seek to introduce a perspective based on recognition of the inequality of deeply divergent outcomes for different people, localities, countries, and regions. Both of the existing narratives on transition are incomplete and politically damaging. The J-curve perspective negates the suffering of millions of people during transition and produces a complacency within the West and Western international institutions. It provides a weak guide to the political and economic challenges of the postcommunist countries. The disaster capitalism narrative strengthens opponents of the West who promote the rise of right-wing populism across the region. One element of this is the nostalgia perspective, which suggests that many things were actually better under communism. This perspective is rooted partially in the memories of many older citizens who grew up under communism and may have a rosy picture of their youth. Some are deeply dissatisfied with the present and therefore romanticize the past (in some cases a past they did not know if they were born after 1989). But nostalgia for the communist past has greater traction in some communities and bodes ill for political stability in the long run.

Another critical perspective—often pushed by contemporary populists— suggests that the transition period represented a conspiracy between old communists and new liberals to seize control and divide society's spoils among themselves. As so well described by the anthropologist Janine Wedel in her award-winning book, *Collision and Collusion*, Western liberals or neoliberals rushed into Eastern Europe to create a capitalist utopia and worked with reformist elites who used the enormous legitimacy of Western advisors to generate great wealth for themselves.[32] The majority of the people, in this view, were disenfranchised during the transition. Others have argued that former communists and reform-minded liberals made a corrupt deal in which former communists were allowed to enrich themselves, while liberals agreed not to prosecute them for past misdeeds. In this narrative, the true anti-communists need to take power and root out these communist and neoliberal influences, for instance, in a Polish "fourth" republic.[33] In Russia, President Putin has put forward a similar and highly effective negative view of the transition, in which outside forces foisted the transition on Russia in a grand conspiracy to defraud and weaken the country. It needs a strong hand to resist these external agents and create a Russian economy that works for Russians.[34]

In our view, however, the perspective that best explains the good and bad sides of transition is an inequality perspective. Rooted in social science research, this perspective suggests that the transition opened up vast inequalities, which have produced two distinct but not mutually exclusive narratives about the transition process. Some prospered greatly; others declined precipitously. Inequalities opened up along a number of socioeconomic lines: regional disparities between capital cities and remote regions, disparities caused by higher returns to education that advantaged educated elites and punished average workers, gender inequalities between women—who tended to be more attached and responsible to families while losing out in employment parity—and men. These inequalities, and others—that are visible on individual, regional, and national levels of analysis—created a situation in which those who could benefit from transition experienced significant gains while the majority of the postcommunist population suffered profound losses. National economic policies did not deliver a positive transition experience to enough of the population to win majority support for the transition to capitalism in most countries. People waited, but ultimately they were disappointed in "the light that failed."[35] Subjective measures, such as public opinion polling and ethnographic case studies, show that although many people advanced during the transition, in only a few countries does a majority express a positive evaluation of the transition to markets and democracy. Many just gave up and left.

Nationally representative surveys and ethnographic case studies clearly show that people initially interpreted Western-oriented economic reforms as a gateway to increased prosperity. Not surprisingly, after the scarcity and consumption restrictions of communism, citizens desired a higher standard of living (in material terms) more than almost anything else. At the same time, they wanted to keep some of the protections of state socialism, such as subsidized housing, medical care, day care, higher education, and low-cost access to food, energy, water, and medicine. This is not, however, what transition delivered. A substantial minority share of the population achieved the promise of a better life, but a vast majority of the population in postcommunist countries suffered over a prolonged (in most countries) recessionary transition period. Just what shape this inequality took and among which populations is explored in the pages that follow.

PART I

The Economic Evidence

I

The Plan for a J-Curve Transition

*"What is needed is nothing short of the orderly closing of
most of the existing production structure and the creation of
a whole new economy."*

ECONOMIST OLIVIER BLANCHARD, 1991[1]

*"Miserable poverty came to exist alongside soaring,
inexplicable wealth."*

ANTHROPOLOGIST CAROLINE HUMPHREY, 2002 [2]

ANY ASSESSMENT OF the social impacts of transition has to begin with economics, since leading Western economists had a direct impact on transition policy, and economic ends were often used to justify various policy means. No other
social science discipline had as great a direct impact on the postsocialist region,
and the discipline predominated because economists controlled (and control)
the three major international financial institutions responsible for overseeing the
transition: the International Monetary Fund (IMF), the World Bank, and the
European Bank for Reconstruction and Development (EBRD). These institutions led the way in developing a program for transforming communist countries into capitalist ones, believing that a short, sharp shock would be the best
approach to achieve growth and recovery. Thirty years later, after a careful review
of the economic data on transition, we find some evidence to support this perspective but much else that shows that for some countries, regions, and people,
transition created an economic disaster of biblical proportions.[3] The bifurcation
of transition realities creates a puzzle: how can transition have created great gains
in some places and great losses in others? The answer is rapidly rising inequality, caused by the workings of capitalism as well as a variety of geographical factors, such as distance to Brussels, possession of natural resources, and geopolitical
competition. These factors determined who won and who lost but were hardly
considered in the initial push for neoliberal reform.

The Push for Reforms

In 1989–91, the IMF took the lead in developing a strategy for reshaping the fundamental economic structures of the postsocialist countries. In doing so, it consulted with top US and European economists. While some discussions occurred in secret—in the context of IMF and World Bank staff meetings[4]—their overall strategy was put on display for all to see. Indeed, some of the top economists in the world produced a thin volume on transition policy, published by MIT Press, which provides a crystal-clear guide to their thinking. This book, *Reform in Eastern Europe*, was co-authored by some of the leading lights in economics at Harvard and MIT: Olivier Blanchard, Rudiger Dornbusch, Paul Krugman, Richard Layard, and Lawrence Summers. This group included the authors of a major economics textbook and Nobel Prize nominees, a future *New York Times* columnist, and a future US Treasury secretary and president of Harvard University.[5] These powerful economists outlined a three-pronged strategy for postsocialist transition including monetary stabilization and price liberalization, enterprise privatization, and institutional restructuring. The approach was strikingly similar to that applied to Latin American countries after the debt crisis of the 1980s.

The Washington Consensus

In the decade preceding the collapse of communism, the international financial institutions designed structural reforms for Latin America to turn countries away from state-managed import substitution industrialization and toward greater openness to the world economy. One economist, who became famous for coining the term, summarized and labeled this approach the "Washington Consensus" in a powerful article entitled, "What Washington Means by Policy Reform."[6] The Washington Consensus consisted of a strong emphasis on stamping out inflation and creating a stable basis for prices throughout the economy, coupled with free market liberalization, free trade with the outside world, and privatization of state-owned enterprises. Opening countries to competition was seen as a way to orient the economy toward production for export. This, in turn, would render these economies attractive to foreign investors, especially when combined with floating currencies and the removal of capital controls that enable countries to limit the amount of capital flowing across their borders.

Since the postsocialist transitions came hot on the heels of the Latin American debt crisis of the 1980s, the first question addressed in *Reform in Eastern Europe*—and in the international financial institutions themselves—was whether the solutions applied to Latin America would be applicable to Eastern Europe and the former Soviet Union. The authors asked, "How much of what we have learned [in Latin America] is relevant for Eastern Europe? Clearly, the issue there is not to repair the damage to an existing market economy but instead to jump-start one. Aren't the initial conditions so different as to require a drastically different approach? We do not think so. Most of the logic behind the standard stabilization package applies to Eastern Europe as well."[7]

It would be wrong to say that leading economists saw no major differences between Latin America and postsocialist Europe and Eurasia. They cataloged these differences carefully but decided they did not matter. These economists believed in the gospel of free markets. They assumed that free trade could integrate both regions into a postnational global economy where the laws of supply and demand reigned worldwide, unencumbered by politics or history. From today's perspective, that appears to have been a mistake. It was unreasonable to expect that all the institutions of developed capitalism would simply spring to life under the pressure of market forces. Postsocialist countries lacked property registers, stock exchanges, and courts with experience adjudicating contract disputes between private parties. The Soviet economy had many unique structural features—for instance, its heavy militarization, geographic dispersion of industries, vertical integration of supply chains, resource dependency, lack of capital and capitalists, and gigantic company towns. So many things were different. Yet the solutions proposed by leading economists mirrored those in Latin America: stabilize prices, liberalize markets, and capitalist economies would come to life. Local context did not matter.[8] In what later came to be known as "market fundamentalism," Western experts proposed that the rules and principles of market economics are everywhere the same. Development strategies also should be one-size-fits-all.

Managing the Transitional Recession

A second issue the authors addressed was the prospect of a deep transitional recession. The authors of *Reform in Eastern Europe* and other leading economists working for international financial institutions (IFIs) understood that liberalizing prices would cause a major economic crisis, resulting in a dramatic drop in real wages, as prices were suddenly liberalized and relative prices shifted. Why? Because many essential items, including food, housing, utilities, transportation, medicine, day care, and medical care, had been either free, subsidized, or price controlled under socialism. Market pricing of basic goods would cause prices to rise dramatically, hitting poor people the hardest. Nonetheless, on balance, the authors of *Reform in Eastern Europe* believed that price liberalization needed to forge ahead regardless of the postsocialist context. "Price liberalization will be painful," the authors stated. "Delaying it, however, will make things worse."[9] Since they believed that prices were the signals that capitalist enterprises needed to operate efficiently, liberalization could not be delayed. In fact, it should happen all at once, if possible, in a single, sudden shock.

Similarly, the authors expected that monetary stabilization would create even more pain, as "the control of inflation often engenders deep economic contraction."[10] Despite the downsides, however, they believed that robust future growth required the policies of stabilization. Inflationary expectations had to be eliminated. Otherwise, price signals would not work. Enterprises would not invest efficiently. The economy would not grow. Therefore, even though leading economists expected a worse transitional recession than elsewhere, since "the distortions in Eastern Europe are much larger, much more widespread, and have been present for much longer,"[11] it was necessary. Economists did not bother to estimate the length or depth of the transitional recession. In another volume published by leading World Bank transition economists, the authors argued that there were no clear models for estimating the effects of transition.[12]

Instead, the authors of *Reform in Eastern Europe* argued for some modest ameliorative measures to help people survive. Specifically, they recommended that "delaying the phasing out of subsidies on some basic necessities, such as coal and electricity, may be justified."[13] They suggested that governments seek to "blunt the worst effects of real wage decreases and the recession through a targeted basic-needs program for the most impoverished parts of the population."[14] This meant replacing subsidies on basic foods with targeted welfare programs, such as cash payments or soup kitchens, for those most in need. This would enable people to get through the deep transitional recession while preventing mass starvation or fatal hypothermia in the long East European winters.

From these economists' point of view, the postsocialist countries had to pay the price for socialism as they transitioned quickly toward market capitalism. There was no other way. Jeffrey Sachs, a leading reform advisor, campaigned for a new Marshall Plan for Eastern Europe and the former Soviet Union, realizing the damage that could be done and how it could be avoided, but this never came to pass.[15] It was too expensive and the West had no desire to pay. Only a few countries received massive transfers from the West, including Bosnia (after the war) and Eastern Germany (after reunification). These transfers did prevent poverty, but at a high cost, particularly for West Germans who paid a special "solidarity tax" to support their Eastern compatriots. In the case of Russia, US president Bill Clinton endorsed and accelerated an essential $10 billion IMF loan and sent special campaign advisors to "rescue" Boris Yeltsin in the 1996 elections, keeping Russia on the path of economic reform. But it was nowhere near sufficient.

Mass Privatization

Western economists acknowledged one unique challenge facing the postsocialist countries: the need to rapidly privatize thousands of state-owned enterprises, representing the bulk of the economy. Such mass-scale privatization had never occurred before in human history, and it created some very real problems for market reforms. Postcommunist countries, by definition, had no capitalists, and most capital was owned by the state. As a result, there were not enough savings in the entire economy to pay even the book value of the companies that needed to be privatized. Relatedly, selling these enterprises all at once, at a time of transitional recession, would depress prices and risk foreign entities buying up the bulk of the economy. There were just too many enterprises and not enough buyers. The market for postcommunist enterprises with outdated technology, poor products, bad marketing, and too many workers was almost non-existent. Therefore, the authors of *Reform in Eastern Europe* concluded that "it is preferable to distribute ownership claims rather than to attempt to sell them."[16] In order to achieve this impossible feat, they proposed a unique approach to mass privatization that involved giving shares for free to all citizens who would then deposit these shares for safe-keeping with holding company intermediaries.

The irony was that leading economists argued fiercely that there could be no deviation from standard stabilization and liberalization practices, but at the same time, they were willing to design a tremendous departure from economic orthodoxy to achieve the goal of privatizing entire postsocialist economies at once. They believed this was necessary because state-owned enterprises would not respond efficiently to market signals. Therefore, enterprises had to be put in private hands as quickly as possible. Indeed, enterprise privatization was made a condition of loans from the IMF and World Bank.[17] In order to achieve this goal in the unique postcommunist environment, in which nearly all enterprises were owned by the state, they invented "mass privatization." Nothing of the type had ever been attempted before. Mass privatization programs, including the one advocated in *Reform in Eastern Europe*, sought to manage the transition from communism to capitalism while avoiding rapacious corruption, rewarding the average citizen, and providing strong corporate ownership and control. These programs provided shares to every citizen for free (or a nominal charge) and allowed people to deposit their shares with an investment company that would monitor enterprises on behalf of shareholders. Since socialist citizens were theoretically the real owners of domestic enterprises (the state was merely the caretaker), this plan made some sense on a moral level. Instead of just receiving a portion of the redistributed profits from these collectively owned enterprises, citizens would receive shares of their newly privatized successors.

At the same time, the authors of *Reform in Eastern Europe* realized that the postsocialist economies required a thorough institutional restructuring. This would be achieved through Schumpeter's concept of "creative destruction."[18] The economist Olivier Blanchard opined: "What is needed is nothing short of the orderly closing of most of the existing production structure and the creation of a whole new economy."[19] Privatization became a way of shifting responsibility from the state to the private sector for shutting down most enterprises in the country. State-owned enterprises in Eastern Europe suffered from multiple inefficiencies, one of which was excess personnel. Because socialist states guaranteed their citizens full employment, state-owned enterprises hired more labor than necessary. This overemployment of workers produced a drag on profits. Citizens had been guaranteed lifetime employment by the state, and as long as the state owned the enterprises, enterprises had to abide by this social contract. Reformers felt that private owners would be best positioned to "rationalize" the workforce so that the newly downsized firms could be resold on the international market for a profit or just liquidated and closed down altogether. In cases where the enterprises remained viable, the old socialist firm ideally would receive necessary infusions of foreign direct investment and new technologies from the West. As Elizabeth Dunn documented in her book, *Privatizing Poland*, foreign investors brought Western managerial techniques and imported new ideas, which allowed select East European enterprises to adapt and remain competitive in the global marketplace, thus preserving and occasionally even expanding employment opportunities. Czech breweries, for instance, consolidated into three large groups bought by major international conglomerates, which expanded export markets and began to drive growth through product innovation.[20]

In other cases, new owners saw an opportunity to make a quick profit. Privatization brought numerous examples of corrupt self-dealing and asset stripping, as owners sought to recoup a profit immediately rather than invest for the long term. Asset stripping was a common practice by both foreign and domestic investors.[21] A state privatization agency would sell an enterprise to a buyer based on an agreement that the buyer would keep the enterprise operational. Once the buyer took possession of the enterprise, however, a fire sale of physical assets bankrupted the firm before anyone knew what happened. The government could seize the enterprise back for breach of contract, but by that time it was too late. Factories were gutted, licenses auctioned off to the highest bidder, and industrial equipment sold for scrap metal. In some places, the process devasted local industries almost overnight.

During the privatization of the tourism sector in Bulgaria, for instance, a Greek investor bought a Bulgarian hotel on the Black Sea, signing a contract requiring the new owners to keep the hotel operating for a fixed number of years.

But after ownership was transferred, the Greek investor drove large trucks over the border in the night and stripped the hotel of all furniture and fixtures that could be sold for scrap—such as windows, toilets, sinks, parquet flooring. When workers arrived in the morning, their hotel was an inoperable skeleton. Since the Greeks had violated the terms of the contract, the Bulgarian privatization agency could only renationalize the now worthless property. Transition economists tended to believe that even predatory practices such as this were part of a creative destruction process that would ultimately reallocate resources in the economy toward more productive uses. But few considered the long-lasting impacts on the ordinary receptionists, maids, waiters, cooks, and tour guides who turned up for work one morning to a building that had been completely pillaged overnight.

Institutional Reforms

In addition, Washington Consensus economists understood that a new capitalist economy would require new labor laws, trade laws, company laws, and a wide variety of state institutions to support functioning markets. In particular, they emphasized the need for new systems of unemployment insurance, which was weak or nonexistent in the postsocialist countries since most people had been required to work and the state guaranteed employment. Since the authors of *Reform in Eastern Europe* expected hundreds of enterprises to shut down or shed labor, they believed that "unemployment will be high during the transition period"[22] and encouraged governments to provide short-term unemployment benefits and public works programs. However, they recognized that this institutional restructuring would not happen overnight. "Putting in place the required laws, rules, and institutions will, by necessity, take time. Some measures, however, must be implemented right away; without them, the dynamics of an uncontrolled rush to the market will lead to failure."[23] In essence, economists advised tearing down the old house before construction on the new house had begun, inevitably leaving some people homeless in the meantime.

2

Plan Meets Reality

THE GRAND DESIGNS of economic reformers encountered two serious problems: the propensity of privatization plans to foster deep and persistent corruption, and an economic collapse far greater than what had been foreseen. Economic disruption proved to be more catastrophic than expected[1] and institutional development far more difficult. As anthropologist Katherine Verdery demonstrated, private property regimes in the West are underpinned by a wide variety of public attitudes, experiences, institutions, and practices that were not common in the newly postsocialist countries. If economists thought that they could establish private economies by distributing company shares to all citizens, "recreating private ownership was vastly more complicated than this."[2]

For one, most individuals did not understand how to be share owners nor did they want to be. During a deep economic crisis, most people preferred to convert the shares they were given into cash. As a result, in Russia and other countries, enterprising individuals and firms went around purchasing share vouchers from average citizens, sometimes on their own, sometimes as representatives of other interests, and ultimately they used the shares they collected to establish ownership in specific firms in which they had insider knowledge or control. Rather than dispersing ownership, mass privatization programs often concentrated it in the hands of a relatively small number of insiders or "investment companies," often affiliated with major banks.[3] Those with preexisting or foreign capital or connections to the previous communist regimes won a decisive windfall, gaining ownership over much of the economy. New oligarchs in the postsocialist region became rich as a result of the privatization process (or through cross-border trading). In many cases, these new private owners found it necessary to grease the palms of government officials in order to get or keep their newly won gains. As Vadim Volkov discovered in Russia, a new order of private security firms arose to protect the new property relations in society.[4]

Rampant Corruption and Criminality

Across the former Eastern Bloc, the creation of free markets and new private businesses coincided with the appearance of new organized criminal networks, which drew from both prison culture and state organizations, including the recently demobilized secret police, Olympic wrestlers, and state trading houses. "The transition to democracy and markets came with an abrupt and extraordinary rise of crime," especially the "interweaving of private-sector crime and public-sector corruption."[5] Table 2.1 shows that homicide rates doubled or even tripled in many countries, with Russia leading the way. The breakdown of order closely tracked the collapse of the formal economy and the concomitant rise of poverty, as shown in Figure 2.1.

Volkov documented the rise of the Mafia in Russia while doing fieldwork and interviewing a wide variety of police, private security contractors, businesspeople, petty thugs, and members of new violent networks. Volkov argues that violence and criminality were foundational to the formation of the market economy in the former Soviet Union. Ordinary people watched helplessly as a new class of "entrepreneurs" robbed and racketeered their way into private property. He explains,

> In big cities, any newly opened commercial enterprise, a shop or a café, would be visited occasionally by various mobile brigades searching for "free objects." All the different scenarios of such a visit can be reduced to the inquiry: "Whom does this business pay?" meaning, "Does it have protection?" The owner's inability to answer the question, that is, to name a group or its leader who collects the fee, determined the outcome of the visit: "From now on you will pay us." . . . The protection fee would start at between three hundred and four hundred U.S. dollars and tended to increase over time until it reached 20–30 percent of the revenue of the client's business.[6]

Volkov argues that the rise of the private security industry and organized crime in post–Soviet Russia was "a story of unintended consequences," but it was also a clear result of "the radical liberalism and anticommunism of the early 1990s." For citizens raised in the Soviet Union and schooled in Marxist-Leninist ideology, most men and women grew up hearing about the supposed evils of capitalism: the immorality of unchecked self-interest; the chaos of economic boom and bust cycles; the vast social inequality, homelessness, and unemployment; and the tendency toward imperialism, war, and aggression. Much of Soviet mythology was crafted by state-supported narratives that lauded the superiority of the

TABLE 2.1 Homicide Rates in Postcommunist Countries (per 100,000)

	1985	1990	1995	2000	2005	2010	2015
VISEGRAD	**2.11**	**1.83**	**2.29**	**2.12**	**1.46**	**1.22**	**1.17**
Poland	1.57	1.79	2.22	2.22	1.45	1.00	0.78
Slovakia		1.76	2.38	2.39	1.72	1.52	0.81
Czechia			1.70	1.86	1.05	0.98	0.83
Hungary	2.66	1.94	2.86	2.01	1.63	1.39	2.26
SOUTHEASTERN EUROPE	**1.97**	**2.50**	**4.66**	**2.66**	**2.37**	**2.32**	**1.66**
Croatia	2.45		3.60	2.28	1.55	1.43	0.87
Slovenia	2.11	1.79	2.21	1.81	1.00	0.73	0.97
Serbia		2.04		2.40	1.60	1.45	1.17
Montenegro					2.14	2.40	1.20
Bosnia and Herzegovina	0.09	1.64		1.64	1.86	1.51	1.66
Romania		3.39	3.30	2.51	2.02	1.30	1.70
Bulgaria	3.23	2.57	5.90	4.15	2.59	1.99	1.75
Albania			8.32	4.19	4.99	4.31	2.21
Kosovo						5.97	2.33
Macedonia			9.26	2.31	7.12	2.08	4.64
CENTRAL ASIA	**4.64**	**8.10**	**9.24**	**7.82**	**4.94**	**9.23**	**3.87**
Uzbekistan	3.58	5.52	5.08	4.31	3.44		1.64
Tajikistan	2.05	3.18	7.55	4.55	2.31	2.40	
Turkmenistan	4.41	9.01	6.39	5.91	4.33		
Kazakhstan	8.08	9.00	15.45	15.58		8.53	4.85
Kyrgyzstan	5.09	13.79	11.72	8.74	9.67	16.76	5.12
BALTICS	**5.99**	**6.20**	**14.16**	**10.26**	**8.35**	**5.19**	**4.21**
Latvia	5.31		11.48	9.98	5.60	3.30	3.35
Estonia	6.61	7.54	17.17	10.22	8.34	5.25	3.42
Lithuania	6.04	4.87	13.84	10.57	11.12	7.01	5.87
EUROPEAN FORMER SOVIET UNION	**5.08**	**6.50**	**10.73**	**9.84**	**8.68**	**5.07**	**4.90**
Azerbaijan	2.39	4.54	5.70	2.78	2.25	2.28	2.34
Armenia	1.47	5.03	3.61	2.96	1.95	1.95	2.56
Georgia	2.62	4.99	7.86	5.48	9.57	4.56	
Moldova	9.05	6.64		10.30	3.57	6.49	2.71
Belarus	4.68	5.00	9.53	10.26	8.63	4.26	3.45
Ukraine	4.94	4.97	8.66	9.05	6.46	4.34	
Russia	10.42	14.33	30.53	28.07	24.80	11.63	11.48

Note: In order of low to high homicide rate in 2015. Correlation between datasets is 0.81.
Source: UN 2020 (https://dataunodc.un.org/content/data/homicide/homicide-rate). 1985 data from World Health Organization (WHO) Mortality Database (https://apps.who.int/healthinfo/statistics/mortality/whodpms/).

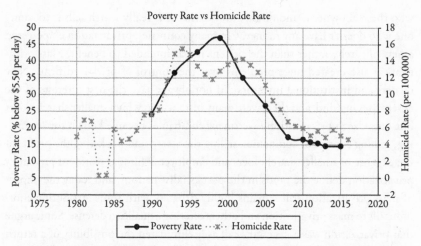

FIGURE 2.1. Homicide Rate (per 100,000) and Poverty Rate (%) during Transition. Correlation between poverty and homicide rates is 0.87.

Source: Poverty rate data from World Bank (2018). Homicide rate data from UN 2020 (https://dataunodc.un.org/content/data/homicide/homicide-rate). 1985 data from World Health Organization Mortality Database (https://apps.who.int/healthinfo/statistics/mortality/whodpms/). Correlation between datasets is 0.81. In order of low-to-high homicide rate in 2015.

socialist system (despite its flaws) over the many ills of capitalism. As Russia rushed to embrace free markets, the now ruling ideology of market fundamentalism "endorsed radical limitations on the role of the state, assuming that the 'invisible hand' of the market would bring about a new economic order as soon as conditions for the free play of economic interests were created."[7] When this new economic order turned out to be a violent and immoral one, postsocialist citizens could not turn to the state for protection since any state interference in the operations of the free market would be considered a return to the socialist past. Private security was the only acceptable answer in Yeltsin's Russia, and the appearance of these violent entrepreneurs shattered social solidarities and undermined previous affective bonds between families, neighbors, and colleagues.

As a result, privatization quickly began to be perceived as a highly corrupt process in which a small elite stole the entirety of what had once been the people's property. Russians labeled privatization "prikhvatizatisiya," which can be translated as "grab-itization." In Bulgaria, the term for "worker-manager privatization" (usually called Management Employee Buy-outs in English) was "rabotnichesko-menidzhŭrska privatizatsiia," but many Bulgarians still cynically refer to it as the similar sounding "razboĭnichesko-mentŭrdzhiĭska privatizatsiia," which means "robber-swindler privatization." Poland's first privatization minister Janusz Lewandowski once said that "privatization is when someone who doesn't know

who the real owner is and doesn't know what it is really worth sells it to someone who doesn't have any money."[8] In many countries, privatization empowered
a new oligarchy rather than the citizens it was intended to benefit. Mass privatization also created huge problems over the control of privatized firms. New
owners and institutional investors did not always have the best interests of the
enterprises in mind, and there were many instances in which smaller shareholders
lost out. Czech privatization investment companies became known for "tunneling," taking control of companies, selling the assets, and pocketing the profits at
the expense of smaller shareholders and employees.[9] Similar stories of predatory
privatization define the 1990s in the postsocialist nations, and today the impact
of mass privatization still remains highly debated, with some attributing enormous ills to mass privatization and others offering a qualified defense. Some argue
that privatization was a necessary evil as it eliminated the possibility of a return
to state control of the economy (though Russia partly renationalized industry
after Putin assumed power in the 2000s). Still, no country has ever adopted a
mass privatization program since, partly due to the controversial results in the
post–Soviet Union.

A Deeper Recession than Expected

The devastating result of applying Washington Consensus policies and rapid
privatization to all postsocialist economies was a deep recession, deeper than
anything experienced in Latin America and, in some countries, deeper than any
recession ever recorded in peacetime. According to economist Jan Fidrmuc in
2003, the "transformational recession was unexpectedly severe."[10] This proved
to be an understatement. While many economists and political figures such as
Polish president Lech Walesa thought the transitional recession would last only a
few months or years, the average postsocialist country did not recover 1989 levels
of economic production for *seventeen years*, until 2006 (see Figure 2.2). In the
average postsocialist country, the transitional recession dwarfed the US Great
Depression of the 1920s and 1930s, a truly epic crisis whose effects will be remem-
bered for generations. One scholar estimates that whereas the average communist
country was ten years behind the West in economic development in 1989, most
of these countries fell ten to twenty years further behind during the transition
period.[11] Maddison Project data show the postcommunist recessions to be the
worst in modern history since 1870.[12]

Figure 2.2 compares the depth of the transitional recessions in postsocialist Europe and Eurasia (starting in 1989) to the US Great Depression (starting
in 1929). It divides the postsocialist countries into three groups—the top ten,

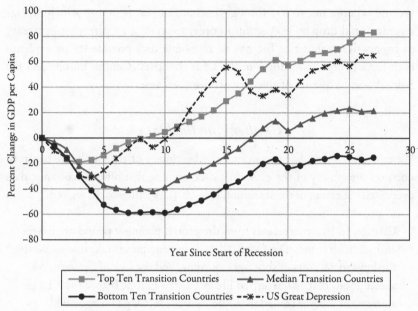

FIGURE 2.2. Postcommunist Transitions Compared to the US Great Depression (percent change in GDP per capita).

Source: Maddison Project Database, version 2018.

bottom ten, and median countries in terms of the length and depth (averaged together) of their transitional economic decline. In the most successful postsocialist economies, a group dominated by the EU member states of Central Europe—Poland, Hungary, Czechia, Estonia, Romania, Slovakia, and Slovenia, as well as Albania, Bosnia, and Belarus—the transitional recession was comparable to the US Great Depression, although somewhat less severe. For the median postsocialist economies, the transition recession was absolutely devastating, exceeding the magnitude of the Great Depression in depth (a 40 percent versus 30 percent drop in GDP per capita) and length (seventeen versus ten years) until recovery. The hardest hit postsocialist countries never recovered the GDP per capita of the late socialist period. Their average levels of GDP per capita remain below 1989 in 2019—thirty years later. In these countries, Ukraine, Moldova, Serbia, Tajikistan, and Kyrgyzstan, but also EU member state Latvia and star reformer Georgia, it is perhaps more accurate to speak of a transition catastrophe. Overall, if one knew the shape of these three curves prior to transition, and assumed that, individually, one would lie in the median of the income distribution, one might choose to endure the J-curve trajectory of the ten most successful states, a 20 percent drop soon followed by an 80 percent increase in income. However, one would probably choose not to live through a seventeen-year period in which average income would drop by 40 percent in order to attain a 20 percent gain twenty to twenty-five years later. The official economic data provide strong evidence both for a J-curve transition—in the CEB countries (Central Europe and the Baltics)—and a disaster of epic proportions elsewhere.

Challenging the Data

Western economists, keen to defend the legitimacy of their policies, began to question the quality of the economic data, arguing that official economic data overstated the extent of the transition recession. As Jeffrey Sachs argued,

> Changes in living standards from the central planning period are inherently difficult to measure. Official data do not adequately take into account the huge social costs of shortages, queuing, and the lack of choice in consumer goods that characterized life in Eastern Europe before 1989. Large amounts of income earned in the new private sector go unreported.[13]

Sachs went on to argue that, at least in Poland, "almost nobody believes that there has been a sharp decline in living standards," pointing to "a veritable boom in ownership of consumer durables (cars, TVs, VCRs, washing machines, refrigerators, personal computers, and the like)" after 1989. Sachs denied the existence of postcommunist recession in Poland by pointing to the inability of traditional economic statistics to adequately measure it.

While few went so far as to deny the existence of a postcommunist recession, many subsequent studies corroborated Sachs's challenges to the usefulness of official economic data. One of the central problems was measuring the size of the "informal," "unofficial," or "shadow" economy that sprang up in the chaos of postcommunist transition. As state enterprises failed, many workers and enterprises left the "formal," recorded, tax-paying economy. They began to work in the informal sector, which encompassed a wide range of activities, from illicit business to cross-border shuttle trading, to any business large or small that sought to evade taxation. Every country has an informal economy, but the postcommunist informal economies grew to be quite large. Rosser et al. estimated the size of the informal sector in the late 1990s at between 15 percent in the case of the Visegrad countries and 40 percent in the case of Russia and Ukraine.[14] Schneider found that the informal economy grew from an average of 31.5 percent in 1990–91 to 37.9 percent in 1999–2000 in the postcommunist countries. The average among rich countries in the Organization for Economic Cooperation and Development (OECD) grew from 13.2 percent to 16.8 percent during a similar time period.[15]

Given this, economists sought to find proxies for the size of the economic decline in postcommunist states that took into account the growth of the informal economy. Initially, several economists focused on electricity consumption. Electricity consumption data were easily available and thought to better reflect actual economic output and household consumption. If factories went out of business, they would not use electricity and if households were impoverished, they likely would use less electricity. Some papers found that electricity consumption collapsed by less than the official economy. However, others found that other factors could drive the relative resilience of electricity consumption.[16] Some analysts tried to estimate output loss using a basket of indicators. While all methods produced some differences, they also showed that postsocialist countries endured a deep depression. Figure 2.3 displays the findings of the most complete dataset, MIMIC, that estimates GDP growth using a variety of regression estimates against "multiple indicators, multiple causes." It suggests that the extent of recession may have been overestimated in official data, but not by much (see Figure 2.3).

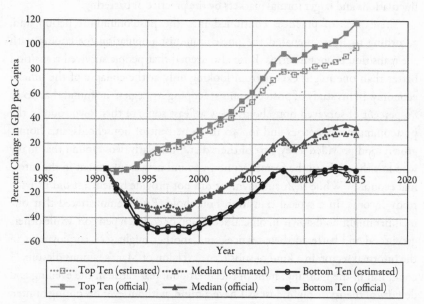

FIGURE 2.3. Estimated and Official Economic Performance (MIMIC). Countries are grouped by economic performance during transition. "Official" curves represent the growth rate in real GDP per capita. "Estimated" lines represent the growth rate in the economy as measured by both official GDP data and estimates of the unofficial economy. Note that the MIMIC database starts in 1991 and excludes six countries for lack of data: Kosovo, Macedonia, Montenegro, Serbia, Turkmenistan, and Uzbekistan, which accounts for any discrepancies with Figure 2.2.

Source: Maddison Project Database, version 2018, Medina and Schneider (2015).

In another attempt to correct the economic data, political scientist Richard Rose used public opinion polling to estimate the extent of income declines after 1989. Rose had a deep knowledge of household coping strategies under communism. In *Understanding Post-Communist Transformations*, he argued that there were at least three types of economies in socialist and postsocialist countries (and presumably elsewhere): (1) household economies, (2) informal economies, and (3) official economies. Households typically relied on all three types, and if one fails, they seek to make up income from the others. Since socialist economies had been dysfunctional for so long, Rose argued, households were already well practiced in hedging between economies and often purposefully diversified their assets and income streams to gain different benefits from each. Under communism, membership in local networks of producers freed households from dependence on the increasingly unreliable system of state rationing. Amid the economic instability of transition, household industries bolstered financial stability, and with diligence, could open up opportunities to participate in the new market economy. Household economies also offered protection from currency fluctuations and larger formal markets by the practice of bartering.

These sorts of practices continued into the postcommunist period and, according to Rose, prepared the postcommunist population for coping with the transition economic crisis. Rose also argued that people survived transition better than one might expect from looking only at the collapse of the official economy. In his study of postcommunist "coping strategies," he found that 70 to 80 percent of surveyed households grew at least some of their own food in the postcommunist countries and for 40 to 50 percent of households, this home-grown food provided a key part of their diet.[17] Similarly, Rose found that many who lost their jobs in the formal economy found new employment in the informal economy. While such employment did not provide benefits, it did provide ready income. In a typical transition household, Rose demonstrated that one member might hold down an official sector job or collect a pension, while others grew food and bartered their services, and another might seek employment in the informal sector, in a kind of subsistence version of Marx's famous dictum, "I could fish in the morning, hunt in the afternoon, rear cattle in the evening and do critical theory at night, just as I have a mind, without ever becoming hunter, fisherman, shepherd or critic." In public opinion surveys in 1992 and 1993, Rose found that only 6 percent of the Central Europe and Baltic populations were "destitute" by his definition, meaning that they "often" lacked necessities such as food, clothing, heating or electricity, while an additional 17 percent "sometimes" lacked necessities. However, Rose's surveys (see Table 2.2) concentrated on the Central European countries, rather than the former Soviet Union, where conditions were far worse.[18]

TABLE 2.2 Percent Often or Sometimes Lacking
Basic Necessities, 1995

	Food	Heating	Clothing
Czechia	10	9	27
Slovakia	12	6	31
Slovenia	13	7	23
Hungary	16	12	34
Ukraine	16	42	46
Poland	19	18	37
Croatia	25	14	50
Bulgaria	36	33	69
Estonia	38	12	49
Romania	41	26	50
Lithuania	50	17	63
Belarus	57	22	71
Latvia	57	22	65
Russian Federation	59	30	69

Note: Percent of households often or sometimes lacking food, heating and electricity, and clothing in response to the question: "Sometimes people have to do without things that people usually have. In the past year has your household sometimes had to do without any of the following?" *Source*: New Baltic Barometer II, New Europe Barometer IV, New Russia Barometer IV.

These studies show that official economic statistics have limitations and do not necessarily provide an accurate measure of well-being. This is why we have made it a point in this book to include data from other disciplines, such as demography and public opinion, and have tried to triangulate data from different fields. Official economic data have serious limitations. But when all is said and done, all point to a deep economic contraction.

Exacerbated by Inequality

The effects of postcommunist economic decline were exacerbated by a concomitant rise in inequality, which appeared for a number of reasons. First, wage controls were dismantled in the formal economy and disparities grew. Second, as state enterprises collapsed and were privatized, unemployment rose. Third, the informal economy grew, with its higher income inequality, lack of benefits and minimum wage protections, and criminality.[19] Official measures, such as Gini coefficients—a measure of income inequality—pick up only part of the increase in inequality for the same reason that all economic statistics are unreliable: because they tend to include only official incomes. Measured Gini coefficients grew dramatically in the postsocialist countries, though they remained lower than in other developing countries due to the legacy of communist redistribution.[20] Table 2.3 displays Gini coefficients of income inequality before taxes and transfers, the mechanisms welfare states use to smooth out market inequalities. Interestingly, tax inequality grew more sharply in the Visegrad countries than in most other regions, likely because of an influx of high-paying jobs connected with foreign investment. Similarly, as Table 2.4 shows, the share of pre-tax income flowing to the top 1 percent increased most sharply in the Visegrad and European former Soviet states, more than tripling between 1985 and 2015. However, *after tax* inequality in these Visegrad countries remained far lower than in any other set of postsocialist countries, thanks to more redistributive tax systems and stronger welfare states in the Visegrad countries, as shown in Table 2.5. But even in the Visegrad countries, measured inequality after taxes and transfers increased by 24 percent from 1985 to 2015.

Rising inequality implied that standard economic measures of well-being, such as GDP per capita, "have little in common with the actual lived experience of most people."[21] To understand why, consider a 2016 paper based on the Luxembourg Income Study household survey data that found major discrepancies between survey-reported income growth and official GDP per capita. The study was inspired by a well-known finding in the United States—that average incomes have stagnated while GDP per capita has grown for several decades. In exploring possible remedies for this, the authors sought out to determine whether the United States was unique. Surprisingly (or not), the study found the biggest discrepancy between household incomes and GDP per capita in postcommunist Central Europe. In several countries, including Poland, *average household income grew at only half the pace of GDP per capita between 1992 and 2010.* In Poland, GDP per capita grew at 4.46 percent per annum, giving the appearance of widespread gains, while household incomes only grew by 1.56 percent. In other words, the average household fell behind in relative terms, even as GDP per capita grew dramatically. In Hungary, GDP per capita grew at a healthy pace of 1.92 percent, but real household incomes actually shrank by an average of 0.22 percent per year between 1991 and 2012. In these Central European countries, the gap between household income and GDP per capita growth exceeded that in the United States by a factor of two.[22] This during a time when pre-tax incomes of the top 1 percent doubled or tripled as a percentage of total national income (see Table 2.4). A different study that corrects household surveys with available data on high-income taxpayers and factors in earnings on capital shows that the top

TABLE 2.3 Income Inequality (Gini Coefficients) before Taxes and Transfers

	1990	1995	2000	2005	2010	2015
CENTRAL ASIA	**38.6**	**40.1**	**40.5**	**39.9**	**38.2**	**37.6**
Kazakhstan	36.2	37.3	37.7	36.9	34.8	33.9
Tajikistan	37.9	38.4	38.8	38.6	38.3	38.3
Kyrgyzstan	41.3	44.2	43.8	43.1	41.5	40.5
Turkmenistan	38.2	39.6	40.5	41.0		
Uzbekistan	39.5	40.9	41.6			
EUROPEAN FORMER SOVIET UNION	**38.9**	**41.7**	**42.5**	**42.1**	**42.2**	**41.4**
Ukraine	23.6	25.1	24.7	23.6	22.6	22.2
Belarus	30.7	31.7	32.7	32.5	32.6	32.2
Azerbaijan	39.4	39.9	39.3	38.2		
Russia	36.3	46.6	47.9	48.0	46.5	44.5
Armenia	47.3	49.8	50.6	49.3	47.9	48.5
Georgia	42.8	45.6	47.8	48.7	50.5	48.7
Moldova	52.3	53.4	54.3	54.2	53.3	52.0
BALTICS	**39.4**	**42.5**	**43.5**	**44.1**	**43.6**	**43.2**
Estonia	45.1	48.0	48.8	48.2	47.4	47.3
Latvia	41.9	43.5	45.6	47.3	47.7	47.4
Lithuania	43.9	46.9	48.8	51.0	52.1	53.3
VISEGRAD	**38.9**	**44.5**	**46.3**	**47.8**	**46.3**	**45.6**
Slovakia	35.4	41.0	43.3	44.0	42.2	40.2
Czech Republic	37.8	41.9	44.2	45.4	44.6	44.3
Poland	38.1	46.1	47.8	51.2	48.1	47.2
Hungary	44.2	49.1	49.8	50.5	50.4	50.8
SOUTHEASTERN EUROPE	**38.5**	**42.9**	**44.9**	**46.3**	**46.9**	**47.4**
Slovenia	37.7	38.4	38.5	40.0	41.1	42.0
Kosovo				42.6	42.7	42.7
Romania	31.7	36.7	38.8	42.5	43.8	44.6
Croatia	42.9	43.2	43.4	43.7	44.7	45.3
Bulgaria	41.5	42.6	43.4	44.3	45.3	46.8
Albania			46.3	46.8	47.1	47.3
Bosnia and Herzegovina				47.7	47.7	47.8
Montenegro				48.3	49.1	50.0
Serbia			49.4	50.7	51.0	51.0
Macedonia		53.7	54.7	56.0	56.6	56.4

Note: In order of low to high Gini coefficients by region in 2015. Gini coefficient is a common measure of inequality. A score of 0 indicates perfect equality and a score of 100 indicates one individual has everything. It can be thought of as the percent of income that would need to be redistributed in order to achieve perfect equality.

Source: Gini coefficient data (before taxes and transfers) from the Standardized World Income Inequality Database, Version 8 (2019) (https://dataverse.harvard.edu/file.xhtml?persistent Id=doi:10.7910/DVN/LM4OWF/4RJPWF&version=4.0).

TABLE 2.4   Percent of National Income Flowing to the Top 1% before Taxes and Transfers

	1985	1990	1995	2000	2005	2010	2015
SOUTHEASTERN EUROPE	**4.72**	**5.67**	**8.24**	**8.51**	**8.80**	**8.57**	**9.66**
Slovenia			6.49	7.33	7.69	7.05	7.03
Montenegro	5.66	5.12	7.56	7.66	6.86	7.02	7.49
Kosovo					7.09	6.82	7.96
Albania				8.31	8.34	7.64	8.06
Croatia	4.24	4.89	6.92	7.56	8.81	7.96	8.16
Bosnia and Herzegovina	5.52	5.03	7.45	8.63	8.59	8.16	8.80
Macedonia		6.74	8.93	9.06	9.53	9.27	9.51
Bulgaria	3.46	5.07	12.82	9.14	10.41	9.97	12.10
Serbia		8.50	9.25	10.50	11.28	11.30	12.78
Romania		5.43	8.23	9.50	11.39	11.95	15.88
VISEGRAD	**3.27**	**4.94**	**8.50**	**8.87**	**10.64**	**10.21**	**10.30**
Slovakia	3.93	4.83	6.06	6.61	7.58	6.94	5.16
Czechia	2.38	4.45	9.45	9.65	10.40	9.80	10.24
Hungary	2.63	5.08	7.13	9.07	11.69	11.40	11.83
Poland	4.16	5.41	11.36	10.16	12.90	12.69	13.98
BALTICS	**4.70**	**6.74**	**11.58**	**11.49**	**13.47**	**9.41**	**10.33**
Lithuania		6.14	8.34	7.73	9.16	8.87	10.18
Latvia		5.47	11.15	11.27	11.10	7.99	10.27
Estonia	4.70	8.60	15.26	15.47	20.14	11.36	10.54
EUROPEAN FORMER SOVIET UNION	**4.38**	**7.04**	**11.48**	**14.87**	**17.22**	**14.65**	**14.88**
Moldova		5.62	7.23	7.96	7.55	7.83	8.35
Russia	4.38	7.34	14.03	20.69	24.91	20.03	20.24

Note: In order of low to high percentage by region in 2015.
Source: World Inequality Database (2020). (https://wid.world/).

10 percent of earners "captured almost two-thirds of post-communist economic growth."[23]

Public opinion polls also produced warning signs that growing inequality was leaving people behind, despite strong aggregate growth. In relatively successful countries like Poland, for example, public opinion polls still took decades

TABLE 2.5 Income Inequality (Gini Coefficients) after Taxes and Transfers

	1990	1995	2000	2005	2010	2015
VISEGRAD	**21.4**	**25.8**	**26.7**	**28.0**	**27.2**	**26.6**
Slovakia	17.5	22.0	25.2	26.6	25.5	24.2
Czechia	20.2	23.9	24.9	25.7	25.3	25.1
Hungary	24.0	27.5	27.4	27.7	27.2	27.7
Poland	24.0	29.8	29.2	31.9	30.9	29.5
EUROPEAN FORMER SOVIET UNION	**30.5**	**32.8**	**33.5**	**33.4**	**32.8**	**32.0**
Belarus	23.1	23.7	24.1	24.0	24.0	23.4
Ukraine	25.9	29.8	29.7	28.8	27.4	27.0
Azerbaijan	31.3	31.8	31.1	30.1		
Moldova	34.5	37.1	38.6	37.7	35.9	33.4
Russia	25.5	36.5	36.8	37.0	35.5	33.6
Armenia	35.5	38.3	39.2	37.7	36.1	37.0
Georgia	32.6	36.1	38.5	38.8	40.8	39.2
SOUTHEASTERN EUROPE	**27.4**	**28.3**	**30.8**	**33.1**	**33.4**	**33.7**
Slovenia	22.5	23.6	23.5	24.0	24.7	25.2
Kosovo				29.0	28.6	28.2
Croatia	28.8	28.6	28.0	27.3	28.9	29.6
Macedonia		31.0	32.2	34.1	34.6	33.3
Romania	21.9	27.2	28.9	32.0	32.6	33.4
Serbia			32.7	34.8	33.3	33.8
Bulgaria	29.3	31.3	32.0	33.1	34.1	36.5
Montenegro				38.4	38.4	38.4
Bosnia and Herzegovina				39.1	39.1	38.8
Albania			38.3	38.9	39.4	40.2
BALTICS	**28.3**	**31.4**	**33.2**	**34.0**	**33.8**	**34.2**
Estonia	29.7	33.6	35.0	33.5	32.2	32.4
Latvia	27.9	30.0	32.8	35.1	35.5	34.9
Lithuania	27.4	30.7	31.8	33.3	33.6	35.3
CENTRAL ASIA	**32.0**	**33.5**	**34.3**	**34.8**	**34.8**	**34.4**
Kazakhstan	28.7	29.2	29.3	28.5	27.0	26.4
Turkmenistan	30.5	31.4	32.0	32.4		
Uzbekistan	31.4	32.2	32.6			
Kyrgyzstan	32.3	35.5	35.8	35.1	34.0	33.2
Tajikistan	36.9	39.3	41.6	43.1	43.3	43.7

Note: In order of low to high Gini coefficients by region in 2015.
Source: Gini coefficient data (post taxes and transfers) from the Standardized World Income Inequality Database, Version 8 (2019) (https://dataverse.harvard.edu/file.xhtml?persistentId=doi:10.7910/DVN/LM4OWF/4RJPWF&version=4.0).

to show that a majority of the population benefited from transition. Although Poland started growing in 1992, a 1999 poll by the leading public opinion polling organization in Poland, CBOS, found that twice as many people reported that · their family had *lost* from transition as gained (29 percent versus 14 percent). Ten years after the revolutions of 1989, there were twice as many losers as winners— in Poland. A consistent majority reported little change in their economic situation. It was not until the poll was rerun in 2009, the twentieth anniversary of the transition, that there were twice as many winners as losers (30 percent reported gains versus 14 percent reporting losses) and it was not until 2019, the thirtieth anniversary of the transition, that a plurality of Poles reported that their families had gained, rather than had simply treaded water. Similarly, a plurality of Poles identified their households' financial situation as poor until 2004 and it was not until 2015 that more Poles said their household financial situation was "good" or "very good" than reported "poor" or "modest."[24] In contrast to what Sachs concluded in 1995, public opinion polls show that transition had a long-term negative impact on households, even in Poland. It took decades for many people to recover. Accession to the European Union in 2004 and the high growth of the 2000s marked a turning point, when a significant minority of Poles finally began to achieve greater prosperity and the number reporting losses began to shrink decisively. Thus, economic averages provide a misleading approach to understanding well-being in the postsocialist states (and probably elsewhere) because of the dramatic growth of inequality. After communism, huge gains flowed to the top 1 percent, while for most households, income grew more slowly than average. The benefits of transition were accrued by someone else.

Growth of Poverty

Along with inequality, poverty increased rapidly in the transition countries. Like all economic statistics, there are a number of ways to measure poverty. Official economic data for the transition period are weak and often incomparable from one country to another. One United Nations Development Program study stated frankly, "All poverty estimates for transition economies, and particularly for the CIS [Commonwealth of Independent States], are subject to major statistical difficulties." Lack of data on incomes from the informal economy presented one obstacle. However, the report also concluded that "the role of the 'shadow economy' in lifting people out of poverty is questionable. Recent studies from Poland and Hungary indicate that the distribution of incomes in the 'shadow economy' is biased toward the rich. . . . The jobs poor people can get are low paid, short-term, and have no social benefits. . . . Incomes from the 'shadow economy' as a main source of income usually only allow poor people to float around the poverty line."[25] The report also found that, "Society became polarized into a rich minority and a poor majority particularly in Russia," and that the "social costs of the transition process are high and persistent, even for the most advanced reformers."[26]

While different international institutions employ varying measures of poverty, few deny the sudden appearance of severe material deprivation in societies that had once sought to meet all basic needs. In order to apply some sort of comparable standard, we use one of the most common measures of poverty, an absolute measure of $5.50 a day, established by the World Bank. This poverty level is higher than that applied in many poor countries worldwide, due to the high cost of heating in cold climates. By this measure, as mentioned earlier, we find 191 million people living on less than $5.50 a day across Eastern Europe and Eurasia by 1999, the peak of the poverty crisis. This means that during the first decade of transition, *poverty impacted 47 percent of the total population of the region*. Essentially half of all people faced substantial, and often drastic, declines in their standards of living compared to 1990. The sudden onset of mass poverty among people who had once lived with most of their basic needs met by the state left deep scars on the national psyche. The extent and endurance of poverty in the median postcommunist country also dwarfed that produced by the US Great Depression of the 1930s, at least according to official statistics.

Figure 2.4 shows that the number of people in poverty peaked in 1999 and only dropped below 1990 levels in 2005. It fell rapidly until the global financial crisis in 2008 and then stabilized at about 60 million people or 15 percent of the population, according to our analysis. In 2014, the World Bank reported that some 80 million people in the region still lived on less than $5.00 per day.[27]

Social Policies

With the deeper than expected transitional recession, the modest ameliorative measures recommended by the international financial institutions failed to meet their poverty-prevention objectives.[28] The authors of *Reform in Eastern Europe* and the IFIs sought to help the worst affected by "targeting" benefits to the poorest of the poor. The idea was quite simple and attractive. Poverty would grow. Budgets would be stretched. The minimal resources available to countries to ameliorate poverty had to be spent wisely and that meant spending money on those who needed these resources the most. In place of the "universal" benefits provided under socialism, in which all citizens qualified for a wide range of social services and transfer payments—including free health care, subsidized day care, free schooling, subsidized housing, subsidized basic food items, paid maternity leave, and even death benefits—the World Bank recommended replacing this system with "targeted" benefits for the poor. Yet poverty skyrocketed. Why?

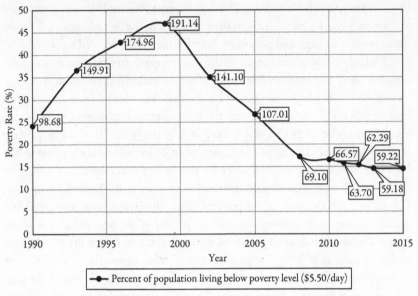

FIGURE 2.4. Poverty in Transition Countries, 1990–2015. Data labels display total number of poor (in millions).

Source: World Bank (2018) (http://iresearch.worldbank.org/Povcalnet/povDuplicateWB.aspx).

A key factor was that reformers removed subsidies on food and essential items. Western economists thought that eliminating subsidies would make enterprises more efficient. Under socialism, the state collected enterprise profits and redistributed them based on a set of government priorities, creating a complex web of cross-subsidization that made it difficult for profitable enterprises to get ahead. Economists believed that this cross-subsidization needed to be eliminated so that more efficient and profitable enterprises would thrive.

However, an unfortunate by-product of cutting subsidies that had sought to achieve various social aims was to drastically increase the prices of many basic goods. Socialist countries had calibrated their welfare states around a "basket" of staple foods and household goods deemed necessities. They ensured that people could afford these necessities in two ways—by calibrating cash benefits to make sure people could purchase these items and by subsidizing their production, so that consumers did not pay the full cost. So, while cars and TVs (not deemed necessities) were almost unattainably expensive under socialism, bread, sausages, sallow, and beer (deemed necessities) were dirt cheap. Overall, the poor benefited the most from these subsidies. While getting rid of subsidies, the IFIs wanted governments to replace them with cash benefits to the very poor, to enable them to eat.

But there was a problem. While targeting social expenditures sounded good on paper, it required a considerable new bureaucracy to determine who deserved benefits and who did not. People had to fill out forms for bureaucrats to process. For a poor and immobile elderly person or a semi-literate herder in a far-flung rural location in Kazakhstan, registering for and qualifying for benefits and accessing services presented serious obstacles. The communist system had made it as easy as possible—just show up at a central location and receive benefits, often for free—for instance, through the post office. "Targeting" systems made benefits difficult to access, *especially for the weakest segments of the population*. Studies show that in Russia, using various different methods of targeting, as many as 25 to 30 percent of the poor were denied their benefits.[29]

Then, there was the lack of money. Governments suffering from a recession worse than the Great Depression and without developed systems of tax collection could not raise enough revenue to pay the multitude of the poor. As a result, the quality and level of social benefits eroded at the same time the official economy shrank in most countries. Of course, the Visegrad countries did more to safeguard the welfare of their populations than did most of the former Soviet Union and Southeastern Europe. Yet the unexpected depth of transitional recessions overwhelmed government services in many countries. Hospitals deteriorated in quality and local polyclinics closed. Kindergartens and crèches shut down and left women scrambling for child care. Sanatoria where the ill and elderly once convalesced were privatized and accessible only for a fee. Enterprise health care centers, subsidized cafeterias, and housing developments were sold, shut down, or charged higher fees. The proud and extensive social systems of communism withered on the vine. People who had enjoyed state provision of a wide range of services suddenly lacked basic goods like heat, electricity, and clean water. Corruption rose as citizens were increasingly forced to pay fees or bribes for nominally free services.[30] Overall, targeted social policies failed to prevent the collapse of social services in a collapsing economy and pushed hundreds of millions of citizens into poverty all at once.[31]

Reform in Eastern Europe author Olivier Blanchard later wrote that, in retrospect, it would have been wiser to maintain many of these poverty-reducing subsidies.[32] Phasing out subsidies gradually as the new private economy grew instead of cutting them all at once, he argued, would have strengthened government budgets and improved the quality of the workforce by maintaining employment while preventing socioeconomic disaster. In short, much transition poverty could have been avoided through different policies.

Effects of Mass Impoverishment

The effects of mass impoverishment in former socialist states have been chronicled by one of the most astute ethnographers of the transition process, British social anthropologist Caroline Humphrey. The rise of this inequality in a once (at least rhetorically) egalitarian society, or at any rate, a society where people were raised to believe in greater egalitarianism, fractured the social networks that might have helped people better cope with the stresses of their new shared reality. Humphrey reports that "these sudden gulfs in pay and security destroyed old relations of easy equality, tearing apart lifelong friendships and breaking marriages."[33] The emotional impacts of these deep gashes in the social fabric are hard to capture in the economic data, but they are the most powerfully felt effects in the lives of individuals who found themselves feeling lonely and abandoned in a world that seemingly had no place for them, as described so vividly by Svetlana Alexievich in her book, *Second Hand Time*.[34]

3

Modifying the Framework

BY THE MID-1990S, the unexpected depth and length of the transitional recessions caused many economists to admit that they had underestimated the "institutional" prerequisites of a market economy.[1] The scholarly journal, *Economics of
Transition*, extended its title to, *"and Institutional Change,"* in 2019. As anthropologist Katherine Verdery pointed out, creating a system of private property in
Romania turned out to be as much a historical and political process as an economic one. It proved very difficult to make market mechanisms work effectively
in the absence of prior institutions or experience.[2] In Bulgaria, Ghodsee found
that ordinary citizens also had little understanding of market mechanisms, leaving them exposed to predatory entrepreneurs and unscrupulous businessmen.
Whereas people raised in capitalist societies are taught to be on the lookout for
scams, con artists, and unrealistic schemes, many East Europeans gullibly invested
their life savings in what they thought were newly created opportunities to get
rich quick or sold off valuable antiques for a pittance to middlemen who then
made huge profits reselling them on the international market.[3]

In Albania, the International Monetary Fund has admitted that Albanians'
"unfamiliarity with financial markets" was a key factor in the nationwide postsocialist pyramid schemes in 1996 and 1997 that accounted for about half of
Albania's GDP and involved almost two-thirds of the entire Albanian population. "When the schemes collapsed," the IMF reported, "there was uncontained
rioting, the government fell, and the country descended into anarchy and a
near civil war in which some 2,000 people were killed."[4] In Russia, the notori-
ous MMM pyramid defrauded between 5 and 10 million citizens,[5] and the 1993
Caritas Ponzi scheme in Romania fleeced tens of thousands of Romanians of
their hard-earned savings because, as the *New York Times* reported, the founders
of the pyramid exploited "the unrealistic expectations of a people who have heard
about capitalism but never experienced it."[6]

While economists had fiercely debated the proper "sequencing" of reform steps,[7] they understood little about how market-supporting institutions and attitudes were created. Launching mass privatization programs in the absence of these institutions and social understandings produced blatant and high levels of corruption, which ultimately poisoned the transition process, creating less than efficient market outcomes and enduring social and political problems. Janine Wedel exposed the processes of "Collision and Collusion" between Western economic advisors and domestic elites seeking to establish an ownership stake in the new market economy.[8] For many ordinary citizens, their high hopes for a prosperous future turned sour; the privatization process looked to them like a way for previous communist elites to extend their privileges into the postcommunist era with the complicity of Western institutions. Moreover, most East Europeans had been educated within a Marxist framework that officially vilified capitalism as an inherently unfair and corrupt economic system, where private profits trumped public welfare. This understanding of capitalism in some ways fueled corruption, because new elites embraced the ethos that markets knew no morality beyond money. For many citizens, capitalism and democracy rode in on a sort of moral vacuum.

In her poignant memoir of growing up in East Germany, Jana Hensel captured how young people experienced this new moral vacuum in their daily lives. Reflecting on her *Jugendweihe*, the old socialist coming of age ceremony, Hensel explained:

> Under the proud eyes of our parents, grandparents, and the entire school faculty, we would pledge to give our all for the noble cause of Socialism, to deepen the bonds of friendships with the Soviet Union and fight for the interests of the international proletariat. In addition to the certificate and the flowers, each of us was given a book entitled *On the Meaning of Our Lives*. It summed up our short existence in five general questions: Who am I? What can I do? What do I want? To whom can I be useful? Who needs me? I loved these books. They initially may have raised some difficult questions, but they always had satisfying answers at the ready. Skill and knowledge, a sense of social responsibility and duty, class loyalty, and a willingness to meet the highest standards in our educational and working lives—these were the characteristics of a true Socialist. Everyone could acquire such qualities as long as he or she, in line with the Marxist-Leninist worldview, emancipated him- or herself from the false consciousness of capitalist exploitation and embraced his or her working-class identity.[9]

After the fall of the Berlin Wall, Hensel spent the rest of her high school and university years in the reunified Germany, and noted with some dismay the withering away of the old socialist morality:

> Few of our former convictions have survived. We no longer believe in the fantasy of a greater sense of community in the East, for instance; something that we were always being told and that we ultimately also ended up telling ourselves.... We like keeping our hands where they are. Most things are none of our business. The key questions in our new lives are: Who am I? What do I want? Who can be useful to me? Whom do I need? It's nice not to have all those people around telling us how much society values us and what our responsibilities are. We don't pitch in anymore. We spend time taking care of ourselves.[10]

Starting in the mid-1990s, policymakers refocused attention on building market-supporting institutions and cultivating the right kinds of entrepreneurial spirit, a process one group of prominent sociologists referred to as "rebuilding the ship at sea."[11] For this new institutionalist thinking on economics, the World Bank's 1996 World Development Report, "From Plan to Market," was a landmark. While expressing support for the market-oriented reforms of the Washington consensus, the report broke new ground by emphasizing institutional development as a key aspect of transition. "Market-supporting institutions will not arise out of thin air," it declared, advising governments to pursue a wide variety of objectives, from ensuring rule of law to fighting corruption and organized crime to promoting education and social security, building a strong financial sector, and regulating markets.[12] The World Bank recognized that the state had an important role to play in supporting market-oriented reforms and laid out a substantial state-led development agenda. In effect, this was an acknowledgment that the strategy of presuming that markets would fix everything on their own had been a mistake. At the same time, the World Bank made clear that, despite everything, countries that moved faster on reform had faced and solved the major issues more adequately.

This new focus on institution-building corresponded with the rise of the European Union as a dominant actor in the transition in the late 1990s, particularly for those countries that hoped to join. As a result, this institutionalist turn in the economics of transition was underlined by the practice of the EU, which required a high degree of institutional effectiveness from its member states to enforce rules decided in Brussels. The EU accession process, launched at the 1993 Copenhagen summit, created three sets of membership requirements: democratic governance, well-functioning market economies, and administrative competence. On the latter point, a key concern was the effectiveness of postsocialist countries' judiciaries. This became a problem for Bulgaria and Romania, whose judicial systems were deemed too corrupt for full EU membership. Both countries remained under a monitoring and verification mechanism after membership was granted in 2007, three years after the first wave of postsocialist countries joined the EU in 2004: Czech Republic, Estonia, Hungary, Latvia, Lithuania, Poland, Slovakia, and Slovenia. In the run-up to accession, all countries were subject to annual "Agenda 2000" monitoring reports that pointed out specific institutional weaknesses and urged or required countries to address them prior to accession.[13]

Impact of Geography

At the same time, the EU accession process made clear that not all postcommunist countries were alike. In fact, they were no longer part of the same world. Some, the most Western among them, had the opportunity to join the greatest common market in the world, the European Union, and others did not. Some had natural resources that made them important sites for investment, regardless of how many reforms they had implemented and whether their country was a democracy or not. Some, particularly in the non-Baltic former Soviet states, came under pressure after 2000 to forge closer ties with Russia. Some, as Orenstein showed in his 2019 book, *The Lands in Between*, ended up subject to a geopolitical tug of war between Russia and the West.

Figure 3.1 displays where the postcommunist economic crisis hit the hardest, revealing which countries experienced the deepest and most prolonged declines in GDP per capita after 1989–91, based on World Bank data. The differences are massive. In one of the least-affected countries, Czechia, GDP per capita declined by 13.4 percent before bottoming out in 1993. In one of the worst-affected countries, Ukraine, GDP per capita declined by 60.3 percent before bottoming out in 1998. On average, the ten worst-off countries suffered a decline of 59.9 percent before bottoming out in 1996. The ten least-affected countries suffered a decline of 24.9 percent before bottoming out in 1992. These were stunning drops that devastated the lives of millions of families. Even the median postsocialist countries suffered a decline of 35.3 percent before reaching a nadir in 1995.

While Figure 3.1 does not show the depth of despair felt by people, it does show where this despair was concentrated. Overall, the Visegrad countries (Poland, Hungary, Czechia, and Slovakia), and other Central European countries such as Slovenia experienced a much milder average drop in GDP per capita. Seven out of the ten least affected by the transitional recession in Figure 3.1 were Central European new member states of the European Union. By contrast,

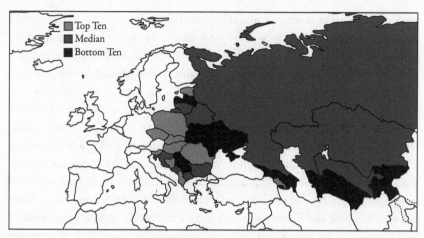

FIGURE 3.1. Drop in GDP per Capita by Country. In order to calculate countries' ranking, first we rank them by % decrease from 1989 to the lowest level of GDP per capita,
length of time from 1989 to the lowest level, and % increase from 1989 to 2016. The overall
ranking is an unweighted average of these three rankings. Top ten are best performing
economies. Bottom ten are worst performing economies.

Source: Real Per Capita GDP in 2010 US dollars (US Department of Agriculture Economic
Research Service and World Bank 2018).

the worst affected was not Russia itself but the countries on the southern tier of
the former Soviet Union, the "stans" of Central Asia and the Caucasus as well
as Ukraine and Moldova. It is fascinating how badly being on the periphery of
the former Soviet Union affected countries, even those, like Ukraine, which
are adjacent to more successful Central European countries. As one scholar
noted, "A new periphery seems to be emerging, formed by SEE [Southeastern
Europe], including parts of the former Balkans and some of the heirs of former Yugoslavia. This is comparable to the periphery of the former Soviet Union
formed by the states of the Caucasus and Central Asia and including some of
the conflict-ridden Russian republics (such as Dagestan, North Ossetia and
Chechnya) and the Republic of Moldova. With few exceptions, these countries
have large (often majority) rural populations, and poverty is mostly more acute
in the rural areas."[14]

Foreign direct investment also concentrated geographically, with the lion's
share coming into the Central European new member states of the European
Union as well as Russia and other countries with abundant natural resources.
This investment revitalized industries for export. For instance, one of the big-
gest surprises was the dramatic growth of the East European automotive industry.
West European, North American, and Asian car companies bought many of their
East European counterparts and invested millions in the relatively under-served

automotive market as well as producing extensively for export. Central Europe has integrated into the West European motor industry "with comparative advantages in the assembly and labor-intensive manufacture of components."[15] Transnational companies now slice up the value chain, locating certain processes in countries best suited to them. Central and East European countries doubled their share of overall European passenger car production from 12 to 24 percent between 1991 and 2007, increasing from 2 million to 4.5 million cars per year. The biggest producers are Škoda, a local brand owned by Volkswagen, as well as Fiat, Toyota, Peugeot, Citroen, Audi, Volkswagen, General Motors, and Suzuki. Russia, Czechia, and Slovakia ranked fourth, sixth, and seventh in Europe in total passenger car production in 2018, not far from the UK, which came fifth.[16] Since many of Central and Eastern Europe's largest industries, including automotive and finance, are foreign owned, Nölke and Vliegenthart labeled these countries "dependent market economies," noting that many of their key political economy decisions were taken outside their borders.[17]

An IMF study found that new member states of the European Union took in $700 billion in foreign direct investment alone from 1994 to 2018. Sixty-four percent of this investment went into services, especially financial services, while only 27 percent went into manufacturing. Manufacturing investment in the Central and East European new member states focused on heavy industry as well as automotive production, including chemicals and petroleum and metals, but also light industries such as textiles, printing, paper, and food and beverage.[18] Russia additionally received $146 billion in foreign direct investment between 2003 and 2011, with the oil and gas industries leading the way.[19]

However, foreign direct investment did not benefit all countries and regions equally. One study showed that among seventy one regions studied in Russia, Moscow received 21,151 times more foreign investment than the Altai Republic. Moreover, only twenty Russian regions received more than $1 billion in foreign direct investment from 2003 to 2011. "Therefore," the authors conclude, "we presume that there was a very limited number of Russian regions in which FDI [foreign direct investment] could have had a significant impact on economic development."[20]

What was true at the regional level was also true at the national level. Some countries prospered while others struggled to receive needed investment and growth. The economically worst affected countries were those on the southern tier of the former Soviet Union, as well as Serbia, Kosovo, and Latvia. Serbia, for instance, was left behind in automotive investment in part due to the Yugoslav wars and resulting political instability. Putin likes to highlight the economic catastrophe in Russia, but as bad as it was, it was only average compared to the deprivations suffered by many of its neighboring states.

Interestingly, some of the countries that experienced the best economic performance after 1989 were countries that received massive subsidies—rather than foreign direct investment—from abroad, such as the former German Democratic Republic, which was absorbed into the Federal Republic of Germany in 1990, and Bosnia-Herzegovina, which received massive postwar aid from the European Union and the United States, enjoying numerous development programs after the Dayton Accords that ended the Bosnian War in 1995. This suggests that Jeffrey Sachs's notion of a massive Marshall Plan for the postsocialist economies could have worked to prevent some of the negative consequences of postsocialist economic decline.

Reform Speed and Growth Revisited

Transition economists and policymakers hypothesized in 1989–90 that countries that reformed quickly would suffer less than gradual reformers. Therefore, if postsocialist countries were experiencing a catastrophic transitional recession, they had only themselves to blame. Countries that adopted neoliberal reforms most completely and quickly initially suffered far less than places like Russia, where reform was more gradual.[21] As the World Bank argued in its 1996 World Development Report: "Economic recovery has been strongly linked to consistent reform, including liberalization and stabilization programs. Growth has typically resumed about three years after the determined implementation of such measures. Later or less committed reformers have recovered more slowly—indeed some have yet to bounce back. These countries have not yet sustained decisive reforms long enough to consolidate macroeconomic stability and resume growth."[22] However, this finding, one of the key tenets of the J-curve perspective on transition, fell apart in the 2000s.

Starting around 2004, academic papers began to find that slow reformers were growing faster than their fast-reforming neighbors. The relation between reform speed and growth disappeared or reversed. One of the key reasons was the rise of oil prices in the 2000s. The postcommunist recession was partly caused by historically low oil prices. When oil prices rose dramatically in the 2000s, the Russian and other post-Soviet oil exporting and transporting economies began to grow. Ultimately, policymakers had to come to terms with the fact that rapid economic reform had not produced better long-term growth. Jeffrey Sachs, an early transition theorist who had previously argued for fast reform found that "economic studies of the transition economies have underestimated the roles of geopolitics, geography and natural resources in shaping each nation's division of labour within the European and global economy." His 2018 paper in *Economics of Transition* found that 85 percent of growth in transition economies to 2015 can be explained by "(1) years of membership in the EU; (2) physical distance from the heart of the EU economy, taken to be Dusseldorf; and (3) annual revenues from oil and gas production, reflecting natural resource deposits." In other words, geography mattered. Institutions mattered. These were the lessons learned by postcommunist reformers, at great cost to populations who suffered through reforms that, at the end of the day, did not produce the outcomes promised.

4

Counternarratives of Catastrophe

DESPITE WESTERN ECONOMISTS' attempts to put a good spin on the post-socialist recessions, the depth and scale of the socioeconomic collapse in many countries gave rise to an alternative narrative of "disaster capitalism." One of the strongest exponents of this approach was Naomi Klein, whose book, *The Shock Doctrine: The Rise of Disaster Capitalism*, argued that neoliberal economic programs had been imposed on countries suffering from deep economic crisis and had not served the interest of the populations but rather benefited a small Eastern and Western elite. In her view, neoliberalism was like a crusading religion, a "closed, fundamentalist doctrine that cannot co-exist with other belief-systems." For disaster capitalist policies to work, "the world as it is must be erased to make way for their purist invention. Rooted in biblical fantasies of great floods and great fires, it is a logic that leads ineluctably towards violence."[1] Klein pointed to Yeltsin's Russia in the 1990s as an example of Western violence toward postsocialist citizens. Russian President Vladimir Putin embraced this worldview and deployed these arguments to turn his country away from the West.

The disaster capitalism perspective corresponded with lived experience in many countries. Fast or slow, all postsocialist countries adopted neoliberal policies to some extent, and the vast majority experienced deleterious effects. For instance, Russia, which received a high score on the EBRD's transition indicators in 1997, endured a decade-long recession. This enabled Vladimir Putin, who won the presidency in 2000, to argue that the economic policies of the 1990s had been a mistake and had been foisted on Russia by foreign powers. They did not correspond to Russian conditions or Russian values. They caused mass impoverishment that only served Western elites, who earned money off advising Russia and created an army of unemployed Russians who could serve Western industry. In Putin's view, foreigners deliberately made his country suffer so that a much-weakened Russia could not challenge the West. Instead, Putin proposed a more nationalist economic policy, whereby he continued to adopt some neoliberal reforms, but combined them with others that were more statist. He wrested the commanding heights of the economy from corrupt oligarchs, put them under the firm hand of the state and exiled, imprisoned, and killed those who refused to go along.

Many watched the deterioration of Russia's once promising market economy with chagrin,[2] yet economic growth returned, in large part because of higher oil prices, but also in part because Putin's centralizing reforms worked. They created an institutional structure to manage a new capitalist economy, albeit in a corrupt and top-down manner. For most citizens of Russia, Putin's form of capitalism functioned well. Growth returned. Poverty rates fell. And as we have discussed, two narratives began to grow out of the transition experience, a J-curve narrative of qualified success—a longer than expected transitional period but overall success—and a disaster capitalism narrative emphasizing the foreseeable and unacceptable impacts of Western neoliberal reforms, which created "new forms of western colonization through transferring expertise, employing Eastern Europe's cheap skilled labor force, and flooding markets hitherto closed to western products."[3]

While this critique of transition economics came mainly from disciplines such as anthropology and sociology, and non-Western leaders like Putin, it had some purchase in the Western economics profession. Jeffery Sachs suddenly resigned from his role as economic advisor to Russia in December 1993 because he found "corruption to be growing and out of control."[4] Nobel Prize–winning economist Joseph Stiglitz found serious faults with the transition process in Russia as well. Stiglitz, who became chief economist of the World Bank after a career at MIT, agreed that the Western economists' transition strategy produced a total disaster for Russia. He reflected:

> Advisers from the West rushed to Eastern Europe to guide those countries through their transitions. Many believed, mistakenly, that "shock therapy" was needed—that the transition to Western-style capitalism should take place overnight through rapid privatization and liberalization. Instantaneous price liberalization brought with it—predictably—hyperinflation.... [It] also brought down the economies, which slid into deep recessions and depressions. Meanwhile, rapid privatizations were giving away hundreds of billions of dollars of the countries' most valuable assets, creating a new class of oligarchs who took money out of the country far faster than the inflow of billions that the IMF was pouring in as assistance. Capital markets were liberalized in the mistaken belief that money would be induced to come in. Instead, there was massive

capital flight, including the famous purchase of the Chelsea football club and numerous country estates in the U.K. by one of the oligarchs, Roman Abramovich. . . . [W]hile a few were driving Mercedes and enjoying the New Russia, millions more were seeing their meager pensions being eroded below even the level of subsistence.[5]

According to Stiglitz, economists and policymakers had created a socioeconomic disaster in the post-Soviet states and much of Eastern Europe, as preconditions were not in place for markets to work, and privatization led to massive theft and asset-stripping.

A set of papers by Lawrence P. King, David Struckler, and Martin McKee on the impact of mass privatization on the demography of postsocialist states played a key role in this debate.[6] In essence, these papers argued that mass privatization had weakened government capacity in those countries where they were implemented and, by doing so, contributed to economic chaos and produced devastatingly high mortality rates. While other economists and political scientists fired back with a stinging critique of the analytic methods used in the paper and its findings, these papers fed into a broader critique of Western transition economics, arguing that neoliberal policies not only led to an economic failure but also to millions of excess deaths. It was an incendiary claim. Conspiracy theorists used it to suggest that Western-backed economic reforms intended to kill off postsocialist populations, reviving (often anti-Semitic) images of bloodthirsty international bankers. Ordinary citizens, suffering and confused about why the promises of free market prosperity had failed to materialize, fell prey to paranoid notions of a coordinated plot to destroy their nations, slowly turning them against the West.

Recovery and Crisis 2.0

During the 2000s, postsocialist countries enjoyed a spate of high growth fueled by high oil prices that lifted the Russian and post-Soviet economies,[7] and the EU accession of ten postsocialist countries in Central and Eastern Europe, eight in 2004 and two in 2007, which set off a massive wave of foreign investment.[8] For a time, it seemed that the promise of transition economics had finally been achieved: foreign investment–driven growth based on export industries. However, the majority of investment poured into consumer finance—the creation of credit cards, mortgage and home equity loans. These fueled a massive housing price bubble throughout the region.[9] As a result, the good times came to an abrupt end with the global financial crisis of 2008–09.

After the collapse of Lehman Brothers in New York, which caused credit to dry up for banks, the postsocialist countries suffered a sudden stop in investment inflows that plunged them into renewed recessions.[10] As the housing bubble burst and currencies in the postcommunist countries devalued, citizens who had taken newly available home equity lines of credit in foreign currencies found themselves owing sums greater than the value of their homes, and banks foreclosed on those who lost jobs and could not make their payments. The global financial crisis precipitated a long Eurozone crisis, which also negatively affected growth in the postsocialist countries and extended a period of recession and low growth.

The global financial crisis revived the debate over the effects of neoliberal economic policies. President Putin used the occasion of the World Economic Forum in Davos in 2009 to launch a head-on attack, arguing that a lack of sufficient government regulation of the Western economies caused the global financial crisis.[11] IFIs lined up to defend the record of neoliberalism and, in particular, explain why neoliberal policies had not been responsible for the new recession that started in 2008.[12] As governments were forced to implement austerity measures across the European continent, popular anger and public dissent flared.

Populist Reactions

Influenced by Russia's return to growth in the 2000s under Putin, governments throughout the postsocialist states began to experiment with a more authoritarian and heterodox approach to economic policy after the global financial crisis of 2008, combining neoliberal policies in some areas with centralization and state control in others.[13] To some extent, these policies represented the willingness of postsocialist states to break with neoliberal orthodoxy and seek policy approaches that would ameliorate some of the negative features of transition. Viktor Orbán's government in Hungary was a case in point.[14] Orbán's FIDESZ party won 2010 elections in a landslide victory over the Socialists who had been discredited by an economic scandal. Orbán's government changed the constitution and dismantled democratic checks and balances in an effort to preserve its single-party rule in Hungary.[15] At the same time, it confronted the IMF and sought to establish greater state control over the economy.[16] It passed laws converting foreign-currency mortgage loans into domestic currency at discounted rates, passing on huge costs to foreign banks and effectively diminishing foreign bank activity in Hungary. The government discouraged foreign investment in the financial and retail sectors but continued to support foreign investment in manufacturing, as part of its jobs and growth strategy. The FIDESZ government also sought to establish a domestic capitalist class loyal to the party. Orbán spoke out strongly against accepting Muslim migrants, and built a fence on Hungary's southern border. While not thoroughly rejecting neoliberalism, Hungary's policies took off in a new direction, where foreign investment was something to be controlled in the interests of a new vision of nationalist goals.

Similarly, Poland elected a nationalist authoritarian majority government in 2015 that sought to distance Poland from the EU. The new Law and Justice Party (PiS) government launched a takeover of the judiciary, limiting its ability to check government policy.[17] It passed a media law that made state media a political tool of the ruling party. After failing to strengthen a law that would have prohibited all abortions (including for those pregnancies that resulted from incest or rape), it passed a massive new family assistance program, Poland 500+, that provided a substantial monthly subsidy to families for each second and additional child (and first child in the case of poor families).[18] The EU and other international financial institutions harshly criticized these policies. However, Polish voters reelected Law and Justice in parliamentary elections in 2019 and narrowly reelected PiS president Andrzej Duda in 2020.

Evaluating the Economics of Postsocialist Transition

Economic evaluations of postsocialist transitions remain quite polarized to this day. On the one hand, advocates of neoliberal policies can point to considerable success stories such as Poland, where rapid reform was followed by relatively brief transitional recessions, significant growth, European integration, and catch-up industrialization. Poland today is a dynamic economy, with skyscrapers sprouting in the center of Warsaw and hundreds of factories scattered throughout the country producing quality goods for export, which are distributed via a network of new highways funded by the European Union.

However, gains from growth even in these success cases have been distributed unequally, with massive differentials between rural and urban areas and between different generations of citizens.[19] These have deep impacts on contemporary politics, with voters in small towns and rural areas electing conservative populists and big cities supporting Western-oriented liberals. Moreover, most other postsocialist countries have experienced much worse economic results. In these countries, the economic crisis following the collapse of communism and the Soviet Union was nothing short of catastrophic, far greater and far longer than the Great Depression of the 1930s, as measured by declines in per capita GDP. Countries will be living with the psychic scars and emotional legacies of the transition period for many decades. As a result, to suggest that we should stop talking about the economic relevance of the transition is analogous to suggesting that we stop talking about the real consequences of the Great Depression on the shape of the American economy. Many economic and social policies and political attitudes that persist in the United States today are direct legacies of the suffering experienced during the 1930s. Similarly, the transitional recessions will continue to influence the societies, polities, and economies of the postsocialist nations for the foreseeable future.

From an economic viewpoint, transition created significant winners and losers, and the key to understanding the polarized narratives of success or failure is to recognize that economic growth was not distributed equally. The lens of social stratification and inequality is essential to understanding the continuing debates. Neoliberal policies set markets free and enabled trade with the rest of the world, especially in the richer Western parts of Eastern Europe. Millions of people in the postsocialist countries took advantage of these opportunities through trade, education, investment, and labor migration. Millions of postsocialist citizens have better jobs, higher life satisfaction, and greater pay than they would have had under socialism—of that there is no doubt. However, the breakdown of socialist welfare states also meant that poor and low-income people in the postsocialist states suffered.[20] Whereas the former socialist states had guaranteed housing, education, employment, and minimum incomes, neoliberal policies dismantled many of these protections, producing high rates of poverty and new problems of homelessness, drug addiction, human trafficking, and despair.

Losses were not allocated equally among countries, regions, families, or individuals. Any way that one could choose to look would show that inequalities increased drastically. Starting with the country level makes sense because studies have shown that between-country inequalities are greater, in most cases, than within-country inequalities.[21] It turns out that where you are born determines your standard of living more than any other variable. When looking at between-country levels of inequality, the contrasts are truly staggering. A country like Czechia survived the transition period fairly well, while a country like Georgia experienced a devastating and prolonged contraction. Largely rural, agricultural countries have again become desperately poor, whereas nations more closely integrated with the European Union have become middle-income countries with great benefits for millions, albeit with exaggerated inequalities.

The China Comparison

When considering the devastation caused by economic transition in the postsocialist European and Central Asian countries, it is hard to avoid comparison with China. China did what many theorists of transition said could not be done: reformed communism.[22] While maintaining harsh communist party rule, sometimes by force, China liberalized central planning, allowed small-scale town and village enterprises, created special economic zones for foreign investment, and created a thriving private sector economy alongside reforming state-owned enterprises. The transition was not sudden; it lasted thirty or forty years, during which time China vastly outpaced Russia and the other countries of the former Soviet Union to become one of the leading economies in the world. It managed this without a massive transitional recession; instead, it had uninterrupted growth, resulting in hundreds of millions of people being pulled out of poverty rather than becoming impoverished (See Figure 4.1).

Given China's experience, which has been emulated successfully by Vietnam, there should be no doubt that Janos Kornai and other critics of communist reform efforts were wrong. Communist economies could have been reformed gradually and gradual reform can be far more successful than the radical transformation attempted in the postsocialist European and post-Soviet countries.[23] In particular, sudden privatization of the entire economy was not necessary. China's dualism showed that it is possible to maintain a large state-owned sector of the economy, directing credits to large enterprises that maintain employment and production levels, while gradually reforming them and forcing them to face competition from a dynamic and growing new private sector. Not only is that strategy possible, but it has proven to be far superior in terms of public well-being, since it avoids a prolonged transition recession and can produce high rates of economic growth and poverty reduction. In 1990, Russia's GDP was approximately 70 percent higher than China's, $1.416 trillion versus $827 billion. By 2018, Russia's GDP was less than one-fifth of China's, $1.7 trillion versus $10 trillion.[24]

Some have questioned whether such a gradual reform strategy was available to postsocialist European and post-Soviet countries after 1989. The Chinese model

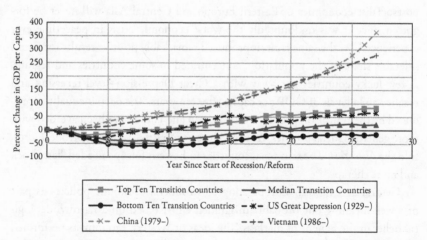

FIGURE 4.1. Postcommunist Transitions and Chinese and Vietnamese Miracles Compared.

Source: Maddison Project Database, version 2018.

was based on a Communist Party maintaining control—by violent force—in the face of reformist pressures (such as those expressed at Tiananmen Square in 1989) and adopting a long-term, relatively consistent policy of economic liberalization. In the Soviet Union and Eastern Europe, Gorbachev's reforms had mixed results, while in Central and Eastern Europe, communist parties lost political control prior to the launch of economic reforms. Could a gradual liberalization strategy have been adopted under more democratic conditions? Perhaps, if it had been recommended and supported by the IFIs at the time. However, since Central and Eastern Europe looked to the West, rather than the East, it applied shock therapy models that some Western advisors had advised in Latin America. It's an interesting counterfactual thought experiment, but we will never know what could have happened. Nonetheless, the China comparison continues to hang over economic debates about the costs and benefits of transition. For while Eastern Europe suffered, China prospered.

Conclusion

From an economic perspective, therefore, transition did not turn out as expected in the postsocialist countries of Eastern Europe and the former Soviet Union. It left prominent economists asking, "Why has output fallen so quickly and sharply in Central and Eastern Europe (CEE) and why has the fall persisted?"[25] Policymakers believed that a sudden stabilization and liberalization, accompanied by rapid privatization would produce the fastest and least painful transition from communism to capitalism. This proved wrong. What occurred in the postsocialist economies of Eastern Europe and Central Asia will never be forgotten since it was undoubtedly the worst economic crisis in peacetime ever experienced. At the same time, it produced remarkably positive results for a considerable share of the population, concentrated in some countries and regions. A few lucky countries got away with a Great Depression–level recession and reached 1989 levels of GDP per capita after ten years. The deep inequalities produced by the transition process were foreseen and could have been avoided with more generous social policies. As Bill Clinton's top Russia advisor, Strobe Talbot, told the *New York Times* in 1993, countries in Eastern Europe needed "less shock and more therapy."[26]

Central and Eastern Europe adopted neoliberal economic policies as part of a well-meaning but probably misguided effort based on a narrow ideological belief in the benefit of markets. The ideas of Western economists performed worse than those of their Chinese counterparts. Western economists knew that neoliberal economic policies would produce widening inequalities, and they did. Under these transition policies, a very sizable proportion of the population in the postsocialist countries did very well indeed, as returns to education increased, as people migrated to wealthier countries, and as free enterprise created new opportunities at home. However, at the same time, these reforms devastated less-educated, less-well-located, and more state-dependent populations, who lost the extensive guarantees of a socialist economy. As the China example shows, development of a vigorous capitalist economy was never going to happen overnight. The transition period was longer than expected by any experts, and many citizens had to wait an entire generation before they saw the positive effects of this "creative destruction."

The human costs of the transition—the collateral damage of building neoliberal capitalism—were the logical outgrowth of imposing capitalism on formerly socialist economies. Successes there were. Yet the scale of the human suffering cannot be denied. Even if one dismisses economic statistics on the basis of inaccuracy, it is difficult to dispute the demographic statistics, which show an alarming picture. The transition was accompanied by large increases in mortality and out-migration, together with immediate declines in life expectancy, fertility rates, and overall population. These crises hit different countries in varying ways, but all postsocialist countries suffered from massive shifts in health, behavior, and population. In many countries, population continues to decline, some thirty years later, creating a perspective on postsocialist transition countries that goes well beyond one based on economic data alone. It is to this demographic data that we now turn.

PART II

The Demographic Evidence

5

Where Have All the People Gone?

MANY DISCUSSIONS OF postsocialist transition begin and end by looking solely at the economic data. Since most experts considered transition primarily an economic process, and economists working within international financial institutions often spearheaded the reforms, this economic focus is understandable. In researching for this book, however, we grew curious about what other academic fields and data could contribute to the overall assessment of the social impacts of transition. In part because one of us is a political scientist and the other an ethnographer, we knew that data from different fields presented sharply opposed views of transition. Indeed, as discussed in the introduction, our collaboration started because we realized that we had different information and perspectives on the two competing narratives about the successes and failures of transition. In our exploration of the demographic data on Eastern Europe and Central Asia, therefore, we became fascinated by the ways these data had been elided or ignored by others proclaiming transition success, especially given that the transition coincided with the worst recorded peacetime population declines in history.

A glance through some recent headlines speaks volumes about the unexpected consequences of the transition. "Eastern Europe is headed toward a demographic crisis," declares Charles Lane in the *Washington Post*, explaining that "instead of feeling like the heroes of the 1989 revolution, or, at least beneficiaries, many Eastern Europeans look at aging, shrinking populations and consider themselves victims."[1] "Eastern Europe Is Shrinking before Our Eyes" and "The Fastest Shrinking Countries on Earth Are in Eastern Europe" are two headlines from *Axios* and *Quartz*, respectively.[2] In *The Atlantic*, Maxim Edwards investigated "Ukraine's Quiet Depopulation Crisis" while Al Jazeera asked "Why Is the Population of Eastern and Central Europe in Freefall?"[3] A 2016 *Financial Times* piece warned that "Eastern Europe has the largest population loss in modern history."[4] Four years later, writing for the same newspaper, Ivan Krastev declared that "depopulation is Eastern Europe's biggest problem," citing UN estimates to claim that the region had lost about 6 percent of its total population since the 1990s, or roughly 18 million people.[5] According to a 2018 report by the United Nations Fund for Population Activities (UNFPA) called "Shrinking Populations in Eastern Europe," the top ten of the world's fastest-contracting populations were all in Eastern Europe. And of the top twenty countries in that category, fifteen of them were also former socialist countries.[6]

Unlike economic processes that show up in short-term data, demographic processes are more complex, and discerning them requires a broader perspective over a longer time period. Furthermore, mortality, fertility, and emigration rates respond not only to economic factors but also to social, political, and cultural norms, as well as to larger structural conditions such as modernization, urbanization, increasing levels of education, and expanding access to health care and birth control, to name but a few. In general, however, demographers agree that lower mortality rates are better than higher ones, and that the increase in life expectancy is one measure by which we can determine the success or failure of a given society. Similarly, high levels of out-migration, especially if dominated by the young and educated, are worrisome trends for any country, particularly if many elderly citizens are left behind. Population graying and high dependency ratios affect most advanced industrialized countries, but in Eastern Europe the massive outflow of working age men and women is compounded by falling fertility rates. Young people make decisions about whether to stay or leave their home country as well as whether or not to start a family based on the perceived prospects of a good life at home. Although certainly harder to measure, a consistent dearth of babies and persistent exodus of youth signal that statistics about rising GDP per capita or surveys showing increases in self-reported life satisfaction are not telling the whole story.

When we started thinking about the relationship between economic data and demographic trends, we initially hoped to look for correlations between the two. But it quickly became apparent that demographic variables behaved independently of economic ones; in other words, countries that were doing relatively well economically (such as Poland) still experienced tidal waves of youth emigration to the West and declining fertility rates. Conversely, some countries, such as those in Central Asia, which suffered the worst economic freefalls after 1991 and had lower GDP per capita, saw rises in life expectancy. As such, we believe that it is disingenuous to evaluate the transition solely on the basis of economic inequality and long-term GDP growth, which anyway do not provide an accurate basis for comparison—not only because the effects of the transition recessions were so deep and unevenly distributed among different subgroups of the population, but also because the economic data do not make sense of the mortality, fertility, and out-migration crises that plagued the region after 1989.

An Overview in Maps

The divergences between the economic and demographic data can be visualized using a few simple maps. To create these maps, we divided the postsocialist countries into three groups for any given indicator: the best performers, the worst performers, and the average performers. To create these categories, we ranked them by the depth of the drop (or increase in the case of mortality), the length of time before they started to improve, and overall improvement from 1989 to 2016, averaged together. Based on this ranking, we identified the ten countries with the least severe crisis, the ten countries with the most severe crisis, and the median countries in each area. Because there are approximately twenty-eight postsocialist countries in Europe and Central Asia, this yields eight to ten countries in each category, depending on data availability. We assigned shading to each set of countries to produce some dramatic maps.

Compare Figure 3.1 to the following maps displaying the demographic impacts of transition. They look entirely different. Figure 5.1 shows the increases in the crude death rate for postsocialist countries after 1989. The postsocialist economic recessions were accompanied by an upsurge in crude death rates that was quite severe in many countries, particularly in Russia. Interestingly, the Central Asian states (among the worst hit by economic crises) did not experience as sharp an increase in mortality rates (due to lower overall levels of alcohol consumption).

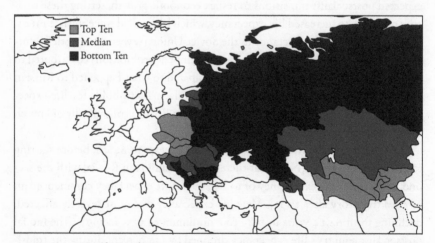

FIGURE 5.1. Crude Death Rate: Best and Worst Performing Postcommunist Countries. In order to calculate countries' ranking, first we rank them by % increase from 1989 to the highest death rate, length of time from 1989 to the highest level, and % decrease from 1989 to 2016. The overall ranking is calculated as an unweighted average of these three rankings. *Source*: Crude death rate (per 1,000 people) (World Bank 2018).

The ten worst-affected countries (including Russia and Bulgaria) suffered a massive increase in mortality, rising by an average of 40.17 percent at the apex in 2011 (and remained above 1989 levels in 2016; see Table 6.1). By contrast, the ten least-affected countries saw their death rates tick up by only 7.8 percent and began to improve by 1992.

What is even more shocking than the massive differences between postsocialist countries on this indicator is their geographic location. Central Asian republics such as Tajikistan and Kyrgyzstan counted among the worst-performing economies during this period, but their death rates did not increase catastrophically. Meanwhile, Russia, many other European republics of the former Soviet Union, and the southern Balkans suffered from the greatest increases in mortality. Some of these countries, like Ukraine, Moldova, and Georgia, had poorly performing economies. However, many others, such as Russia, Bulgaria, and Lithuania, were average in the extent of their economic collapse. Albania and Bosnia were among the least affected economies but experienced some of the highest mortality rates. For Bosnia, there is an obvious explanation: the war, which produced high death rates and, subsequently, massive amounts of foreign aid to stop the fighting. But not so for Albania.

Life expectancy can be understood as a measure of overall well-being, and in most developed countries, it increases gradually from year to year, as societies work to produce a better life for their people. Declines in peacetime happen rarely, and such declines provide a warning sign for an economy. Economists expected postsocialist transitions to restart economic growth, setting these societies on a path to increased life expectancy, which had stalled since the late 1960s. Indeed, declining life expectancy in the Soviet Union (reversed only briefly during the mid-1980s because of Gorbachev's attempt at prohibition) contributed to its ultimate collapse, but it was nothing compared to what happened to Russian citizens after 1991. Figure 5.2 shows that a similar pattern holds for life expectancy. Some countries that performed worse than Russia economically did much better in life expectancy.

Life expectancy in Russia dipped from 69.71 years to 64.46, before starting to grow again in 1994. [Note that there are two minima in Russia, with the second being 2003 (life expectancy of 65.05 years). Life expectancy commenced an upward trajectory after 2003]. Male life expectancy was most severely affected, declining from 64.24 years in 1989 to a minimum of 57.55 in 1995.[7] The modal postsocialist country's life expectancy dropped by 1.32 percent during the transition, before beginning to recover, reaching 1991 levels again in 1996. Strikingly, the mildest declines in life expectancy sometimes occurred in countries with the worst economic performance, such as Serbia, Georgia, and Turkmenistan. The worst declines in life expectancy were concentrated in the European former

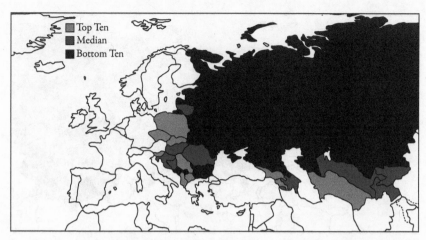

FIGURE 5.2. Life Expectancy: Best and Worst Performing Postcommunist Countries. In order to calculate countries' ranking, first we rank them by percent decrease from 1989 to the lowest level of life expectancy, length of time from 1989 to the lowest level, and percent increase from 1989 to 2016. The overall ranking is calculated as an unweighted average of these three rankings.

Source: Life expectancy at birth, total (years) (World Bank 2018).

Soviet Republics plus Kazakhstan, Bulgaria, Kosovo, and Montenegro. Estonia, an economic high performer, also suffered one of the worst declines in life expectancy. As explained later in this book, policy decisions (such as the speed or type of privatization) and the growth of informal and household economies, as well as cultural factors (such as religion, levels and types of alcohol consumption, and levels of social cohesion) help explain some of this variability.

Rates of out-migration force us to consider another set of factors, often related to geography and cultural or diasporic ties as well as membership in the European Union or historic ties to Russia. Countries that suffered high rates of out-migration were not always those with the biggest mortality or economic crises. Figure 5.3 shows that Russia, whose mortality crisis was among the largest, experienced net *in-migration* during the transition period, largely from the former Soviet republics. Countries on the borders of the European Union, as well as Central Asian countries with strong circular migration patterns to Moscow and St. Petersburg experienced the highest rates of out-migration. According to our own calculations, the average postsocialist country saw a population decline of 8.22 percent from 1989 to 2017.

Even relatively successful EU member states lost population at a dramatic rate. Croatia lost 14 percent of its population between 1990 and 2017—from 4.78 to 4.13 million—and continues to decline. Bulgaria lost 20 percent of its population between 1989 and 2017—from 8.88 to 7.08 million and is forecast to continue

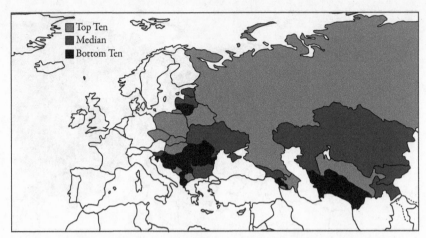

FIGURE 5.3. Net Migration Rate: Best and Worst Performing Postcommunist Countries. In order to calculate countries' ranking, first we rank them by percent decreases in net immigration rate from 1989 to the lowest level, length of time from 1989 to the lowest level, and percent increase from 1989 to 2016. The overall ranking is calculated as an unweighted average of these three rankings.

Source: Net migration rate (per 1,000 population) (UN 2017).

on this downward trajectory. Although some countries, such as Tajikistan and Turkmenistan, saw both high out-migration *and* population growth, many European postsocialist countries have yet to return to pre-1989 population levels and continue to decline, leading to all of the incendiary headlines noted earlier in the chapter. Indeed, existential worries about the population decline of titular majorities (Poles in Poland, Hungarians in Hungary) have fueled the rise of populist leaders promising to increase birth rates while resisting in-migration from non-Christian populations (e.g., Syrian refugees). This refusal to accept immigrants (largely for cultural reasons) means that many of these countries may have entered a potentially irreversible demographic death spiral.[8]

In the next chapters, our goal is to examine some of the endogenous and exogenous factors affecting mortality, fertility, and out-migration across the postsocialist region. Although we recognize the importance of diverse historical and cultural factors underpinning some of the long-term trends we hope to investigate, in general, socialist-era policies of universal access to health care (through the Semashko system), supporting women as both mothers and workers (through the provision of generous child allowances, extended paid parental leaves, and state-funded crèches and kindergartens) as well as severe limits on out-migration (through often draconian travel restrictions) conspired to create a relatively homogenous demographic situation in the region before 1989-91.

Where necessary, we look at longer historical trends beginning either before or during the communist era to elucidate the sudden and dramatic changes that shook the region after the transition began. Our goal is not to be comprehensive (that would be impossible in a book of this nature) but rather to highlight some of the demographic findings that further complicate the economic data presented in the previous chapters and relate them to some of the factors driving the recent increase of populism across the region.

6

The Mortality Crisis

TO ANYONE WHO lived through the 1990s, it should be no surprise that social-ist countries experienced a massive mortality crisis after the collapse of commu-nism, since this fact was widely reported in the media and scholarly literature. Moreover, anyone traveling to the postsocialist countries throughout the 1990s would have noticed scores of homeless men, mostly drunk, living in railroad sta-tions. Russia was the worst hit, with crude death rates climbing 53.27 percent to a peak of 16.4 deaths per 1,000 people in 2004 (see Table 6.1), primarily among men.

It is of course necessary to understand changes in Russia's crude death rate in historical context, since Russia has always seen vast fluctuations, and historically Russia started out with significantly lower life expectancies than those found in the West. In 1915, for example, while the Russian empire was still ruled by the tsar, life expectancy at birth was 34 years[1] (compared to 47 years in Germany[2] and 46 years in France[3]). In 1920, after the dual catastrophes of World War I and the Russian Civil War, Russian life expectancy fell to only *26 years* (compared to 43 years in both Germany and France). After 1920, with the expansion of the new commissar for health's universal health care system (eponymously called the Semashko system) based on state provision of basic care, free at point of service, the new Soviet government set about eradicating common infectious diseases. Life expectancy shot up 12 years to 38 by 1930, only to fall back down to 33 years in 1935 due to the widespread devastation wrought by Josef Stalin's purges and famines. By 1940, average life expectancy increased again to 41 years (compared to 62 years in Germany and 57 years in France), but then the Soviet Union took another massive population hit, losing an estimated 27 million citizens during World War II. At the end of the War in 1945, average Russian life expectancy was 24 years (compared to 46 years in Germany and 54 in France) (see Figure 6.1).

TABLE 6.1 Percent Change in Crude Death Rate since 1989

Country	Percent Increase (1989–Max)	Maximum Year	Percent Decrease (1989–2016)
Tajikistan	0.0	1989	47
Turkmenistan	0.0	1989	20.4
Slovakia	1.0	1990	5.9
Czechia	1.6	1990	17.1
Poland	5.0	1991	−1.0
Uzbekistan	4.8	1993	22.2
Hungary	5.1	1993	5.8
Slovenia	6.4	1993	−1.1
Kosovo	4.3	1999	−1.4
Kyrgyzstan	13.9	1994	23.6
Azerbaijan	14.1	1994	9.4
Estonia	28.8	1994	0.8
Latvia	36.1	1994	−19.7
Moldova	17.1	2007	−11.5
Armenia	18.0	2011	−17.1
Croatia	17.3	2015	−11.8
Kazakhstan	40.8	1995	3.0
Romania	23.4	2015	−21.5
Serbia	24.8	2015	−22.2
Bulgaria	27.5	2015	−25.8
Belarus	46.1	2002	−23.5
Ukraine	43.1	2005	−26.7
Lithuania	38.5	2015	−37.5
Albania	24.8	2016	−24.8
Montenegro	45.1	2006	−39.1
Georgia	42.2	2015	−41.9
Russian Federation	53.3	2003	−20.6
Macedonia	31.6	2016	−31.6
Bosnia-Herzegovina	49.6	2016	−49.6

Note: Percent increase measures the percent increase in death rate from 1989 to the maximum year. Percent decrease measures the percent decrease from 1989 to 2016, with negative values representing a percent increase.
Source: Death rate, crude (per 1,000 people) (World Bank 2018).

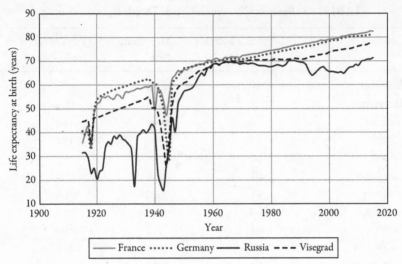

FIGURE 6.1. Life Expectancy in Russia, Germany, France and Visegrad Countries, 1915–2015.

Source: Gapminder (2020).

But after 1945, Russian life expectancy skyrocketed, peaking at about 68 years in 1970. The Semashko system had been quite successful at eradicating infectious diseases and lowering infant and maternal mortality rates. For example, in 1915, Russian mortality for children under the age of 1 was 267 per 1,000; by 1990 the rate was only 24 per 1,000.[4] But increasing life expectancy, diets richer in dairy and meat, and more sedentary urban lifestyles led to an increase in cancers and cardiovascular diseases. The Soviet health care system lagged behind the West in the provision of new treatments and preventative care, and as a result, life expectancy began a slight peacetime decline, falling to 67 years in 1985 (compared to 74 in Germany and 74 in France). Recognizing the ill effects of alcoholism, particularly on Russian men, the last Soviet premier, Mikhail Gorbachev, instituted a short-lived policy of prohibition in the late 1980s, which increased life expectancy to 69 in 1990. After 1991, life expectancy plummeted again, and Russia's mortality crisis "turned out to be the worst drop in life expectancy in the past half-century in any country that wasn't an active war zone or experiencing famine."[5]

The life expectancies of the so-called Visegrad countries of Czechoslovakia, Hungary, and Poland were historically closer to the experiences of the West European economies and rapidly closed the gap after the Second World War. Less developed countries such as Romania, Bulgaria, Albania, and Yugoslavia, however, started the twentieth century with average life expectancies far below those of countries like Germany and France, but they saw rapid increases in life

expectancy after 1945 due to modernization programs, the spread of universal
health care systems based on the Semashko model, and more attention to the
control of infectious diseases. For example, average Bulgarian life expectancy in
1935 was 50 years and rose to 52 years in 1945 when the country became part of the
Eastern Bloc and began building a socialist economy. By 1990, after 45 years of
communism, life expectancy steadily increased to 71 years, and, unlike in Russia,
did not begin to fall until after the transition period began.[6] Bulgarian infant
mortality rates fell from 130 per thousand in 1945 to 14 per thousand in 1990.[7]
In Albania, average life expectancy in 1945 was 40 years. After the 1946 estab-
lishment of the People's Republic of Albania, life expectancy steadily climbed
to 72 years by 1990, a massive gain of 32 years in just over four decades (see
Figure 6.2).[8]

As in the Soviet Union, these poorer, largely peasant countries rapidly industrialized and modernized during the communist period, allowing them to almost
close the gap with the West. But in most cases, life expectancies in Eastern Europe
began to plateau in the 1980s while the Western countries continued their
upward trend. Johan Mackenbach argues that this differential resulted from the
failure of socialist societies to cope with the onset of "degenerative and manmade
diseases." Basically, once a population begins to live long enough, a new set of
maladies begins to affect men and women who used to not survive long enough
to get cancer or suffer from strokes and heart attacks. Mackenbach concludes
that "autocratic governments are equally or more effective in reducing mortality
from conditions which can be controlled technically through the deployment of

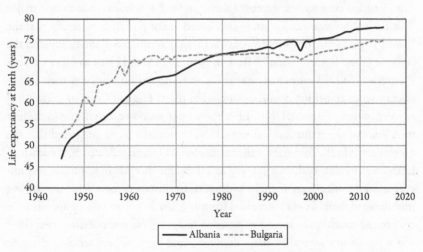

FIGURE 6.2. Life Expectancy in Bulgaria and Albania, 1945–2015.
Source: Gapminder (2020).

the state apparatus (e.g. infectious diseases). Alternatively, democratically elected governments may be more effective in reducing mortality from conditions which can only be controlled with the active participation of the citizens," through diet, exercise, and voluntary reductions in smoking and alcohol consumption.[9]

The transition period coincided with falling life expectancy. Most East European countries saw increases to the crude death rate after 1989, but they were much smaller than in Russia and other successor states of the Soviet Union. For instance, the crude death rate rose only 1.62 percent in Czechia, 5.07 percent in Hungary, 4.95 percent in Poland, and 0.98 percent in Slovakia, with mortality rates peaking one to four years after 1989 and then declining (see Table 6.1). By contrast, in nineteen post-communist countries, mortality rates remained above 1989 levels in 2016, in some cases very substantially. In 2016, Bulgaria's crude death rate was still 26 percent higher than in 1989, which could in part reflect the massive out-migration of young people and the higher death rate of the older population that remained. Life expectancy dropped sharply in certain countries, as shown in Table 6.2, though again the extent of these drops varied widely, from 6.8 percent in Russia to only 0.1 percent in Albania and 0 percent in Slovenia, Serbia, and Macedonia. Six former Soviet countries saw life expectancy drop by more than 5 percent after 1989. We now turn to an examination of the factors underpinning these declines.

Interrogating the Causes of Excess Mortality

The causes of the postsocialist mortality crisis are still hotly debated among epidemiologists, economists, demographers, and other scholars, but as one major World Health Organization study concluded in 2014, there is no doubt that the "health of people in the former Soviet countries deteriorated dramatically after the collapse of the Soviet Union."[10] Back in 1999, the United Nations Development Program (UNDP) estimated that there were 9.7 million missing men in the twenty-seven transition countries studied in their "Human Costs of Transition" report,[11] whereas in 2001, UNICEF reported 3.26 million excess deaths in the first nine years of the transition.[12] A 2010 UNDP research paper suggested that the excess deaths in the countries of the former Soviet Union reflected an epidemic of heart and circulatory diseases as well as a dramatic increase in homicide and suicide among working-age men. In Lithuania, for instance, the suicide rate among middle-aged men (45–54) increased from 109 deaths per 100,000 population in 1985 to 160 deaths per 100,000 population in 1995.[13] No one questions that there was a significant mortality crisis after 1989 and 1991. Where scholars disagree is how much of this mortality crisis can be laid at the feet of the psychosocial stresses caused by the rapid reform process. In other words, could these excess

TABLE 6.2 Percent Change in Life Expectancy at Birth since 1989

Country	Percent Decrease (1989–Min)	Minimum Year	Percent Increase (1989–2016)	Attained 1989 Level
Macedonia	0	1989	6.7	1989
Slovenia	0	1989	11.1	1989
Serbia	0	1991	5.2	1991
Slovakia	0.2	1991	7.8	1992
Albania	0.1	1992	9	1993
Armenia	0.2	1991	9.7	1993
Czechia	0.4	1990	9.3	1991
Georgia	0.2	1992	4.2	1995
Poland	0.6	1991	9	1992
Azerbaijan	0.3	1992	10.9	1994
Turkmenistan	0.1	1993	8	1995
Uzbekistan	0.3	1993	7.2	1997
Croatia	0.8	1992	8.6	1995
Bosnia-Herzegovina	0.9	1992	8	1995
Hungary	0.5	1993	8.8	1994
Tajikistan	1.2	1993	12	1997
Romania	0.8	1997	7.9	1998
Lithuania	4.1	1994	4.1	1999
Estonia	5.1	1994	11	1999
Kyrgyzstan	3.1	1995	4.5	1999
Moldova	1.3	1997	5.9	2004
Kosovo	0.9	1999	6.1	2000
Bulgaria	1.9	1997	4	2001
Latvia	6.4	1994	6.2	2000
Russian Federation	6.8	1994	3.5	2011
Ukraine	5.2	1996	1.3	2011
Kazakhstan	6.1	1996	5.9	2009
Montenegro	1.7	2000	3.5	2009
Belarus	5	1999	3.3	2012

Note: Percent decrease measures the percent decrease in life expectancy from 1989 to the minimum year. Percent increase measures the percent increase from 1989 to 2016.
Source: Life expectancy at birth, total (years) (World Bank 2018).

deaths have been avoided? If so, why didn't policymakers take more seriously the potential human costs of their programs? Or were these deaths an unavoidable cost for the construction of democracy and free markets in the region?

A large body of research focuses on identifying the specific causal pathways, which we will only briefly discuss here. In the epidemiological literature, scholars have studied the role of increased alcohol consumption, loss of jobs, loss of social status, stress caused by rapid change, declining spending on health care and social services, and fraying safety nets. The WHO estimates alcohol consumption in the former Soviet states to be among the highest in the world, though some countries, particularly the European former Soviet states, have far higher alcohol consumption than others.[14] It is also important to recognize that specific patterns of alcohol consumption (i.e., binge drinking) and the type of alcohol consumed (i.e., vodka, moonshine [*samogon*], or substitutes instead of wine and beer) also contributed to higher mortality rates. In 2001, Shkolnikov et al. showed that cardiovascular deaths of men in the Urals are strongly associated with binge-drinking.[15] In Barnaul, forensic autopsies conducted on 25,000 corpses between 1990 and 2004 showed that in 21 percent of male deaths attributed to circulatory diseases, the autopsied bodies had deadly or near-deadly levels of ethanol concentration in the blood. The researchers suggested that more than 50 percent of male mortality in Russia could be attributed to excess alcohol consumption.[16]

Increased alcohol consumption also helps to explain why the European former Soviet republics experienced sharper spikes in mortality than the Central Asian republics. Muslim men generally drank less and were therefore less likely to die during the transition, despite more severe economic crises in several countries. Ethnic Russians living in Central Asia also drank more than ethnic Kyrgyz, Kazakh, and Uzbek men despite the Russians' higher social status and lesser likelihood of being poor. While ethnic Russian males always had higher mortality rates than Central Asians, differences between the two groups spiked during the transition period.[17] Not surprisingly, therefore, Rechel, Richarson, and McKee concluded in 2014 that alcohol was the "principal cause of the rapid fluctuations in mortality that have characterized the Russian mortality crisis."[18]

But this just pushes the question back further. Why did Russian men, already known for their high alcohol consumption, suddenly begin drinking themselves to death? In 2010, political scientist Daniel Treisman suggested that the sudden uptick in alcohol consumption resulted from a dramatic decrease in relative prices for alcohol in the early 1990s.[19] During the communist era, alcohol was sold by a state monopoly with strict controls on store hours. With free market reforms, countries radically liberalized the market for alcohol production and sales, allowing unlimited consumption after a period of relatively strict control. The World Health Organization agreed that "governments in the Soviet and post-Soviet eras have contributed substantially to the alcohol problem through the production and distribution of cheap alcohol, as well as weak alcohol control policies."[20] However, during the brief attempt at prohibition in the late 1980s, the home production of cheap *samogon* as well as the increased use of alcohol substitutes (aftershave, etc.) undermined and ultimately forced the government to reverse its policy. So, there was more going here on a mere change in relative prices.

Today, many experts believe that increased binge-drinking was caused by the "stress of transition," measured as a dramatic drop in social security, an increase in crime, and a widespread fear of poverty and unemployment. Furthermore, social bonds were shredded by the sudden move to a market economy, although this process varied across the region. Indeed, Stuckler, McGee, and King argued that spikes in postsocialist mortality caused by mass privatization were mitigated in societies where citizens enjoyed stronger social ties, such as in Poland or the Czech Republic.[21] Being a member of a church group or a local soccer club provided valuable support for the newly unemployed, and the collapse of GDP per capita affected different communities in different ways. Whereas the recession brought some societies closer together, in places like Russia the economic turmoil also tore communities apart, devastating the social bonds that could have helped people cope with the chaos and upheaval of the early transition years (as we will see in the ethnographic chapters). Falling minimum wages also contributed to the psychosocial stress of the transition. In 2005, Brainerd and Cutler argued that "in Russia, the minimum wage fell from 30 to 35 percent of the average wage in the late 1980s to less than 6 percent of the average wage by 2000." They posited that the level of psychosocial stress in Russia was far higher than in the East European countries that "maintained a relatively high minimum wage throughout the 1990s," such as Poland (34 percent) and Hungary (42 percent).[22] Russia's mortality levels only began to improve in 2004 after Putin assumed power and the Russian economy began to stabilize thanks to higher oil prices.[23]

One case often overlooked—and not included in most datasets—is that of Eastern Germany, which ceased to be an independent country in October 1990. In 1998, however, researchers confirmed increased mortality rates for East Germans in 1990 and attributed these excess deaths to the "drastic social, political, and economic changes that took place during the transition from the socialist to the market economy."[24] The German authors of the study argued that the rise in deaths from alcoholism, heart and circulatory problems, and suicide *was causally related to the reunification process*, and mostly affected middle-aged men, as in other countries. In the former GDR, thousands also lost their lives prematurely from the psychosocial stress associated with the transition, but their suffering is invisible in our data because they became part of a reunified Germany and therefore were considered West Europeans. The World Bank and United Nations did not include East Germany as a transition country.

While alcohol consumption and psychosocial stress were probably the two key interrelated factors contributing to the postsocialist mortality crisis, gender, geography, and cultural factors also played important roles. During the transition period, it was predominantly men—in particular, poor and less-educated men— who turned to alcohol when they lost their jobs and could no longer support their families. Other unhealthy behaviors, such as smoking and poor diet, also contributed to men's worsening health. By contrast, women did what they could to earn and take care of their family.[25] One study attributed "59% of deaths among working-age men and 33% of deaths among working-age women in the 1990s to alcohol."[26] Social norms played a major role in this, as loss of social status clearly affected men differently and "heavy alcohol consumption was stigmatized among women."[27] Geography also mattered. Soviet single-company towns (*monogorodi*) suffered greatly from rapid privatization, as unemployed or underemployed workers in such towns could not easily find alternative employment and were more likely to drink as a form of entertainment. Monotowns also tended to be remote, making it difficult for people to travel elsewhere for work.[28]

As mentioned above, religious discourses also played a role, as this pattern of unemployment, despair, and men drinking themselves to death was far less pronounced in Soviet Central Asia, even though the economic collapse was equally or more severe. Muslim men did not drink as much as their Orthodox Christian counterparts (even if both populations were generally quite secular). One study comparing lifestyle factors in mortality in Kazakhstan and Kyrgyzstan, which has a higher Sunni Muslim population, found that "Muslims in both countries were significantly less likely to drink frequently and smoke," and that people in Kyrgyzstan had healthier lifestyles and five additional years of life expectancy despite being much poorer. In the 2001 survey that was the basis of this study, only 3 percent of Kyrgyz survey respondents indicated that they could afford a major purchase such as a new car or apartment. The vast majority of the population lived below the absolute poverty line of $4.15 per day as set by the World Bank. This survey also found that women had much healthier behaviors than men.[29] Another study looking at Russia, Kyrgyzstan, Armenia, and Georgia found that mortality patterns in Armenia and Georgia were more similar to those in Kyrgyzstan, despite Armenia and Georgia being majority Christian countries. "These more favorable mortality patterns occur even though these countries have been poorer than Russia and have in many ways been more severely hit by the post-Soviet economic crisis."[30] The authors posited that drinking patterns, particularly the leisurely consumption of locally made wine and cognac rather than the binge drinking of vodka, could explain these differences. They concluded that cultures of alcohol consumption "may largely trump macro-economic factors in generating specific adult mortality patterns in the region."[31]

Different policies of postsocialist liberalization also played a role. Some observers suggested that the excess mortality in the former Soviet Union and Eastern Europe resulted from a breakdown of health care infrastructure, but Brainerd and Cutler found little evidence to support this thesis.[32] Although studies confirm that the Soviet Semashko health system effectively collapsed after 1991, radically reducing the availability of free care for the majority of the post-Soviet population, many countries did at least try to introduce some form of a social insurance scheme based on Germany's Bismarck model. But outcomes varied widely across the region. In Kyrgyzstan, for example, the health insurance systems introduced after 1991 proved insufficient; they provided as little as 4 percent of total health expenditures.[33] The rest was made up by direct state funding and especially fee-for-service payments.

The slow and often unintentional privatization of the health care system happened because the old Semashko system had been funded from the central state budget and provided universal access for all citizens based on local catchment zones determined by residency.[34] After 1989 or 1991, the central government tried to devolve funding to local municipalities, to employers, or to privately managed social insurance funds. But municipalities lacked the resources, and employers often proved unwilling to contribute. The owners of private social insurance funds sometimes absconded with the monies collected, leaving hospitals and polyclinics without funds. In 1994, 14 percent of survey respondents reported paying a fee for medical care while in the hospital in Russia. That number increased to 45 percent in 1998. The informal fees paid also increased dramatically, from 40 to 66 percent of the average monthly salary.[35] But since many excess deaths were related to alcohol consumption, and most binge drinkers could not have been saved by seeking medical help, the haphazard privatization of health care systems was not as important as other social determinants of health, particularly the speed of enterprise privatization and the psychosocial stresses caused by sudden unemployment.

Did Mass Privatization Cause Mortality?

While most epidemiologists reached a consensus about the role of stress and alcohol consumption in the postsocialist mortality crisis,[36] the *role of government policies* in causing the millions of excess deaths after the collapse of the Soviet Union remains deeply controversial. In 2009, Stuckler, King, and McKee published one of the most incendiary articles about the demography and economics of transition.[37] "Mass Privatisation and the Post-Communist Mortality Crisis"

used regression analysis to show that countries that adopted a radical shock therapy strategy (including rapid mass privatization) experienced higher mortality
rates—by about 15 percent. This article received a stern rebuke from economists
of transition. Some argued that the methods were problematic and found that
adding lagged variables and changing the specifications slightly eliminated the
positive results.[38] Jeffrey Sachs, as quoted in the *Financial Times*, called the paper
"analytically profoundly flawed" and claimed that it "did not establish a causal
link."[39] Others suggested that the vast increase in alcohol consumption had more
to do with the end of the Gorbachev-era campaign for sobriety and the reduction
in alcohol prices in the 1990s.[40]

However, a team of epidemiologists led by the authors of the original paper
subsequently won the grant funding necessary to conduct a new set of face-
to-face interviews and surveys in Russian monotowns. They found that those
monotowns that experienced faster rates of privatization did, in fact, also have
higher rates of alcoholism and male mortality.[41] These surveys were bolstered
by others conducted in Hungary that showed that rapid privatization there was
also correlated with increased mortality. Although it remains controversial, this
work is part of a growing body of scholarship showing that neoliberal economic
reforms, and rapid privatization in particular, worsen health outcomes in transition and developing countries[42] —scholarship that is endorsed by the World
Health Organization.[43] For instance, "IMF economic reform programs are associated with significantly worsened tuberculosis incidence, prevalence, and mortality rates in post-communist Eastern European and former Soviet countries."[44]
Unlike alcoholism, tuberculosis is easily treated with increased access to medical
care. But the quasi-privatization of health services does little to diminish tuberculosis rates. Instead, tuberculosis rates drop dramatically in countries that increase
public health spending.

While some economists and policymakers blame the poor health of postsocialist populations on the legacies of communism or the cultural characteristics
of certain populations, the evidence suggests a more complex picture. This debate
is important to us because it posits that the excess mortality was avoidable. If
neoliberal economic reforms caused or exacerbated the mortality crisis in postsocialist countries, a different set of policies might have reduced the human cost.
The original article by Stuckler et al. argued that mass privatization alone may
have cut postsocialist population levels by a million citizens. It tried to provide a
clear link between the economic policies of neoliberalism and changes in mortality rates, work continued by looking at the effects of austerity and mortality in
Greece after the 2008 financial crisis.[45]

At the same time, we understand the resistance to drawing too strong a causal
link between neoliberalism, austerity, and human health outcomes. We admit

that there are many possible confounding factors, but it is also obvious to us that the proponents of neoliberal reforms—as well as those vested in the narrative of the transition as an economic success—often dismiss these findings. To even propose a causal link is to hint that the transition to free markets had real, and in some cases severe, human costs. Rather than admit that these human costs were necessary (and thus perhaps parrot early Soviet leaders who made similar claims about the necessity of the human costs for the transition to socialism), many economists either question the reality of these human costs or argue that they had nothing to do with the reform process.[46] These debates may never be settled, but the perception of victimhood on behalf of the populations of former socialist states had real political consequences today. The ongoing fertility crisis further compounds this idea of victimhood.

7

Collapse in Fertility

"Listen to me, we did not know where we stood after re-unification. Many people lost their jobs and did not have any money. And if you had a child, how is that supposed to work? After re-unification almost nobody has babies. It was really noticeable."

—33-YEAR-OLD SALESPERSON FROM
EASTERN GERMANY IN 1998[1]

"Before the Turn [the collapse of Communism in 1989], things were much simpler. It is a pity: now, one has to think of questions of survival, when thinking about having a baby. It wasn't like that before."

—25-YEAR-OLD EAST GERMAN WOMAN IN 1995[2]

"Even if I wanted another child, the first problem is that there is no place for it to live. To get pregnant with a second child, I have to live with my mother and bring my husband here or else go live at the home of a mother-in-law and father-in-law. I cannot afford to live in a rented apartment, to live on my own with anyone. It's very complicated. I don't know."

—28-YEAR-OLD BULGARIAN WOMAN LIVING IN
A FOUR-GENERATION HOUSEHOLD IN 2004[3]

ACROSS THE POSTSOCIALIST region, the onset of the transition period coincided with women's individual decisions to delay or forgo childbearing altogether. Although birth rates began to decline before 1989, the sudden introduction of free markets accelerated this process dramatically. In the 1990s, Russian demographers lamented about a graph they called the "Russian cross," a steeply rising curve representing mortality rates overlaid by a precipitously downward curve representing fertility rates. In the immediate years after reunification, the former German Democratic Republic experienced the lowest fertility rate in recorded history. Between 1989 and 1992, while Russia, Bulgaria, and Poland saw their fertility rates fall by 23 percent, 20 percent, and 5 percent, respectively, the fertility rate in the former East Germany dropped by 47 percent.[4] In this section, we examine some of the economic and cultural factors that may have caused the sudden drop in birth rates in Eastern Europe, recognizing the many challenges inherent in establishing a definitive causal link between the onset of free markets and individual choices to delay the start of a family.

In 2000, the United Nations Population Division estimated significant declines in populations for most of the European Union countries. The total fertility ratio (TFR) for the pre-accession fifteen member states stood at 1.5 children per woman in the period from 1990 to 1995—well below the replacement level of 2.1 children per woman (although this number hid significant variations among member states). After the accession of the first eight Eastern European countries in 2004, the EU average stayed the same, even though most East European countries had relatively higher fertility rates prior to 1989.[5] But it is also important to note that East and West European fertility patterns declined for different reasons in the second half of the twentieth century. Whereas Western European fertility declines resulted from the increasing age of mothers at first childbirth and the growing number of women who decided to forgo family formation altogether, almost all East European women had their first babies quite young and did not have subsequent children. Explaining the demographic puzzle of the near universality of childbearing and a relatively low maternal age at first birth with the phenomenon of lowest-low fertility in Ukraine in 2005, Brienna Perelli-Harris proposed that "when faced with such hardships as unemployment or lack of housing, couples do not usually delay first births, although they may delay or forgo additional childbearing. Because they do not believe that their economic situation will improve later, Ukrainian women decide to give birth close to the optimal physiological age. On the other hand, economic factors may make a second child prohibitively expensive for the average family."[6]

This marked difference in fertility patterns reflected different types of state policies toward family formation. In most socialist countries, for instance, governments provided explicit incentives to encourage early marriage and early childbearing, largely because, unlike in Western Europe, women were expected to be both mothers and full participants in the formal economy, due to both male labor shortages and at least a theoretical commitment to women's emancipation.[7] According to one 30-year-old bank teller interviewed by Susan L. Erikson in East Germany:

> We were 20 when re-unification happened. Usually you would have been married at 18 or 20 and had children then. It was a prerequisite to be

married in order to get an apartment. You married and had a child first, and then you built your own life. Now it is completely the other way around. First you live your life, and then you have children when you are about 30.[8]

Indeed, Eastern Germany had some of the most generous maternity benefits among the Warsaw Pact countries. As early as 1950, the East German state granted working mothers with more than two children special maternity grants and child allowances (*kindergeld*) as well as eleven weeks of paid maternity leave (with a guarantee that a woman's job would be held in her absence). In 1952, the state also granted married women a monthly paid day off of work to deal with their household duties, and in 1958, the maternity grant was increased and extended to all families, even those with only one child.[9] It is important to remember that most of these policies were in place in Eastern Germany before West German women even earned the legal right to work outside the home without their husband's permission in 1957![10]

East German maternity benefits got a massive boost in 1972. In that year, the socialist government increased the maternity grant, and introduced interest-free marriage loans for young couples. Job-protected, paid maternity leaves grew from eleven to eighteen weeks, and working mothers of more than two children earned extra paid holidays from work. Single parents were granted special sick leaves to care for children, and universities and workplaces built special onsite nurseries and kindergartens to make it easier for students and apprentices to combine their studies with parental responsibilities. In 1976, the GDR granted mothers a job-protected *babyjahr* (baby year) for their second and subsequent children (with the first 26 weeks at full pay and the second 26 weeks at a lower rate). Maternity leaves were increased to a year and a half if the mother had a third child or more in 1984, and by 1986 the *kindergeld* became even more generous and the *babyjahr* was extended to all women, even those having their first child.[11]

In Bulgaria in 1989, 84.7 percent of women were employed as wage workers outside the home.[12] As in the GDR, Bulgarian women benefited from a wide variety of social policies designed to ease their dual responsibilities as mothers and workers. Women here also enjoyed job-protected maternity leaves, which began a month and a half before delivery with the option of continuing until the child turned three. For a woman's first three children, this leave was fully paid by the state until the child was two years old. Employers could not refuse to grant it if it was requested, and the state recognized the leave as labor service and counted it toward a woman's pension. In addition to the paid maternity leave, new parents also received monthly child allowances until a child was 16 (or 18 if the child was still in school), with amounts that increased after the birth of second and third children. Moreover, rather than taking all of the leave herself, the woman could grant permission to the father or to his or her parents to take any unused portion of her leave, a provision that was often used by grandmothers to care for their grandchildren while mothers returned to work.

In 1949, only 35 percent of Hungarian women worked in the formal economy, but by 1970, 65 percent were employed outside the home.[13] As in East Germany and Bulgaria, Hungarian women enjoyed generous paid maternity leaves of up to three years by the late 1960s.[14] After women returned to work, they had access to a wide network of state-funded child care facilities. Between 1953 to 1965, the number of public nurseries (for babies under the age of 3) increased by almost five times. The state also constructed new kindergartens, increasing the number of facilities by 40 percent through the 1950s. Municipalities built nurseries and kindergartens in both residential neighborhoods and in workplaces allowing women to choose to drop off their children before or after the commute.[15] Similarly in the GDR, by 1989 the state had dramatically increased the number of child care facilities. In 1949, only 17 percent of children had child care places, but by the late 1980s, 100 percent of women who wanted a place for their children had access to one. Thus, before the reunification, 95 percent of children between the age of 3 and 6 attended kindergarten and 80 percent of children under the age of 3 had a *Krippenplatz* (crib place).[16] In Bulgaria, too, the state guaranteed working women heavily subsidized child care facilities, and as in Hungary, individual enterprises in Bulgaria often had onsite crèches and kindergartens, so that women could bring their children to work.[17] Similar policies were instituted across the socialist bloc, including in the Soviet Union, which actually experienced an uptick in its birth rate between 1980 and 1990 as a result of a new comprehensive maternity leave law passed in 1981.[18]

After the transition began in 1989, the once extensive state system of kindergartens and maternity supports imploded across Eastern Europe. Newly privatized enterprises closed their child care facilities. So did municipalities facing budget shortfalls. Furthermore, the liberalization of prices and the dismantling of public services often accompanied liberal economic reforms, pushing women out of the labor force. In Bulgaria, for example, there were 1,151 public crèches (*detski yasli*) offering 77,369 places for children under the age of 3 in 1980. By 2003, there were only 637 crèches offering 21,542 places, a 45 percent decrease in the number of facilities, and a 72 percent decrease in the number of places offered.[19] For kindergartens (*detski gradini*), there were 6,185 public facilities offering 420,804 places for children between 3- and 6-years-old in 1980 but only 3,278 facilities offering 201,145 in 2003, a 47 percent decrease in twenty-three years. As the public facilities closed across the country, private kindergartens did not replace them. In 2004, there were only twenty-six private child care centers offering a mere 708 places.[20]

Indeed, the dire lack of urban crèches and kindergartens caused great frustration for Bulgarian women after 1989 and was the subject of occasional popular protests in Sofia and Varna. On the other hand, as reported by Meurs and Giddings, high female unemployment, particularly in rural areas, also led to a severe decrease in demand for facilities. Falling enrollments caused more facilities to close.[21] In the former GDR, Susan Erikson heard a litany of complaints about the lack of child care facilities in re-unified Germany. One 39-year-old female computer programmer told her: "[Now] there is always the problem of child care and preschool openings, they are lacking everywhere, and that was never the case in [East Germany] times. Then you knew you'd get support, but nowadays, you have to fight for everything."[22] Another East German woman, a 30-year-old bank teller, explained that during the socialist years, "people lived calmer because they did not have to think about things. They knew they would get daycare, they had their jobs somewhere. Even if it was not exactly what they wanted, they had a job."[23]

It should be no surprise that once these provisions for child care, maternity leave, cash payments disappeared, women had fewer babies. With the exception of Central Asia, where fertility rates have always been higher than in Eastern Europe, almost all postsocialist countries saw sudden declines in their total fertility rates in the 1990s. In Russia, TFR fell from 2.85 children per woman during the baby boom in 1955 to 1.94 in 1980 before recovering to 2.12 in 1990. Russian TFR plummeted to 1.25 between 1990 and 2000.[24] In Hungary, TFR fell from 2.9 in 1950 to a low of 1.81 in 1963 before recovering to 2.1 in 1980. During the 1980s, the Hungarian birth rate fell to 1.81 in 1989, but after the collapse of socialism, it began decreasing to 1.4 children per woman until 2015 when it slowly began to recover in part because of Viktor Orban's pronatalist policies.[25] In Bulgaria, TFR declined steadily from 2.89 in 1950 to 1.95 in 1990. After the onset of the Bulgarian transition, TFR bottomed out at 1.2 in 2000 before ticking back up.[26] Figure 7.1 below shows the historical development of TFRs for selected countries between 1950 and 2015.

Although the reasons for the declines were complex, and part of the fall reflected a convergence with West European fertility patters and economic factors, new government policies also played an important role. In Central Europe, for instance, post-1989 governments pursued deliberate policies of "re-familization" to encourage women to stay home. As state enterprises closed down or were sold to private investors, unemployment rates skyrocketed. At the same time, displaced workers competed for jobs on newly competitive labor markets and new governments were encouraged to slash their public expenditures by defunding crèches and kindergartens. Some states compensated for closing kindergartens by extending parental leaves for up to four years, but at far lower rates

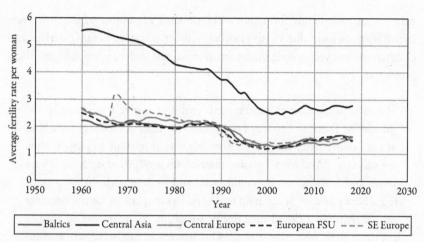

FIGURE 7.1. Total Fertility Rate, 1960–2018.
Source: World Bank (2020).

of wage compensation and without job protections.[27] As birth rates fell, demand for kindergartens decreased and more child care centers closed, creating a vicious cycle that some governments have tried to reverse with aggressive state policies to reintroduce generous family benefits in places like Russia, Poland, and Hungary and specifically in Poland, to limit women's reproductive rights.[28]

Of course, economic factors are not solely responsible for depressing fertility. In Central Asia, the Islamic religion and more traditional gender roles have contributed to higher birth rates despite poorer economic outcomes. In Russia, Cynthia Gabriel has argued that many forces—the cultural idea that women should have their babies before the age of 28, the lack of sober partners, early male mortality rates, the small size of urban apartments, the growing unavailability of grandmothers to help with child care, and the widespread social expectation that parents will provide their children a home—all contribute to suppressed fertility rates.[29] In the Czech Republic, Rebecca Nash attributes the low birth rates of the 1990s to the desire of young Czechs to enjoy their youth like their counterparts in Western Europe. Rather than starting families early, many young Czechs want to study, travel, and become established in their careers before settling down to parenthood.[30] The early age of first births common before 1989 is considered a distortion forced on them by the brutality of the planned economy and the one-party state during a time when men in the politburo tried to control the private lives of individual citizens through state policy.

Indeed, across Eastern Europe, particularly in the new member states of the EU, young people have become far more individualistic than their parents and believe that early family formation will limit their life options. Like their peers in the West, postsocialist youth prioritize self-actualization before marriage and children. As one young Bulgarian woman explained to the anthropologist, Maria Stoilkova:

> The most important thing for me is really to evolve intellectually and spiritually. There was no way I could drop my plan in exchange for a kind of cozy domesticity that my mother felt was important to pursue when she was 25. . . . And who is getting married anyway? All of my friends were single and it was great, we could travel and look into all that was exciting. There was a lot of catch up to do and to compensate for the times we missed living in a closed state during socialism. Many people decided to continue their education abroad. Our parents in fact were very encouraging of all this. I guess, though, if you live in a small town there's really not much to do but to go for marriage. What bothers me most about the culture of marriage here in Bulgaria is that people get married and they simply stop growing. It is another issue altogether with a child in your hands, obviously, you no longer can experiment with choices.[31]

As this quote shows, young people in Eastern Europe also looked at the new opportunities available to them after 1989 and considered early marriage and children an anachronism forced on previous generations by their living in closed societies. Remaining carefree and unattached, many of these same young people understandably set their sights on emigration to the West. Thus, without question, the most salient explanation for the collapse of birth rates in Eastern Europe and the European portions of the former Soviet Union have to do with the massive exodus of young people of childbearing age who set out to make new lives for themselves outside the countries of their birth.

8

The Out-Migration Crisis

WHILE IT IS well accepted that the effects of the prolonged recession, the mortality crisis, and the fertility crisis were negative, discourses about the large out-migration flows (see Figures 8.1 and 8.2) from the postsocialist countries remain controversial. Western Europe suffered from a spike of in-migration after 2015, and this was accompanied by a political crisis in several countries. But is it also a crisis when too many citizens leave? When the population declines? According to the Bulgarian scholar, Ivan Krastev, the out-migration crisis is one of the most important, if not the most important, legacies of the collapse of socialism.[1]

Some scholars argue that out-migration has positive impacts on the sending country, since most migrants go for economic reasons and enjoy a higher living standard inside the European Union or in other Western nations or in Russia than at home. Young people also have more opportunities for self-actualization and more educational and professional opportunities in wealthier societies. Furthermore, migrants send remittances, which raise the household consumption of those left behind. If and when migrants return, they may bring much needed skills and experience of working in the Western economies, leading some to talk of "brain circulation" rather than "brain drain."[2] As a result, Adrian Favell claims that "East European movers cash in on the premium of working in the higher-paid West, and East European economies develop through the two-way circulation of talent and capital."[3]

This talent and capital may lead to "modernizing" attitudes and social behaviors in the sending country as well as significant improvements to capital stock.[4] One group of researchers concludes that East European "societies are now much more like societies in Western Europe" as a result of return migration.[5] Economists theorize that exporting labor may also raise wage rates in sending countries.[6] Furthermore, one group of Polish researchers concludes that since men in rural areas more commonly migrate for work, poorer women in small

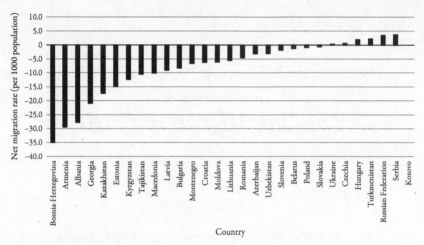

FIGURE 8.1. Net Migration Rate (per 1,000), 1992.

Source: United Nations (2017).

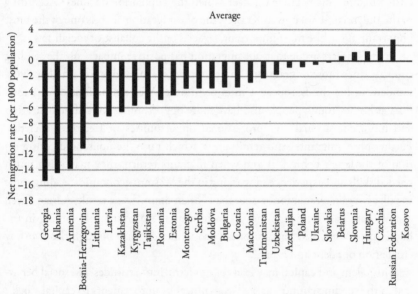

FIGURE 8.2. Average Net Migration Rate (per 1,000), 1992–2012.

Source: United Nations (2017).

towns tend to learn how to drive. Therefore, "Women's increasing equality in particular often seems to be an unintended result of migration."[7] While there is certainly a positive story to be told about the many new possibilities for travel, adventure, and emigration after decades of onerous travel restrictions, there are also some significant downsides.

East Europeans in the West

Although it is true that some East Europeans who have migrated to Western Europe enjoy higher living standards than they would at home, many work in the lowest paid sectors of the local economy and their presence is often unwelcome. For example, ethnographer Martina Cvajner spent years studying a group of ex-Soviet illegal immigrants in northern Italy and investigated the subjective experience of migration through the eyes of Russian, Ukrainian, and Moldovan women whose lives were disrupted by the sudden economic collapse of the 1990s.[8] Many of these women were formerly middle-class mothers and once enjoyed what they considered "normal" lives. As administrators, teachers, pharmacists, or doctors, they used to have their own apartments, spent weekends gardening at their dachas, took annual holidays at the seaside, and enjoyed the relative stability and security of the clumsily planned Soviet economy even as they struggled with constant consumer shortages. After surviving the chaos and upheaval of the 1990s, these women gave their children over to their own parents and struck out to make a better life for themselves and their families in the West, looking to earn money to pay back their debts and send remittances to their families back home. Cvajner details the deep sense of humiliation these women felt as they were forced to care for Italy's working-class elderly. The Italians often had less education and professional experience than their new caretakers, and the former Soviet women ironically called themselves *lavaculi* (literally: ass-washers), and felt that their lives had not improved much through migration to the West even as they enjoyed new opportunities for consumption and recognized the value of the remittances they sent home."[9]

In addition to these women from the former Soviet Union, Romanian migrants are the largest foreign national population in Italy, and tens of thousands of Romanian women work as domestic caregivers for elderly Italians. Despite the fact that Romanians can legally migrate to and work in Italy, they often labor for long hours for low wages and face discrimination and harassment. Because of a high female unemployment rate in Romania and the linguistic similarities between Italian and Romanian (both Romance languages), Italy attracts many Romanian women to take up these caregiving jobs. They leave behind their own children and elderly parents in Romania, creating a care deficit in their own homes. Romanian caregivers are so deeply exploited in Italy that many return to their own country with something that two Ukrainian psychologists dubbed "Italy syndrome" in 2005. Women who live-in with elderly wards are on call twenty-four hours a day, and they can lose their ability to feel emotion.[10] "Italy syndrome" describes women who return to Romania or Ukraine unable to express emotions or interact with their own families; they are apathetic, despondent, and drained of their ability to care.[11] For Romanian women working in agriculture, the situation is far worse. A 2017 exposé in *The Guardian* found that Romanian women working on farms in Sicily were routinely raped, beaten, and unable to leave.[12] They lived in conditions the investigative reporters likened to "21st-century slavery," citing a local police figure of about 7,500 Romanian women being held by their employers against their will.

In the United Kingdom, which opened its labor markets to EU citizens earlier than most Western EU member states, Polish migrants are the largest foreign minority and Polish is the second most spoken language after English. Largely concentrated in the low-wage construction, hospitality, and food-packing industries, Polish migrants generally do jobs that British citizens do not want to do.[13] The lead-up to the Brexit vote precipitated a palpable rise in harassment and hostility toward East Europeans: men have been punched and stabbed in the street for speaking Polish, and in the community of Huntingdon, Cambridgeshire, pro-Brexit fliers in English and Polish stated, "Leave the EU/No more Polish vermin" and were distributed in schools and delivered through local mailboxes.[14] Many Poles had lived in the UK for fifteen years or more prior to Brexit, worked and paid taxes, and were both shocked and outraged at a loss of EU status. In January 2019, Polish prime minister Mateusz Morawiecki issued a statement trying to lure Poles in Britain back to their home country to support the growth of the Polish economy, but many migrants have bought homes and had children in the UK.[15] These children have never lived in Poland and consider themselves British.

In the Netherlands, after a massive influx of migrants from Central and Eastern Europe, Geert Wilders and his far-right Freedom Party created a website so that Dutch citizens could write in to complain about the former socialist citizens who had settled in their country. In 2012, the website, called "Hotline Central and East Europeans," stated: "Do you have trouble with EU nationals? Or have you lost your job because of a Pole, Bulgarian, Romanian or other Central or Eastern European? We would like to hear."[16] Although widely condemned in the Netherlands as discriminatory, the website received 32,000 complaints in just forty-eight hours, showing the deep resentment many native Dutch felt toward the influx of EU nationals from the East.[17]

The anthropologist Leyla Keogh followed worker-mothers from Moldova to Istanbul where they also cared for the elderly parents of middle-class Turks but struggled against their illegal status and the derisive stereotype of the so-called "Natashas." According to the anthropologist Banu Nilgün Uygun, the Turkish media represented women from the former Soviet Union "at best, as tragic heroines created by the collapse of a system—as beautiful, educated and civilized women who, out of economic despair, are forced into the laps of uneducated, uncivilized, vulgar Turkish men. At worst they are portrayed as cunning, manipulative entrepreneurs who break homes, take away 'our money' and spread STDs."[18] Thus, although we recognize that there are many individual success stories of East Europeans making happy and healthy lives for themselves in the West, it is also important to acknowledge that, generally speaking, Western populations often have been hostile toward East European migrants, even those who come legally. Moreover, many East Europeans are concentrated in professions that West Europeans do not want to do, and they are poorly paid and living in precarious circumstances.

The Impacts on Those Left Behind

In addition to the discrimination that many East European migrants face in the West, there are clear indications that high rates of out-migration can be disastrous for sending countries and their populations, particularly when it leads to the loss of educated workers. In a February 2020 editorial for the *Financial Times*, a Romanian Member of the European Parliament (MEP), Clotilde Armand, argued that "Eastern Europe gives more to the west than it gets back."[19] Angry that the Western countries never account for the many profits Western corporations have earned by their expansion into previously inaccessible East European markets and by their exploitation of cheaper East European labor costs, she also highlighted the unaccounted for value of educated East European professionals working in the West. Reflecting on impending EU budget discussions in Belgium, Armand noted:

> The budget talks are often miscast as a showdown between whining eastern and central European countries asking for more cash and frugal northerners insisting their generosity has limits. . . . But look at the bigger picture and a different story unfolds. Much of the wealth in Europe flows from poorer countries to richer ones—not the other way around. Start with the brain drain. Europe's periphery is hemorrhaging young bright workers whose education was paid for by taxpayers in their home countries. Between 2009 and 2015, Romania lost half of its doctors. Every year, around 10 per cent of those that remain are actively recruited by human resources agencies seeking practitioners to treat greying western European

countries. This is not just a Romanian affair. Poland lost at least 7 per cent of its nurses and physicians in a decade. Surveys of Polish medical students show that more than half plan to leave after graduating. In Bulgaria that figure is 90 per cent. Croatia, which joined the EU in 2013, has already lost 5 per cent of its health practitioners. This exodus is a de facto transfer of wealth—and a big one. A single doctor's education costs the Romanian public coffers around €100,000. That spending does not appear in the EU budget negotiators' spreadsheets but it should. The annual drain of doctors alone represents more than a quarter of the funding that the EU sets aside each year to help Romania catch up with the rest of the club.

Armand concludes her editorial by pointing out that East and West Europe forged a social contract when the East European countries joined the EU: the East would open its markets to Western goods and services and the West would provide the funds for much needed infrastructure modernization and development in the East. In 2020, Western nations seem to want to enjoy the benefits without having to shoulder the costs.

Another negative impact of out-migration is on the elderly citizens whose adult children migrate abroad and are left behind to care for themselves. Under socialism, retirement ages were generally lower than in the West and grandparents often played an important role in helping to raise their grandchildren. In exchange, adult children would provide comfort and care to their parents as they aged, and in some countries, children are constitutionally obliged to look after their parents in the same way that parents must take care of children. But high levels of out-migration have upended this arrangement. In his ethnographic fieldwork in Romania, for instance, the anthropologist Bruce O'Neill narrates the story of a woman named Ana, a homeless senior citizen who had once worked as an accountant. After the coming of democracy, her firm was privatized, and she was laid off at the age of 48. Because she had been working for over twenty-five years, she was eligible for a full pension from the state but couldn't legally start collecting the pension for almost a decade. Ana tried to find work, but no one wanted a middle-aged woman. "I couldn't get hired," Ana told O'Neill. "After the revolution companies looked only for the young: girls and boys they could train. They didn't want to deal with people like me. . . . Time and again, companies saw me walk through the door, and they just looked the other way."[20]

For the first time in her life, she became dependent on her husband's income, but it wasn't enough to cover their expenses. They tried to sell their apartment but got swindled out of a large portion of the proceeds through a scam. Romania's corrupt postsocialist legal system offered no assistance. Her three adult children had emigrated to Cyprus, where they were starting their own families and had no extra income to send to their parents. Then Ana's husband died, and she could not afford the rent on their small apartment, so she moved into a homeless shelter for the elderly where she subsisted on her small pension. Ana was only one of hundreds of elderly Romanians who found themselves homeless after the traumas of the 1990s, their adult children having left the country in search of better economic opportunities in the West.

Some migration scholars from the global South also regard out-migration as a damper on development, noting that out-migration countries "experience a convergence between depopulation and the abandonment of productive activities in areas of high emigration."[21] Positive effects of return migration assume that there is a place left to return to. To some extent, the depopulation of rural areas was not necessarily a result of out-migration but of "metropolitanization," or mass movements of people from rural areas and small towns to the major metropolitan areas that experienced the greatest benefit from the liberal economic policies of the 1990s.[22] Under communism, most states had some form of address registration system that prevented migration from rural areas to the cities. Socialist economies did their best to industrialize rural areas, even when these industries were inefficient. In Bulgaria, for example, earnings from the profitable tourism industry on the Black Sea coast were reallocated to subsidize unprofitable rural industries to maintain full employment commitments.[23] With privatization and liberalization in the 1990s, most of these rural industries could no longer compete on global markets and were forced to shut down.[24]

In his history of Europe since 1989, Philipp Ther found that after a few years, the economies of "the capital cities Prague, Warsaw, and Bratislava . . . reached the average size within the [European] Union. The western parts of Poland, the Czech and Slovak Republics, and Hungary also profited from the upswing," attracting foreign direct investment in factories. However, the GDP per capita of poorer, eastern regions in Poland, for instance, was only about one-fifth of that in the capital. It was from these regions that out-migration was more likely, both to the metropoles and abroad.[25] After decades of having party leaders tell people where they could and couldn't live, is it any wonder that ambitious individuals struck out to take their chances in the big city? In Ukraine, for example, "the gap between Kyiv and the poorer regions widened to more than 6 to 1."[26] In poorer regions of Ukraine, average living standards were similar to those in developing countries such as Morocco or India and far behind the average for Turkey. "Scenes in the unspoiled Ukrainian Carpathians would fill any organic food enthusiast or hiking tourist with joy," Ther reports. "But local farmers perform arduous, back-breaking work. Few are able to sell their products in the nearest town because of the poor state of the roads. Almost all the dairies and mills have closed. The residents of the Carpathians are in a similar situation to the Alpine farmers before the construction of the railroad. They have just enough to survive."[27] Is it any wonder that young people flee the rural areas in droves?

Long-Term Impacts of the Migration Crisis

The scale of out-migration from Central and Eastern Europe has been extremely high in global comparison, with one IMF discussion paper claiming that it was "unprecedented in speed, scale, and persistence compared with emigration experiences elsewhere."[28] Another study found that Poland lost 3.3 percent of its population in the immediate aftermath of EU accession, from 2004 to 2007. These losses were particularly concentrated among young people aged 20 to 29 years, where as many as one-quarter of this demographic departed from some regions of the country.[29] In 2007, it was estimated that 6.6 percent of the Polish population was living temporarily abroad. "Migration from Poland became [the] domain of young and relatively well-educated persons coming mostly from relatively backward regions of the country."[30] As one major IMF report put it, "Emigration from Central, Eastern, and Southeastern Europe (CESEE) has been unusually large, persistent, and dominated by educated and young people." The report estimates that 20 million people have left the region since 1989, or 5.5 percent of the population, making this migration the "largest in the world in modern times as a share of sending country population." Southeastern European (SEE) countries were even more affected, losing 16 percent of their population. While acknowledging that emigration has had a positive effect on migrants themselves and on the EU as a whole, the IMF report found that "large-scale emigration—through its externalities—may also have slowed growth and income convergence in CESEE economies." The authors wrote:

> The significant outflow of skilled labor has reduced the size of the labor force and productivity, adversely affecting growth in sending countries and slowing per capita income convergence. With this trend, emigration appears to have reduced competitiveness and increased the size of government, by pushing up social spending in relation to GDP, and made the budget structure less growth-friendly. These effects are particularly strong in SEE and Baltic countries.[31]

While neoclassical economic theory would posit positive effects from emigration because of tightening labor markets, more recent endogenous growth theory "suggests that [the] welfare and productivity of those left behind may indeed decline if there are externalities associated with emigration. Specifically, emigration of high-skilled workers may lower the stock of human capital as well as the rate of return on capital and labor."[32] Furthermore, enterprises may not invest in high-skilled jobs in countries that are hemorrhaging high-skilled workers to the West.[33] Left-behind areas with lower-skilled workers may become less productive as a result. And these effects could be self-reinforcing over time. An IMF report also found evidence of a "negative feedback loop from permanent high-skill emigration to weaker governance that, in turn, has likely fueled more outflows of better educated people."[34]

The 2016 IMF report also claimed that "about two-thirds of CESEE countries witnessed lower GDP growth either on account of migration-induced loss of labor or worsening skill composition."[35] In addition, the IMF found that remittances, which are often said to improve standards of living in receiving countries, can also reduce recipients' willingness to work, increase wages, and increase the exchange rate in ways that depress growth. The authors report that "countries that have experienced significant outflows of skilled workers (the Baltics and SEE countries) have also seen greater upward pressures on domestic wages. . . . Real labor productivity has also been negatively affected by skilled labor outflows. A counterfactual analysis indicates that cumulative real labor productivity growth in CESEE countries would have been about 6 percentage points higher in the absence of emigration during 1995–2012."[36]

Thus, the statistics are clear: millions of workers have left the postsocialist countries, killing villages and small towns, and putting entire countries face to face with the prospect of an irreversible downward demographic spiral as they export human capital to the West. Out-migration, which occurs primarily in the relatively well-educated and capable working-age population, leaves a hole in domestic economies. It harms economic growth in the sending areas, just as it boosts it in recipient countries. In our view, countries that lose a significant proportion of their population are suffering from a crisis. In essence, one can view migration as people voting with their feet on the viability and desirability of living a life in their home countries.

In their book on the broken promises of democracy in Eastern Europe, *The Light That Failed*, Ivan Krastev and Stephen Holmes argue that East European elites brought this crisis on themselves by uncritically holding up the West as an ideal to imitate in the 1990s. If becoming like the West was the ultimate goal of the political and economic reforms after 1989, why would young people make the decision to stay in a country striving to become a perfect copy of the West rather than just moving to the West itself?[37]

It is also important to recognize that in a global perspective, future prospects for population decline in the postsocialist countries are also extreme. Not only have these countries lost 10 to 20 percent of their population in the last thirty years, but they are expected to lose *a similar or greater proportion* in the coming decades.[38] Obviously, this is not sustainable. According to United Nations projections, and as already mentioned, the ten fastest-shrinking populations in the world are all in Central and Eastern Europe. These populations are projected to decline by an additional 15 to 23 percent by 2050. Bulgaria's population is expected to fall from 7.08 million in 2017 to 5.42 million in 2050, a 23 percent drop. Those outpacing the world in population loss also include Latvia, Moldova, Ukraine, Croatia, Lithuania, Romania, Serbia, Poland, and Hungary.[39] As Ivan Krastev has emphasized, "Depopulation and demographic decline are the true tragedy of central Europe."[40]

Furthermore, there is reason to believe that, at least for some countries, official population data underestimate the extent of decline. One group of researchers, for instance, shows that census data from Armenia and Georgia reported population levels much lower than official annual population estimates, probably because of out-migration; however, authorities did not adjust the official data.[41] Moreover, many East Europeans remain formally registered in their home countries even if they have lived abroad for many years. They may return for visits in the summers and for important holidays, but they are making their lives elsewhere. Out-migration from the postsocialist countries is the flip side of the so-called in-migration crisis of Western Europe.

The Importance of Regional Differences

When considering the economic, mortality, and out-migration conditions together with the help of the visualizations (see Figures 3.1 and 5.1 through 5.3), one comes face to face with the regional dimensions of these crises. First, one cannot help but conclude that Central Europe, particularly the Visegrad countries of Poland, Hungary, Czech Republic, and Slovakia, plus Slovenia, did relatively well on the economic and mortality measures, as with other measures of the social impacts of transition. None of the three major transition crises hit these countries as strongly as elsewhere. There are many potential explanations. The Visegrad countries were not part of the Soviet Union and spent only forty rather than seventy years under communist rule, and Hungary, Czechoslovakia, and Poland all attempted to reform communism and faced brutal interventions or martial law before 1989. They are predominantly Catholic and Protestant rather than Christian Orthodox or Muslim. People in these countries tend to drink wine and beer rather than vodka and other spirits. The Visegrad countries also lie to the West and have closer historic ties and trade relations with Western Europe. They were quick to recognize themselves—and to be recognized—as European and be integrated into NATO and the European Union.

All other transition countries beyond these five were affected more severely by at least one or two postsocialist crises. The postsocialist mortality crisis hit the European post-Soviet countries more severely than others, including countries with average economic crises like Russia, countries with severe economic crises like Ukraine and Moldova, and countries with relatively strong economic performance like Estonia. Leading scholars have identified a "mortality belt" in the western post-Soviet countries. Yet other countries that border this "mortality belt" and experienced similar economic shocks "recorded negligible increases in mortality rates during their transition from communism."[42] Similarly, most East European countries registered drastic fertility declines, but in Central Asia higher birth rates supported natural population increases. Geographic and cultural factors may help to explain the diverse social impacts of transition.

The migration crisis appears to have hit Southeastern Europe particularly hard, despite increases in life expectancy and lesser mortality crises. Countries with higher than average life expectancy like Croatia or relatively strong economic performance like Romania still experienced above average rates of migration. It appears that migration was driven by cultural ties and geographic proximity to the European Union. This may explain why relatively richer countries experienced dramatic out-migration even when the length and depth of their economic and mortality crises were not as severe. People leave when they perceive the chance for better lives elsewhere and the relative differences in standard of living or pay are greater.

The differences in Central Asia are pronounced. Many Central Asian countries were among the worst affected by economic crises, but their demographic responses have been sharply different. Fertility rates remained higher in Central Asia, and as life expectancy improved more quickly, population surged, particularly in Tajikistan (from 5.15 million in 1989 to 8.92 million in 2017) and Uzbekistan (from 19.98 million in 1989 to 32.39 million in 2017).[43] By contrast, the average European postsocialist country saw its population decline by 8.22 percent in the period from 1989 to 2017. Central Asians also migrated for work, primarily to Russia, but because of the population boom, out-migration did not have the same devastating effects on their domestic economies back home. Although this diversity of outcomes makes it difficult to posit one clear set of causal mechanisms, there is no doubt that the onset of transition in the 1990s had largely negative impacts on mortality and fertility and significant effects on migration whether for better or for worse.

Conclusion

When we consider the economic, mortality, fertility, and migration crises taken together, we find further evidence that the social contract was shattered in the former socialist countries. While this social contract may have been based on unsustainable and repressive political and economic programs, it functioned (at least rudimentarily) for over four decades in Eastern Europe and for over seven decades in the USSR. After 1989, policies that had been in place for generations simply disappeared overnight, leaving people to fend for themselves. Nurseries and kindergartens closed, and health care became less accessible. Child allowances and public subsidies for rents, utilities, and basic foodstuffs vanished. While many succeeded in market competition, winning for themselves and their families a much brighter and more prosperous future, many women, rural dwellers, pensioners, and people at the lower end of the income distribution lost things that they once considered basic rights. Now, electorates in the postsocialist countries are clamoring for a social system that puts the majority of the people and national development at the center of public concern. Even IFIs have become worried that their policies may not be sustainable if they do not enjoy widespread support and are seeking ways to rebuild social trust after the economic, mortality, and out-migration crises of the transition period. To understand the full scale of the damage done to social trust, we now turn to evidence on public opinion, democracy, and markets, which has fluctuated throughout the transition period.

PART III

The Public Opinion Evidence

9

Disappointment with Transition

IN 2006, THE European Bank for Reconstruction and Development (EBRD) and the World Bank undertook the first massive public opinion survey that covered all twenty-eight postsocialist transition countries from Central and Eastern Europe to Central Asia (minus Eastern Germany).[1] Up to that point, international financial institutions (IFIs) had not regularly inquired about public opinion on the ongoing process of transition. But in 2006, IFIs thought it important to evaluate the successes and failures of economic reforms and adjustment in the eyes of the public. Unlike previous surveys such as Eurobarometer or the New Europe Barometer, the EBRD and World Bank's new Life in Transition (LiT) surveys included Russia and all of the former Soviet republics, making it possible to finally compare public opinion on transition throughout the postsocialist states.[2]

If this had happened much sooner, the feedback from the affected populations might have been useful for policymakers. LiT's first wave consisted of 1,000 face-to-face interviews in each of the twenty-eight postsocialist countries for a total sample of 28,000 respondents. In a dedicated report, the EBRD broke the countries into three regions: Central Europe and the Baltics (CEB), Southeastern Europe (SEE), and the Commonwealth of Independent States and Mongolia (CIS+M). Yet, in contrast to what its sponsors might have hoped for, the LiT produced surprising, even jolting, results. Postcommunist populations showed a surprising level of discontent with markets and democracy. Despite the rapid economic growth of recovery from postcommunist transitions, the majority of people remained disappointed.[3]

This disappointment surprised the researchers because they conducted the 2006 Life in Transition (LiT1) survey at a relatively good time for the economies of Central and Eastern Europe and Central Asia. Fifteen years into the transition process, the chaos of the 1990s was behind them, and most countries were experiencing rapid economic growth in the early years of the twenty-first century. Poverty rates had peaked in 1999 and had started to fall. Between 2000 and 2007, Central Europe and the Baltic (CEB) countries, as well as Bulgaria and Romania, joined the European Union and gained access to credit with which to purchase homes, cars, and other consumer goods previously beyond their reach. As a result, the EBRD perhaps sought to use the LiT survey as an opportunity to publicize the encouraging results of transition. Although the EBRD recognized that the goods of the new consumer society were being distributed unevenly, their report accentuated the positive and expressed optimism about the future. For instance, of those adults surveyed, 54 percent agreed that children born in 2006 would have a "better life" compared to their own generation. Furthermore, as with previous public opinion studies conducted in individual countries (as discussed in Chapter 11), the young, urban, and educated felt good about their future prospects. Given the generational disparities, it made sense to downplay the sentiments of those too old or undereducated to take advantage of the new opportunities.

But even the EBRD chief economist, Erik Berglöf, admitted that the LiT revealed that not all was well in the postsocialist region. In 1999, roughly 191 million people in the region had been living on less than $5.50 a day, many who were working full time but not earning enough to meet their most basic needs, leaving significant legacies of poverty.[4] Citizens coped by growing their own food in summer dachas or garden plots and not shopping at convenient supermarkets but at open air markets where prices were cheaper.[5] In countries such as Russia or Ukraine with brutally cold and long winters, $5.50 a day was barely enough to cover heating costs and the number of calories necessary to fuel an ordinary metabolism in sub-zero temperatures. For many East Europeans, postsocialist winters meant "heat or eat." During the communist era, heat had often been free and basic foodstuffs heavily subsidized, highlighting a visceral contrast between past and present. In his preface to the report, Berglöf opined: "It is important to keep in mind that the damage done during the hard times, not only to material well-being but also to general levels of trust and subjective well-being, should not be underestimated. All of us who strive to promote transition have some work to do to convince people in the region of the benefits of transition and to restore trust in public institutions and in each other."[6] Berglöf's concern stemmed from worrying trends in the survey data that showed a deep fissure between how economists measured the economy and how average people felt about it, which is the subject of this part of our book.

In the first place, only 30 percent of those surveyed believed that the economic situation in their country in 2006 was better compared to "around 1989," though few economists would have guessed this from World Bank and IMF data, which showed that most countries had recovered and exceeded their 1989 levels by that point. Fewer than 40 percent reported that the political situation in 2006 was better compared to the period before the transition. Although younger and richer subgroups were relatively more optimistic about the political and economic situation, the overall results were not what the EBRD hoped to find after fifteen years of "successful" transition. Fewer than half of the respondents reported that they were satisfied with their lives in 2006, with over a third reporting that they were dissatisfied with their lives (the others were neither satisfied nor dissatisfied). In Western Europe, only 11.6 percent of citizens reported being dissatisfied in 2006, according to Eurobarometer.[7] In terms of support for the free market and liberal democracy, attitudes toward democracy were more positive than those toward the free market, and nowhere did more than 50 percent of respondents agree that "a market economy is preferable to any other form of economic system." About a fifth of the respondents agreed that "under some circumstances a planned economy may be preferable to a market economy," and the rest claimed that "for people like me, it does not matter." By contrast, nearly two-thirds (62.4 percent) of Western Europeans expressed being "very" or "fairly" satisfied about the way democracy worked in their countries.[8] A postcommunist social contract based on markets and democracy had failed to win the confidence of a majority of the population.

Indeed, support for "democracy and a market economy" combined only reached 37 percent in the LiT, with about 10 percent advocating a return to "authoritarianism and a planned economy" and another 4 percent hoping for "authoritarianism and a market economy" (the Chinese model). Interestingly, in both Southeastern Europe and the Commonwealth of Independent States plus Mongolia, 12 percent of respondents wanted "democracy and a planned economy."[9] The LiT showed that only a minority bought into the J-curve narrative about the success of markets and democracy. A majority of citizens did not, at least not fully. In part, this was because of the contingent nature of some of the questions asked, such as asking whether a planned economy might be better "under some circumstances." But still, in 2006, the report seemed to show that democratic capitalism commanded the support of only a *minority* of the population.

Even more troubling, though, were the findings about faith in public institutions and general attitudes toward fellow citizens. When asked whether there was less corruption in 2006 than there was in 1989, only 15 percent of respondents agreed, with a full 67 percent saying that they disagreed. Young people between the ages of 18 and 34 were particularly affected by this corruption. The EBRD noted, "In Russia, the corruption in schools is thought to be ubiquitous. As one citizen remarked, 'You have to pay for everything now. Even in secondary schools;

everything appears to be free but at the same time the school is asking for money all the time—for renovation and other things. From secondary school onwards parents pay for good marks and for their kids to pass their exams. A child needs good marks in their school diploma in order to go further. Schools take money from parents, they do everything for money. Certainly teachers need to feed their children. But if corruption starts in secondary school, what kind of professionals will we get as the result?' "[10]

Another striking result of the 2006 Life in Transition survey was the low level of trust people reported in their fellow citizens; whereas two-thirds of respondents believed that most people could be trusted before 1989, only about a third agreed that most people could be trusted in 2006. This result was consistent across the sub-regions, and in no age group or income category did fewer than 50 percent of the respondents believe that people were generally "more trustworthy" under the old regime. Again, it is important to remember that the first wave of the Life in Transition was conducted in the fall of 2006, well before the effects of the global financial crisis made themselves felt in the postsocialist countries. The EBRD sought to put an optimistic spin on these results by emphasizing the positive, seeing hope in the more strongly pro-democratic and pro-market opinions of the young, urban, well-educated, and relatively well-off. The EBRD's report concluded that things were still heading in the right direction. The transition process just needed more time. However, the global financial crisis was right around the corner. Support for markets and democracies dipped in 2010, the second time the LiT survey was conducted, before recovering in 2016 in LiT3. But the troubling question remained: if postsocialist economies had improved as much as average economic figures suggested, why was the majority of the population disappointed?

One answer was the growth in inequality. More specifically, the public opinion literature shows that people evaluate political and economic systems from two different viewpoints: egocentric and sociotropic. From an egocentric or self-interested perspective, people evaluate economic and political institutions by asking: what do these institutions do for me? Not surprisingly, we find that after 1989, when some became billionaires while others were cast out on the street, "winners" and "losers" of the transition developed sharply different views of how political and economic systems were functioning. Their views mirrored individual self-interest. Those who suffered were more critical. Those who benefited were satisfied. As inequality widened, however, citizens felt losses more intensely. Whether average incomes were going up or down, those at the bottom of the income distribution sank relative to others and those at the top rose. The distance between groups was increasing, giving those lower down the income distribution the sense that they were falling further behind. Thus, inequality may have weakened support for reform by giving a greater proportion of people the impression that they were relative losers.

But perhaps more important, postcommunist populations were not only thinking about themselves. Like other populations, citizens of the postcommunist countries also evaluated their new political and economic institutions in sociotropic terms. They evaluated the shocking changes of the 1990s through the lens of how they reshaped society as a whole and whether the new system overall was good or bad and whether it accorded with their values. Since the vast majority of the postcommunist population grew up under communism and continued to support socialist values of government redistribution and job guarantees, postcommunist populations often regarded their post-transition societies as unfair and unjust.[11] As Pop-Eleches and Tucker concluded in the most exhaustive book to date on communist legacies for public opinion, "Citizens of post-communist countries are more likely to think the state is responsible for individual-level welfare."[12] Rising unemployment and inequality offended their sensibilities. Since hustlers, black marketeers, and former communists seemed to take advantage of new opportunities to a disproportionate extent, postcommunist populations came to believe that the new capitalist elite had gained its wealth through corruption and greed. As a result, people lost faith in public institutions and trust in their compatriots. As one Russian citizen remarked, "Russia doesn't have a future. The country is heading for collapse and the Russian people will be destroyed, thanks to our authorities—a load of thieves with large amounts of money in the bank."[13] The bottom line: for both egocentric (self-interested) and sociotropic (society-related) reasons, rising inequality produced more disappointment with markets and democracy than one might expect by studying average economic growth rates alone. If the IFIs had been looking at public opinion all along, they might have been better equipped to address the deep resentments that linger in the region to this day.

Collecting and Using Public Opinion Data

In our attempts to use public opinion data to analyze postcommunist transition, we encountered a few problems. First, in contrast to economic data, which are readily available because they are collected annually by the World Bank, the European Union, the EBRD, the IMF, and the other agencies of the United Nations system, public opinion data were considered so marginal to problems of transition that international financial institutions did not bother to collect it systematically. Second, while postcommunist public opinion data are not entirely lacking, we found coverage to be spotty in our extensive efforts to collect cross-national comparative data for all countries of the postcommunist period.

Institutions and researchers often studied only a subset of postcommunist countries in large, cross-national projects—surveying Russia, for instance, or European
Union members and candidates rather than the Western Balkans or Central Asia.
Even the EBRD's Life in Transition surveys included different sets of countries
in each of its three iterations in 2006, 2010, and 2016, making it difficult to track
changes over time for the whole region.

Third, different institutions used different survey questions to assess public
feelings about the transition process, and even the same institutions changed the
questions of their surveys over the years. For example, some key questions, such as
popular support for the market economy, were dropped from the Eurobarometer
surveys after 1997, making it difficult to contrast popular support for democracy
with support for capitalism. Also, the way the EBRD's Life in Transition asked
about support for a market economy differed sharply from Eurobarometer's
formulation. As a result, broad, cross-regional comparisons of public attitudes
toward transition rest on limited data, indicating the lower priority international
organizations placed on learning what people thought. Somewhat ironically,
the international financial institutions seem to have embraced a rather Marxist
materialist mindset, believing that public attitudes would follow economic performance. The superstructure of popular opinion did not warrant systematic
examination until problems arose.

Fourth, as with any international surveys, there is also the problem that different populations interpret the same questions through the lens of their own cultures and societies. Questions about happiness and life satisfaction are notoriously
subjective, as are people's feelings about the future. Michael Mutz, for instance,
has shown that for a significant subset of the German population, self-reported
life satisfaction noticeably increased during the 2016 Union of European Football
Associations (UEFA) European Cup but returned to baseline within two months
of the football (soccer) championship.[14] Similarly, the annual Eurovision Song
Contest seems to marginally increase life satisfaction in the countries that compete when compared to those that do not compete, thus leading researchers to
consider more seriously the public health benefits of national participation in
international events.[15] These methodological challenges often result in a devalua-
tion of public opinion surveys.

Finally, international surveys also face problems of interpretation. Some of
these arise from the way that different agencies and international institutions
report on the data they produce and the public relations function that data
reporting from surveys can serve. For example, the World Bank and the EBRD
are two international financial institutions with a vested interest in the narrative of transition as a success because they designed the policies implemented in
the former communist countries after 1989–91. The three large Life in Transition

surveys conducted by the EBRD investigated public opinion in the region but interpreted the results to highlight the *successes* of its work in the region and downplay the failures.

But combined with economic, demographic, and ethnographic data, as we do in this book, public opinion data can contribute to a more holistic picture of the transition and provide a valuable window onto the thoughts and moods of the wider populace. The following chapters therefore examine a sample of the public opinion data produced over the last three decades, but they also explore the interpretation and dissemination of those data. Despite the overall rosy picture of transition success painted by international financial institutions, public opinion data have consistently shown limited commitments to democracy and free markets that present an important challenge to the J-curve narrative. In deeply divided societies, such as Russia of the 1990s, these issues of interpretation may matter more.

Public Opinion of Winners and Losers

IF CITIZENS EVALUATE transition from an egocentric or self-interested standpoint, one might anticipate that winners of transition, more than losers, would support economic reforms. This would be particularly true in a country with rapidly increasing inequality, such as Russia, where winners became billionaires and losers were forced to beg on the streets. To evaluate just how differently winners and losers might evaluate reforms, political scientists Judith Kullberg and William Zimmerman examined public opinion surveys of Russian elites and ordinary citizens in two parallel surveys conducted in 1992–93 (among Russian elites and the population of European Russia) and in 1995–96 (among Russian elites and the population of all of Russia).[1] The elite samples were carefully constructed to elicit opinions from five strategic sectors of the economic, political, and cultural elite; the researchers interviewed (1) journalists and editors, (2) high-level enterprise managers, (3) elected and appointed politicians, (4) academics, and (5) military officers.

In their 1999 paper, "Liberal Elites, Socialist Masses, and Problems of Russian Democracy," the authors hypothesized that the economic losses associated with transforming a centrally planned socialist economy into one based on free markets would inevitably reduce popular support for democracy because in Eastern Europe, democracy and free markets were inextricably intertwined in the 1990s. The economic pain necessary to establish markets fell *unevenly* across society as the creation of private sector employment could not keep pace with the collapse of public sector jobs. Without meaningful opportunities for reeducation and training, the categories of people who lost social status and experienced extreme economic hardship were vast. These included women and minorities (such as Roma)[2] newly discriminated against in competitive labor markets; middle-aged professionals and workers with decades of experience unable to retool their skills for the new economy; and pensioners forced to live on fixed incomes in a world of newly liberalized prices. Because citizens understood that the transfer of previously state-owned wealth would accrue to the Westernizing elites in the best position to benefit from privatization, many former Soviet citizens turned against the ideals of liberal democracy and free markets, clinging instead to their old communist ideologies or grasping for newly emerging nationalist ones. The marginalized voices of these so-called losers of the transition process would not be represented if researchers had spoken only with elites in Moscow or St. Petersburg. Kullberg and Zimmerman argued that these voices mattered and that they would "pose a long-term challenge to the postcommunist order and the legitimacy of Russian democracy."[3]

The authors found significant discrepancies not only between the elite and the mass public, but also between different sectors of the public. Those most likely to reap the rewards of political and economic liberalism—the young, the well-educated, and the well-connected—were more likely to support democratic and free market reforms. For example, in the mass survey of 1995–96, respondents were asked what type of political system would be most suitable for Russia: the old Soviet one, the present political system (of Russia in the mid-1990s), or a Western-style liberal democracy. Almost half of the respondents preferred the old Soviet regime (49 percent). Just over a third (34.4 percent) preferred the present order, and only 17 percent believed that a Western representative democracy would be suitable for Russia, showing deep discontent with the objectives of transition. When the authors dug into the public opinion data further, they found that women, the elderly, the less well-educated, and those living in smaller towns and villages were more likely to prefer the old Soviet regime, and they suggested that these populations understood that they would be economically disadvantaged in a more liberal political order. Kullberg and Zimmerman claimed that the

> ideological variation—both between elites and the masses and within the mass public—is largely the result of differences across groups and individuals in the postcommunist structure of economic opportunity. Support for liberalism is causally related to the ability of individuals to participate in the new economic order: those who are "locked out" of the new economy are constrained by circumstances and context from improving their conditions will be more likely to express antiliberal attitudes. Thus, what largely accounts for the elite's embrace of liberalism, and conversely, its non-acceptance by a considerable portion of the Russian mass public *is not simply economic decline, but the differential impact of economic restructuring on opportunities, and, therefore, long-term material prospects of groups and individuals* [our emphasis].[4]

In their conclusion, Kullberg and Zimmerman postulate that the democratic transition in Russia in the 1990s was being led from above, spearheaded by liberalizing elites who perceived opportunities for personal gain in the new system. The vast majority of the Russian public was opposed to Western style liberal democracy and felt that the economic and political reforms were being imposed · on them. The authors urged their colleagues in political science not to ignore the importance of the sentiments expressed in the public opinion data. They believed (back in 1999—before the first election of Vladimir Putin) that these anti-liberal tendencies would not disappear with time but would deepen and spread if the economic rewards of liberalism were not more evenly distributed throughout Russian society.

In our own analyses of the Russian Longitudinal Monitoring survey, we find further evidence of low support for reform in Russia in the 1990s. Life satisfaction remained below 20 percent overall until 2001, when the economy began to improve after Putin's election. The data show that men and urban residents were more satisfied than women and rural residents by 4 to 5 percentage points on average. By 1999, only 11 percent of respondents believed their family would live better in a year, a number that only rose above 20 percent in 2001. Again, men and urban residents were more hopeful about their financial situation by about 3 to 4 percentage points. Economic decline clearly damaged perceptions of transition, but some groups were more despondent than others, based on their perceived prospects in the new capitalist economy and the growth of relative inequality.

Declining Support for Markets in Central and Eastern Europe

At the same time, public opinion in Russia differed greatly from views in Central and Eastern Europe, where opportunities for trade with the West were greater and a decisive majority of the population supported market reforms during the 1990s. Still, the transition recession also caused support to drop in some of the countries with the best economic prospects. As in Russia, research pointed to a divergence of opinions among prospective winners and losers. In 1997, the scholar Bernd Hayo used the European Union's Central and East European Eurobarometer surveys between 1990 and 1992 to examine citizens' subjective perceptions of the transition process, specifically whether they approved of the change to a market economy.[5] Although Hayo understood that the data were preliminary, he identified three key trends that would prove important in later public opinion surveys throughout the region. Concentrating on Poland, Hungary, and Czechoslovakia/Czech Republic and Slovakia, Hayo found (1) that East Europeans linked political liberalization with economic liberalization; (2) that the initial enthusiasm for the free market economy appeared to decline over time; and (3) that wealthy, young, urban, educated men were more in favor of democratization and the creation of a competitive, capitalist economy than the poor, the elderly, the less well-educated, rural dwellers, and women.

Reflecting on the declining support for democracy/market economy, Hayo noticed that not only were the numbers of people against the market economy growing, but the number of those who previously had "no opinion" on the question was decreasing. As the early transition years went on, people who had once been agnostic about the changes were increasingly in opposition. Hayo suggested that most East Europeans responding to survey questions did not initially understand the concept of "free market economy." They assumed that "free market economy" meant "higher living standards" such as those found in the capitalist, democratic West. Once they better understood the trade-offs that a capitalist economy entails, they began to turn against the concept:

> In the beginning, people think that the creation of a free market economy is a clean and easy way to economic progress. Soon it becomes clear that this will not be the case, and people who support the market economy only for these reasons begin to rethink their position. Over time, they realize that there will be winners and losers and that the allocation to either of these categories is not necessarily based on equity grounds. This learning process leads to a decline in the number of people who have no opinion on the question. A polarization takes place with an increasing number of people rejecting the changes.[6]

As in the case of the liberal elites and socialist masses in Russia, Hayo's early examination of public opinion data in Central Europe suggested that there were large swaths of the population that intuited that they were ill-equipped to thrive in a market economy and liberal democracy (since the two were always conflated). They expressed negative opinions of the transition from its onset, but their preferences were mostly ignored. Liberal elites could easily cast these populations as socially weak and ideologically backward, an all too easy accusation to level at those living in rural areas with little education, at the elderly who lived most of their lives under state socialism, and at women who were supposedly more risk-averse and suspicious of drastic political or economic changes. But as younger, well-educated, urban men began to understand that capitalism did not automatically grant economic rewards to those more deserving or willing to work the hardest, they too could begin to lose faith in the transition process, an outcome that Hayo saw possible even in the mid-1990s, well before the first EBRD Life in Transition survey.

What is particularly relevant in these early public opinion studies is the extent to which East European populations were told—both by their own leaders and by the West—that the transition process would be painful at first but would be worth it in the end—that there was a bright capitalist future just a decade or so away (see Part 1 of this book). We know from ethnographic studies in the region (which will be explored at length in Part 4) that many East Europeans harbored "market dreams" for their futures.[7] And even if they were too old to benefit from capitalism and democracy, they believed that their children would one day reap the rewards and that this was worth the short-term pain and social displacement. These early studies of East European public opinion recognized the political risks associated with the divergent economic impacts of transition on different socioeconomic groups. But many observers believed that the prosperity and freedoms to come would slowly prevent or erode any mass opposition to the transition process. They also relied on social policies to ameliorate the worst effects, policies that were better applied in the Visegrad countries than elsewhere. Pieter Vanhuysse, in his landmark study, *Divide and Pacify*, showed that Central European governments used social policies such as early retirement deals to prevent outbreaks of protest against reform.[8] Social policy responses were far more vigorous in Central Europe, with its Bismarckian welfare state traditions that predated the communist period,[9] than in Russia and the former Soviet Union or Southeastern Europe.[10]

Dissatisfaction with the transition to democracy and free markets waxed and waned over the following decades, often in line with trends in the economy (see Figures 12.2 and 12.3). This suggests that people evaluated transition in egocentric terms, in terms of what it did for them. Eurobarometer polls show that support for a market economy declined in the Visegrad and Baltic countries from a high of around 80 percent at the outset of transition in 1990–91 to 65 percent and 55 percent, respectively, in 1994, the worst year of the transitional recession for many countries (see Figure 12.2). As the economic situation improved, support for markets slowly began to rise to around 65 percent by 1997. Southeastern Europe, where the economic effects of transition were particularly severe in some countries, support for markets rose to around 70 percent by 1992 and stayed relatively constant. Yet still, respondents displayed a meaningful difference in support by gender, location, and education, with male, urban, and college-educated respondents more likely to support markets by 5 to 10 percentage points than their female, rural, and less-educated co-respondents.

Satisfaction with the development of democracy (see Figure 12.3) followed a similar U-shaped pattern in all three sub-regions of Central and Eastern Europe (Baltics, Balkans, and Visegrad), declining from 45–50 percent in 1990–91 to around 30 percent in 1994 and rising again thereafter. However, gender and urban/rural differences mattered less to support for democracy than support for markets, with men more likely to support democracy by about 3 percentage points. Rural residents, in fact, were more likely to support democracy than urban residents, although the sample size is small, and the difference is only 1.5 percentage points.

Support for markets and democracy clearly followed a logic of self-interest, with some countries and regions exhibiting strong support and others weaker support. Cultural factors also mattered. Russians exhibited limited enthusiasm for democracy and markets throughout the 1990s, despite having a similar transitional recession to other countries that exhibited far higher levels of support. But egocentric economic evaluations were strong. Within countries, for instance, we find significant evidence that groups that expected to do better under market reforms and democracy supported these reforms to a greater extent. Others became nostalgic for the communist past.

Red Nostalgia

While the J-curve narrative that a short transitional recession would be followed by great economic success was believed by some, others began to see the transition as an epic disaster. This can be found specifically in the growth of the phenomenon of communist nostalgia or what Ghodsee called "red nostalgia" in 2004.[11] In 2005, Joakim Ekman and Jonas Linde worried that policymakers and scholars of democratic consolidation in Central and Eastern Europe were too focused on "skillful institutional engineering and elite-level maneuvering."[12] In their view, the new democracies in Eastern Europe could not be consolidated without popular support, and they warned that leaders ignored public opinion at their peril. Ekman and Linde used data from the 2001 New Europe Barometer (NEB) and two previous surveys, the New Democracies Barometer (1991–98) and the New Baltic Barometer (1993–2000). They combined these surveys into a single data set containing 62,000 respondents in ten postsocialist countries in the process of joining the European Union: Bulgaria, Czech Republic, Estonia, Hungary, Latvia, Lithuania, Poland, Romania, Slovenia, and Slovakia. For each year of the surveys, roughly a thousand face-to-face interviews were conducted with stratified sub-samples in each country, making for a robust sample. Furthermore, what was novel about the 2001 NEB survey was that it explicitly asked respondents about the desirability of a hypothetical return to communist rule, a question not found on other Eurobarometer or World Values surveys but reprised later in the EBRD's Life in Transition surveys starting in 2006.

In 2001, in the seven Central and East European countries, the share of nostalgic respondents ranged between 15 to 30 percent (as shown in Table 10.1), a significant minority, but the authors found that the "general tendency throughout the region is one of increasing support for a return to communist rule."[13] In the three Baltic countries, this figure was much lower, never reaching above 15 percent of the population, most likely because Baltic citizens associate "communist rule" with Soviet imperialism. What makes these findings so significant is that these were not just people responding to questions about whether they approved or disapproved of a market economy or the move to liberal democracy. These were citizens who told the researchers that *they wished to return to the authoritarian rule of the past*. Before 2008, one hypothesis about communist nostalgia was that it was something primarily found among the elderly who were wistful for their youth, but Ekman and Linde found that "nostalgia" for communist rule had less to do with age and more to do with a general dissatisfaction with postcommunist rule and its destabilizing effects on everyday life. Younger citizens who

TABLE 10.1 Red Nostalgia (percent of respondents)

	1993	1995	1998	2001
Latvia		7		7
Estonia		6		8
Lithuania		8		14
Hungary	18	20	23	16
Czechia	7	9	17	18
Romania	13	10	18	18
Poland	17	8	13	23
Slovenia	12	13	14	23
Bulgaria	27	28	26	24
Slovakia	16	18	29	30

Note: Percent who agreed with "return to communist rule" to the question, "Our present system of government is not the only one that this country had. Some people say that we would be better off if the country was governed differently. What do you think?"

Source: Joakim Ekman and Jonas Linde, "Communist Nostalgia and the Consolidation of Democracy in Central and Eastern Europe," *Journal of Communist Studies and Transition Politics* 21, no. 3 (2005): 354-374, doi: 10.1080/13523270500183512.

were only children in the 1980s also reported a desire to return to communist rule. The authors suggested that these nostalgic sentiments represented a growing discontent with the free market economy's ability to deliver the goods, what the authors called "system output."

Writing in 2005, before the onset of the global financial crisis and the Great Recession, Ekman and Linde believed that the growth of communist nostalgia in Eastern Europe was not incompatible with democratic consolidation. As long as enough of the public had faith in democratic and free market institutions (roughly 70 percent), the liberalization of Eastern Europe would not be threatened by the nostalgic sentiments of what they called the "losers" of the transition. Indeed, the authors admitted that the transition process had been particularly brutal for many segments of the population, and that it was completely understandable that some citizens would long for the social security and economic stability of the past. But Ekman and Linde also argued that it would be foolish to ignore "the *potential* danger" of the persistence and growth of the desire to return to communist rule. They wrote in 2005 that "if nostalgia is the result of disappointment in the democratic system's ability to produce output, and at the same time this kind of discontent is increasing, it may in the end constitute a substantial challenge to the legitimacy of democracy in postsocialist Europe. Former communist parties may or may not gain from such public dissatisfaction, but it would be more accurate to say that protest parties in general may capitalize on such sentiments."[14] As Kullberg and Zimmerman warned in the Russian context, both far-left communist and far-right nationalist parties could benefit from economic discontent with free markets and nostalgia for the pre-1989–91 past, thus predicting the rise of politicians like Putin, Orbán, and the Law and Justice Party in Poland.

II

Attitudes Shift over Time

FOR THE TWENTIETH anniversary of the fall of the Berlin Wall, the Pew Charitable Trust conducted public opinion surveys in nine postsocialist countries in Central and Eastern Europe between August and September 2009. They compared the results with a 1991 survey to measure changes in the attitudes toward the transition to democracy and free market capitalism throughout the region. The surveyed countries were East Germany, Czech Republic, Slovakia, Poland, Hungary, Lithuania, Russia, Bulgaria, and Ukraine. Although the Pew survey excluded the former Yugoslav Republics and the majority of the successor states of the Soviet Union (where public opinions, according to the 2006 Life in Transition survey were more pessimistic than in the Central European and Baltic regions), the findings were still enlightening. The Pew report, "End of Communism Cheered but with More Reservations," was still generally positive because the researchers found that "majorities of people in most former Soviet republics and Eastern European countries endorse the emergence of multiparty systems and a free market economy."[1] Compared to 1991, self-reported life satisfaction had risen in most countries, although there were important regional variations. The Pew report found that younger people remained optimistic compared to their elders and argued (like the EBRD) that this boded well for the future consolidation of democracy and capitalism in the region.

A key part of the report's title, however, was the phrase "but with more reservations," because what the Pew survey found was a decrease in the initial enthusiasm reported in the 1991 survey. This mirrors Bernd Hayo's early hypothesis that people would begin to turn against democracy and capitalism once they understood that a free market economy would widen economic inequality and possibly create more losers than winners. The Pew researchers reported that "the initial widespread enthusiasm about these changes has dimmed in most of the countries surveyed; in some, support for democracy and capitalism has diminished markedly. In many nations, majorities or pluralities say that most people were better off under communism, and there is a widespread view that the business class and political leadership have benefited from the changes more than ordinary people."[2]

Indeed, of the nine countries surveyed, five of them (Hungary, Lithuania, Russia, Bulgaria, and Ukraine) saw declines in popular support for the change from authoritarianism to democracy between 1991 and 2009. In the case of Bulgaria and Ukraine these declines were 24 and 42 percentage points, respectively (dropping from 76 percent to 52 percent in favor in Bulgaria and from 72 percent to only 30 percent in favor in Ukraine). All nine countries surveyed between 1991 and 2009 saw declines in support for the change to capitalism, with a 34 percentage point drop in Hungary, a 26 percent drop in Lithuania, and a 20 percent drop of support in Bulgaria. But overall, the survey still found widespread endorsement and support for the demise of communism and growing levels of self-reported life satisfaction between 1991 and 2009 for all countries (see Table 11.1).[3]

Even if the levels were relatively low, the vast majority of respondents in all countries reported that their life satisfaction was higher than it had been two decades earlier. Respondents were asked to rank their life satisfaction on a scale of 1 to 10 with 10 being the most satisfied with life and 0 the least satisfied. The percentage of citizens who ranked their life satisfaction with a score between 7 and 10 (i.e., the most satisfied) grew from 12 percent in 1991 to 44 percent in 2009 in Poland, 13 to 43 percent in Slovakia, 7 to 35 percent in Russia, 13 to 35 percent in

TABLE 11.1 Life Satisfaction by Country

	1991	2009	2019
East Germany	15	43	59
Czechia	23	49	57
Poland	12	44	56
Slovakia	13	43	49
Hungary	8	15	47
Lithuania	13	35	44
Bulgaria	4	15	29
Russian Federation	7	35	28
Ukraine	8	26	25

Note: Percent who chose 7–10 on a ladder of life where the top of the ladder represents the best possible life (10) and the bottom the worst possible life (0).
Source: Pew Research Center (2011, 2019).

Lithuania, and 8 to 26 percent in Ukraine. The Czech Republic had the highest levels of life satisfaction with 49 percent of respondents placing themselves in the highest category up from 23 percent in 1991. In Western Europe, the most satisfied grew from 45 to 57 percent in the United Kingdom, 41 to 54 percent in Italy, 36 to 52 in France, 31 to 53 in Spain, 52 to 64 in West Germany, and 15 to 59 in East Germany.[4] These results were consistent with the emergence of a significant minority of the population who felt that they had been winners of transition. Even in Bulgaria and Hungary, where only 15 percent of respondents ranked their life satisfaction with a 7–10 in 2009, these numbers were up from 4 and 8 percent, respectively. In terms of self-reported personal well-being, therefore, the overall trend was definitively positive. Many East Europeans reported significant increases in their subjective well-being, something that the IFIs rightly celebrated and took as evidence for the success of their shock therapy policies.

But once again, there was significant regional and demographic variation, with young people reporting higher life satisfaction than older citizens. Most respondents were also cognizant that there had been many losers of the transition process. When asked about the economic situation for "most of the people" in the respondent's country, and whether "most people" were better off, worse off, or about the same as they were under communism, in none of the nine countries surveyed did more than 50 percent agree that "most people" were better off in 2009 than they were before the onset of transition. In the case of Hungary, 72 percent of respondents claimed that "most people" were worse off, and 62 percent of both Bulgarians and Ukrainians felt the same. Even in the relatively more successful countries of the Czech Republic and Poland, 39 percent and 35 percent of Czechs and Poles believed that "most people" in their countries were worse off in 2009 than they were under communism.

The Pew Survey confirmed the continued salience of the diversity of outcomes during the earliest years of the changes. Twenty years of transition to liberal democracy and free markets had not mitigated inequalities between urban and rural populations, younger and older, educated and less well-educated, or wealthy versus poor. The Pew Report explained:

> The demographic gaps in well-being among the publics of former Iron Curtain countries were suggested by reactions to the end of communism two decades ago. It was the young, the better educated and the urban populations who were cheering. How older, less well educated and rural people would adapt was then identified as one of the principal challenges to acceptance of democracy and capitalism. This remains the case, especially in Russia and Ukraine, where people who now rate their lives well voice the strongest support for democratic values, while those less satisfied are the least disposed to the new values.[5]

And those "least disposed" to support "democratic values" could still vote. The Pew Report, like some of the previous reports already discussed, worried that popular discontent with democracy and free markets would make itself felt at the ballot box through the support of illiberal parties. The 2009 Pew report was particularly concerned about the situation in both Hungary and Ukraine where high levels of dissatisfaction and frustration with the transition process could threaten long-term political stability. Hungary's subsequent turn toward the illiberal democratic policies of Viktor Orbán and Ukraine's ongoing civil war could have been predicted from the mixed signals in the public opinion data, but the Pew researchers, like the EBRD and the World Bank in the first wave of the Life in Transition survey, concentrated on the positives in hopes that the opinions of the losers would fade with more time. Capitalism would reward hard work and perseverance, and it was expected that losers would blame themselves and their lack of effort, rather than the caprices of the free market, for declining living standards.

After the Global Financial Crisis

But disaster struck again. Collectively, the global financial crisis of 2008 that radiated from the West devasted the transition countries of Eastern Europe and Central Asia. Whereas the period between 1999 and 2006 had seen 55 million people emerging out of poverty, GDP contracted by 5.2 percent and unemployment skyrocketed across the region in 2009.[6] In Latvia, GDP contracted by 18 percent, and few households in Central and Eastern Europe or Central Asia were unaffected by the crisis, either through job losses, reduced wages, or a fall in remittances from abroad. To measure the impact of the crisis on public opinion, the EBRD and the World Bank conducted a second wave of their Life in Transition survey (LiT2) in 2010, which included the original countries surveyed in 2006 and five Western countries for comparison: France, Germany, Italy, Sweden, and the UK. What they found was widespread social dislocation and economic hardship, with more than half of the respondents in seventeen countries reporting that their households had been affected "a great deal" or "a fair amount." More than 70 percent of the population in the transition region that reported being affected by the global crisis said they had to cut back on basic foodstuffs or health expenses as a result.

Despite the severity of the crisis in many countries, overall support for democracy and capitalism declined, but not as much as the EBRD expected. When asked about their preferences regarding political and economic systems, a plurality of respondents in the transition region still preferred the liberalizing tendency:

As in 2006, more people (about one-third of the sample) prefer the combination of market economy and democracy to any other combination of responses. Barely 10 per cent of respondents said that both a planned economy and an authoritarian government may be preferable under some circumstances. The data also show that more people unequivocally prefer democracy as a political system than a market economy as an economic one. Almost 45 per cent of respondents choose democracy over any other political system, whereas less than 40 per cent would opt for a market economy under any circumstances. Nearly one-quarter of respondents feel that the type of economic system that they live under is not important to them and over one-fifth think similarly about the political system.[7]

What is fascinating about the EBRD report is that the economists doing the analysis considered that the support of about *one-third* of the population was enough to shore up national commitments to democracy and free markets (compared to the 70 percent that Ekman and Linde thought necessary for political stability). While they mentioned the importance of regional diversity, they tended to skate over the fact that support for democracy and free markets was waning; popular support for democracy rose in eleven but fell in eighteen nations. Mass approval of capitalism rose in thirteen countries and declined in sixteen. While only one in ten people reported a desire to return to authoritarianism and a planned economy, an additional 35 percent believed that some other combination of political and economic system was more desirable than Western democracy and capitalism. And one of every four people in the transition region said it didn't matter what kind of political and economic system they lived under.[8]

The presence of five West European countries in the data set also allowed for some interesting comparisons. In the first place, Western countries were far less affected by the global recession than the transition countries, with only 15 percent of German households claiming that the global recession had affected them "a great deal" or "a fair amount."[9] Overall life satisfaction was also markedly higher in the West than in the transitioning East, signaling an important "happiness gap."[10] After two decades of transition, the former socialist countries had not yet caught up to their Western neighbors, and the ongoing reverberations of the financial crisis exacerbated these differences. Still, the overall message of the report remained hopeful. In his preface, Berglöf concluded that the second Life in Transition survey "confirms the resilience of transition—but also that transition is a work in progress. . . . Diminishing expectations in the aftermath of the crisis and relentless negative demographic trends will no doubt put these systems under renewed pressures. But while markets and democracy come with their own baggage, they are more likely to provide constructive answers to these pressures than any plausible alternative."[11] In other words, given the options available to transition countries, the EBRD concluded that the path laid out for them by EBRD experts remained their best choice.

Thus, if you read the entire EBRD report on the Life in Transition II survey, what emerges is a sense that the *right types of people* are still supporting democracy and capitalism, and so (at least implicitly) the opinions of the rest of the population can be discounted. Policymakers and bankers were assured that the young, educated, urban, well-to-do continued to support the economic and political system that best guaranteed their long-term economic and political success. It also turns out that those households with high levels of income and education in the urban areas were less affected by the global financial crisis than those who were already poor before the crisis hit. Despite the hardships facing the region, EBRD chief economist Erik Berglöf reported that postsocialist elites were still on board with the liberal democratic and capitalist program. Yet the postsocialist countries clearly still had a lot of work to do to make the economic and political system effective for the majority of citizens.

In a follow-up to their 2009 study, "Twenty Years Later: Confidence in Democracy and Capitalism Wanes in Former Soviet Union," the Pew Research Center examined public opinion in Russia, Lithuania, and Ukraine between March and April 2011.[12] Once again using the 1991 survey as a baseline, the Pew Research Center compared support for democracy (see Table 11.2) and capitalism (see Table 11.3) twenty years after the breakup of the USSR. In terms of support for the change to a multi-party system, all three countries registered steep declines over the two decades. In Russia in 1991, 61 percent of respondents were

TABLE 11.2 Satisfaction with Democracy by Country

	1991	2009	2011	2019
Poland	66	70		85
East Germany	91	85		85
Czechia	80	80		82
Slovakia	70	71		74
Hungary	74	56		72
Lithuania	75	55	52	70
Bulgaria	76	52		54
Ukraine	72	30	35	51
Russian Federation	61	53	50	43

Note: Percent who approve of change to a multiparty system.
Source: Pew Research Center (2011, 2019).

TABLE 11.3 Satisfaction with Markets by Country

	1991	2009	2011	2019
Poland	80	71		85
East Germany	86	82		83
Czechia	87	79		76
Slovakia	69	66		71
Hungary	80	46		70
Lithuania	76	50	45	69
Bulgaria	73	53		55
Ukraine	52	36	34	47
Russian Federation	54	50	42	38

Note: Percent who approve of change to a market economy.
Source: Pew Research Center (2011, 2019).

in favor of the transition to democracy, but only 50 percent remained in favor by 2011 and this fell to 43 percent in 2019. In Lithuania, this percentage dropped from 75 percent to 52 percent (although it recovered to 70 percent in 2019, and while 72 percent of Ukrainians were satisfied with democracy in 1991, this percentage dropped to 30 percent in 2009, but then rose to 35 percent in 2011 and to 51 percent in 2019, after the election of Volodymyr Zelensky, the comedian, as president. In none of the three countries did a majority express satisfaction with the change to a free market; in 2011 only 45 percent of Lithuanians, 42 percent of Russians, and only 34 percent of Ukrainians said they supported capitalism (although these percentages rose in 2019 to 69 percent in Lithuania and to 47 percent in Ukraine in 2019; in Russia the percentage continued to decline to only 38 percent in 2019).[13] In Bulgaria, the percentage of the population supporting democracy fell from 76 percent in 1991 to 54 percent in 2019 and for support of free markets the percentages also fell from 73 percent to 55 percent in the same period. If you look at Table 11.3, you will notice that only in Poland and Slovakia did satisfaction with markets increase between 1991 and 2019; in all other countries surveyed by Pew it declined.

When asked "who has benefited from the changes since 1991?" (Table 11.4), only 11 percent of Ukrainians, 20 percent of Lithuanians, and 26 percent of Russians believed that the transition to democracy and capitalism benefited "ordinary people" in 2011. When Pew did a follow-up survey in 2019, 21 percent of Ukrainians believed that ordinary people benefited from the changes, but the percentage fell in Russia to 22 percent. Looking at the region more broadly, however, all countries surveyed between 2002 and 2019 saw increases in the

TABLE 11.4 "Has Transition Benefited Average People?"

	2009	2011	2019
Poland	42		68
Czechia	53		54
Slovakia	21		42
Hungary	17		41
Russian Federation	21	26	22
Lithuania		20	
Ukraine	10	11	21
Bulgaria	11		19

Note: Percent who say ordinary people have benefited a great deal or a fair amount from the changes since 1989/1991.
Source: Pew Research Center (2011, 2019).

percentage of people who believed that ordinary people had benefited from the changes, although only in Poland and Czechia did a majority of respondents feel that ordinary people had benefited.

So, who did benefit? In Russia, Lithuania, and Ukraine more than three-quarters of the respondents reported that business owners had benefited from the changes, whereas 82 percent of Russians, 91 percent of Lithuanians, and 95 percent of Ukrainians believe that politicians were the primary beneficiaries, exactly those elites identified in the research by Kullberg and Zimmerman at the end of the 1990s. Those who were most in favor of the transition were widely perceived in 2011 to be those who had benefited the most from the social, political, and economic upheavals of the previous two decades. The Pew survey also found overwhelmingly negative assessments of the impacts of the transition on society; respondents believed that social relations between citizens had been badly damaged by the changes, as had law and order, public morality, and their standard of living.[14] Since Russia and Ukraine are two of the most populous countries in the region (with almost 189 million people between them in 2011), this widespread breakdown in social trust was a profound finding.

Finally, when considering the ideal role of the state, respondents were asked whether people in their country should "be free to pursue their life's goals without interference from the state" or "that the state play an active role in society so as to guarantee that nobody is in need." After two decades of transition, 76 percent of Lithuanians, 75 percent of Ukrainians, and 68 percent of Russians believed that it was more important for the state to look after the needs of the socially weak than to ensure the individual freedoms necessary for people to pursue their own personal goals. Since the 1991 survey, support for individual freedoms declined in all three countries, and although the young were still more likely to support a more limited role for the state, solid majorities of citizens in all three countries believed that their governments should be doing more to expand social safety nets. Survey data revealing the perseverance of anti-liberal attitudes complicates early ideas that postsocialist populations would catch up to the liberalism of their Western-oriented elites.[15]

Country-level studies confirm the majority disenchantment with the results of transition. Although we do not have the space to do an overview of domestic polling in all of the postsocialist countries, just two examples highlight the persistence of frustration with the hardships of the transition to democracy and free markets. For instance, in 2011 in Poland, one of the undisputed success stories of the transition process (at least in terms of economic growth), a national poll found the widespread belief that most Poles lived more comfortable lives "before 1989." Researchers asked Polish citizens: "When was life easier for you—before 1989 or at present?" The choice of 31 percent of respondents was before 1989, and only 19 percent said: "at present." A further 21 percent didn't answer the question and 30 percent were too young to remember Polish life under communism. According to the authors of the study: "This means that 44.2 percent of respondents who remember those days think that life was easier for them then [before 1989] while 26.7 percent said that it is better at present. [Thus], in the half of the adult population who have an opinion in this respect, clearly more numerous are those who think that their own—and thus probably also other people's—lives were easier before 1989."[16] Two years later in 2013, a poll of 1,055 Romanians over the age of 18 found that only 34 percent reported that their lives were *worse* off before 1989. When asked if their lives were better before 1989, under the dictator Ceaușescu, 44 percent agreed. A further 16 percent said their lives were no better or worse than before 1989.[17] Since Romania was one of the most brutal and restrictive communist countries, it is astonishing that only about a third of respondents claimed they were better off after over 20 years of democracy and free markets.

The EBRD's Life in Transition (LiT) III survey confirmed the persistence of this nostalgia for the economic stability and social security of the previous era. By 2016, slightly more Croatians supported a planned economy than a market economy: 32 percent versus 31 percent. The EBRD found huge declines in support for transition in Azerbaijan: from 60 and 56 percent in favor of democracy and a market economy in 2010 to 28 and 16 percent in 2016. In Hungary, survey respondents were asked "whether they would rather live in a country with full political liberties but weak economic growth (country B) or in one with limited freedoms and stronger growth (country A)." In 2016, 70 percent of Hungarians chose the country with strong economic growth. When asked the same question, 82 percent of Slovenes and 83 percent of Russians said they would trade political liberties for economic growth. In Romania, 22 percent of respondents said that an authoritarian system would be preferable in some circumstances and 26 percent favored the planned economy. About a third of Ukrainians said they would prefer (in some circumstances) to live under an authoritarian regime or in a planned economy. By March 2019, in the run-up to the presidential elections in Ukraine, a Gallup survey found that only 9 percent of Ukrainians had confidence in their government, the lowest confidence level in the world for the second year in a row. Moreover, just 12 percent of the Ukrainian population believed in the honesty of the electoral process and 91 percent claimed that their government was rife with corruption.[18] Eastern Europe is not Denmark, but something was definitely rotten in this part of the world as far as popular support for democracy and capitalism were concerned. And all of this was before the novel coronavirus pandemic, which had widely disparate effects on countries of the region, but everywhere brought large economic disruptions.

The Good News: Life Satisfaction

Despite the declines in support for multi-party elections and free markets, which suggests that a growing number of people were buying into the disaster capitalism narrative on transition, the data clearly show that subjective well-being *increased* throughout the region (albeit from relatively low initial levels and with large variability between countries) (see Figure 11.1). In July 2011, the prime minister of Bhutan suggested to the General Assembly of the United Nations that rather than just measuring Gross Domestic Product, the UN should also measure "Gross Domestic Happiness."[19] The first World Happiness Report used Gallup World Poll data to examine happiness in the member nations of the UN. An initial set of rankings based on 2010–12 data showed that the former socialist countries of Central and Eastern Europe and Central Asia lagged way behind the Western capitalist countries in terms of happiness.[20] Out of 156 nations, the highest ranked postsocialist country in Eastern Europe was the Czech Republic at position 39, followed by Slovenia at 44, Slovakia at 46, and Poland at 51. Way down the list were Serbia at 106, Bosnia and Herzegovina at 107, Hungary at 110, Macedonia at 118, and Bulgaria at 144 (sandwiched between Afghanistan and Botswana). In the Commonwealth of Independent States, Moldova was the highest ranked at 53. Russia ranked 68, Ukraine ranked 87, and Azerbaijan, Armenia, and Georgia (often singled out as a success case of transition) ranked 116th, 128th, and 134th, respectively.

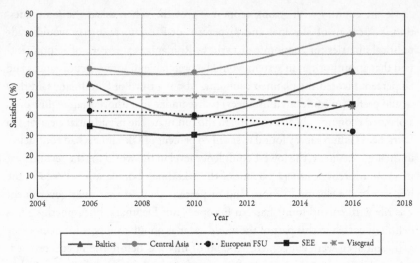

FIGURE 11.1. Life Satisfaction (LiT). The survey question asked respondents to what extent they agreed with "All things considered, I am satisfied with my life now," ranging from 1 ("strongly disagree") to 5 ("strongly agree"). The figure reports the percentage of respondents that agreed or strongly agreed with the statement.

Source: LiTS—Life in Transition Survey (WorldBank/European Bank for Reconstruction and Development), 2006, 2010, 2016.

But if you compared the 2015–17 World Happiness Report rankings to the 2010–12 rankings for the twenty-eight countries in the EBRD's Life in Transition surveys, the news was definitely good.[21] In the years between the 2013 and 2018 World Happiness Reports, eighteen countries saw their rankings increase and only ten countries saw their rankings fall. In some cases, however, the fall was precipitous, as in the case of Ukraine which fell from 87 to 138, no doubt because of war. The Czech Republic had climbed up to 21st place and, perhaps thanks to Viktor Orbán, Hungary had moved from 110th up to 69th place on the list. Things even seemed to be looking up for dour Bulgaria, moving up 44 places to 100, finally shedding its status as the most miserable postsocialist nation (at 112, 128, and 129, Albania, Georgia, and Armenia were now more miserable, with Ukraine at the lowest point).

How to explain this relative surge of happiness in the region? On the one hand, while other public opinion polls did provide evidence that self-reported life satisfaction was increasing, one significant reason for the reshuffling in the rankings was that Central Asians suddenly were reporting much higher levels of life satisfaction. Additionally, a lot of people in the Western world were getting more miserable relative to the former communist countries, including people in the United States, Greece, and Italy, which all fell in the rankings between 2010–12 and 2014–17. Indeed, when the EBRD released its third Life in Transition survey (LiT3), it made much of the fact that the happiness gap between the transition countries and the comparator countries had finally closed. If you only read the press release, the executive summary, and the foreword, you would think that the East had finally caught up with the West. It is only when you dig into the specific chapter on life satisfaction, that the EBRD explains that a rise in regional life satisfaction wasn't the only reason for the closing of the happiness gap:

> "Life satisfaction" is higher in 2016 than it was in 2006 in almost all the surveyed countries. Life satisfaction has particularly increased in Central Asia, where about 70 per cent of respondents are currently happy with their lives overall. Similarly, life satisfaction among respondents in central Europe and the Baltic states has increased since 2006 and now compares well with Germany and Italy. . . . Taken together, these results indicate that the life satisfaction gap between the transition region and western European comparator countries has finally closed. The reason for this apparent "happiness convergence" is twofold: between 2010 and 2016, life satisfaction has, on average, increased in the transition region while it has declined in both Germany and Italy.[22]

The irony of the EBRD findings is that life satisfaction surged in Central Asia in countries least committed to the principles of democracy, and that the closing of the happiness gap with Western Europe reflected declining life satisfaction in only two of the original five comparison countries. France, Sweden, and the UK were dropped from the 2016 survey, and "Western Europe" was now represented only by Germany and Italy. One wonders whether the happiness gap would have closed between Eastern and Western Europe if all five of the comparison countries used in the 2010 survey had been included in the 2016 survey (especially Sweden). Still, the message of increasing life satisfaction was one of the most optimistic findings of the report, and the EBRD confidently proclaimed that the transition had been a success, more or less.

More recent 2019 surveys demonstrate the same upward trends. Central Europe and the Baltics have almost caught up with Western Europe after thirty years. In other parts of the postcommunist region, life satisfaction is up dramatically since 1991, but a "happiness gap" still exists between East and West. Pew's 2019 survey showed that Czechia and Poland had caught up with West European countries. Slovakia, Hungary, and Lithuania are not far behind. However, Bulgaria, Russia, and Ukraine (29, 28, and 25 percent) still report half the level of high satisfaction (a 7–10 on a 10-point scale) as Western Germany, Poland, and Czechia (64, 57, and 56 percent).[23] Using a different scale, Eurobarometer asked all EU member states and some candidate countries (Serbia, Macedonia, Albania) about life satisfaction since expanding membership to Central and East European countries in 2004. Survey data from November 2019 showed that 32 percent of West European respondents reported that they were "very satis- fied" with their lives, compared to an EU average of 25 percent. In contrast, only 17 percent of Central Europe and Baltic countries reported being "very satisfied," while only 7 percent of Southeast Europeans (including Hungarians) concurred. Of course, it depends how one asks the questions, but data from 2019 show that postcommunist countries still experienced a happiness gap with the West, though it has decreased significantly over time and it is far smaller in the Central Europe and Baltic member states of the EU.[24]

Data interpretation issues aside, one thing is clear: had transition not produced so much inequality, there would have been fewer losers; and with fewer losers, the new economic and political systems probably would have enjoyed more public support. Yet self-interest—whether conceived of as people's individual financial situation, future prospects, or life satisfaction—was not the only factor driving public opinion in transition countries. Postsocialist populations also carried with them certain European values and the legacy of socialism. Vast majorities of the postsocialist population continued to believe that governments should play a sig- nificant role in the economy, particularly in tax and spend redistribution and the provision of social services and job guarantees. Yet rapidly increasing inequality produced societies that many saw as corrupt, unjust, and even oppressive. It was not only the poor who held these views, but the well-off as well. Inequality thus corroded sociotropic evaluations of transition—undermining people's sense of living in a just and well-functioning society. This too was clear from the outset, but only if one looked at public opinion.

Toward a New Social Contract?

IN MARCH 1989, an international group of scholars met in London to launch a research project to compare social justice values in capitalist and communist countries, just a few months before the fall of the Berlin Wall. Inspired by the work of political theorists such as John Rawls, their ultimate goal was to understand the nature of what Jean-Jacques Rousseau called "the social contract," and how it was grounded in public beliefs about fairness and justice. Led by David Mason of Butler University, the International Social Justice Project (ISJP) conducted an initial 1991 survey in capitalist countries, including the United States, Japan, and Germany, and communist (or former communist) countries including Russia, Poland, and the Czech Republic. Their study provided a baseline for public opinion in the immediate postcommunist period, with a follow-up in 1996. Given the fortuitous timing, the survey allowed the ISJP to study whether public attitudes in the former communist countries would support transition or oppose it. As Kluegel and Mason predicted, "The political legitimacy of the new regimes in East-Central Europe can not be taken for granted. . . . [S]uch legitimacy must be based not just on democratic political institutions and capitalist economic growth but also on a popular sense that the political system and the economic order are fair."[1]

Fast forward to 2020 and the ISJP's concerns seem prophetic. Democracy is under siege in countries that were once forerunners in reform. Freedom House has declared Hungary an authoritarian regime. Poland is moving in the same direction. Most of the former Soviet states are authoritarian regimes, often dominated by a single leader for dozens of years. President Vladimir Putin has justified his strongman role with reference to the damaging effects of market reforms in the 1990s and is now eligible to remain in office until 2036, longer than Stalin. Whether economic growth lifted all boats or not, even international financial institutions are beginning to acknowledge that postcommunist transition

countries failed to create a new social contract.[2] Most citizens express disappointment with what their societies have become. In a recent book, scholars Ivan
Krastev and Stephen Holmes call liberalism in Central and Eastern Europe "the
light that failed."[3] Rising inequality caused societies with strong socialist values
to fall apart. Some individuals rose to great heights; others sank. These outcomes
were not perceived as fair, in part because of the corruption that accompanied
market transition and the perception that the wealthy rose to power through
illegitimate means. Even if their own living standards were rising, citizens of the
postcommunist countries disliked what their societies had become.

One of the most important insights of the International Social Justice Project
was that people responded differently to ideological labels like "markets" and
"democracy" than they did to more specific propositions like "government should
guarantee that everyone has a job." Belief in abstract concepts did not easily map
onto public opinions about the role of government in the economy. In the postcommunist countries, belief in abstract concepts of liberalism often masked a
continuing commitment to the values of socialism.[4] When pressed on the details,
such as whether the government should guarantee jobs or redistribute incomes,
ISJP found that socialist values died hard. For instance, in both their 1991 and
1995–96 surveys, around 90 percent of the population in Hungary, Bulgaria, East
Germany, and Russia believed that the government should guarantee jobs. The
rate in the Czech Republic was lower, at 78 percent in 1991 and 75 percent in
1995, closer to West Germany, which had the highest rate of the West European
countries surveyed, where 71 percent believed the same in 1991. The United States
registered 50 percent support, for comparison.[5] Most citizens of the postcommunist countries continued to desire strong government guarantees, similar to
those of socialist times. In some countries, such as Hungary and East Germany, a
majority of the population even supported establishing upper limits to individual
incomes, a common feature of the communist era (see Table 12.1).

Second, while the ISJP revealed that potential "losers" of transition—namely,
the poor and less educated—held to socialist values more frequently than rich
people, it also found majority support for socialist values among the likely "winners" of transition. For people with less than a primary education, support for
socialist values approached 90 percent, but even 50–60 percent of those with
higher education believed that the government should take a strong role in providing social guarantees. Postsocialist populations wanted an economic system
that was fair, not only one that worked for them. People care about what kind of
society they live in, not only their own self-interest. And while the ISJP revealed
that postcommunist populations shared many similarities with social justice
norms of Western capitalist countries, socialism also left them with an enduring
legacy of pro-socialist attitudes that differed to a significant degree from attitudes

TABLE 12.1 Attitudes about Justice and Fairness: What the Government Should Provide

	Minimum standard of living		Upper limit on income		Job	
	1991	1996	1991	1996	1991	1996
Bulgaria	90.11	91.32	40.43	42.85	84.98	87.78
Eastern Germany	93.03	87.69	58.59	53.03	95.49	88.83
Western Germany	83.67		31.57		70.33	
Hungary	89.60	69.53	55.60	54.95	86.40	88.91
Japan	79.41		32.69		82.88	
Netherlands	74.93	50.38	31.86	35.06	53.39	44.94
Poland	85.28		44.23		86.06	
United Kingdom	82.03		37.91		66.19	
United States	55.66		16.62		50.00	
Russia	84.14	90.79	31.43	39.50	92.45	93.12
Slovenia	90.47		58.25		86.91	
Czech Republic	86.30	85.23	26.30	21.51	78.02	74.16
Estonia	91.90	86.34	30.60	29.27	74.80	75.61
Slovakia	89.19		35.41		89.73	

Note: Percept of respondents answering "yes": Left question is "The government should guarantee everyone a minimum standard of living." Center question is "The government should place an upper limit on the amount of money any one person can make." Right question is "The government should provide a job for everyone who wants one."
Source: International Social Justice Project (1996).

in most capitalist countries, with the possible exception of Germany and its "social-market" values. The dilemma, therefore, was that the economic reforms that postcommunist governments launched after 1989 did not correspond to the social-market values and expectations of postcommunist populations. ISJP revealed that majorities believed that postcommunist countries were already too unequal in 1991. In Bulgaria, 80 percent of the population in 1991 thought that inequality was already "much too large." That number exceeded 90 percent in 1996.[6] What would happen when capitalism widened inequalities further?

Yet rather than embracing the social-market values of voters, postsocialist governments competed to outbid each other to implement the most market oriented (and inequality generating) economic policies, through a process that Hilary Appel and Mitchell Orenstein have termed "competitive signaling."[7] Desperate for foreign investment to renovate their lagging economies, postsocialist countries adopted most of the policies of the Washington Consensus on economic reforms, those recommended by the European Union as a requirement for membership, and even went beyond them to implement avant-garde neoliberal policies such as pension privatization and the flat tax. By implementing the most market-oriented reforms, postsocialist countries could rise up in ranking systems developed by international financial institutions, such as the EBRD's "Transition Index" or the World Bank's "Ease of Doing Business Index." But these reforms ran roughshod over public attitudes about fairness and justice, creating a disjuncture between increasing life satisfaction and sociotropic evaluations of the transition.

Corruption: Bane of Transition

One of the key reasons that postsocialist populations saw the economic structures in their country as unfair was corruption. Many postsocialist citizens believed that their societies were led by politicians and businessmen, not to mention organized crime groups, who unfairly took advantage of their position and the chaos of market transition for personal gain. They stole privatized assets, used their ill-gotten wealth to influence politics, and now control access to lucrative careers and opportunities. As a result, corruption perceptions have become probably the biggest political issue in the postsocialist countries. Many elections in postcommunist countries (for instance, Slovakia in 2019) are fought and won on anti-corruption platforms.[8] Studies have consistently found that corruption in postcommunist countries is higher than elsewhere.[9] These studies are based on public opinion surveys that ask about individuals' experiences or perceptions of corruption, conducted either among elite groups such as business leaders and experts or the general population. In some cases, indexes are compiled from various sources, as in the case of the Transparency International Corruption Perceptions Index, the most widely publicized measure (see Table 12.2). In this area of public opinion, the World Bank has been active, producing its own index of corruption perceptions based on business surveys, the Business Environment and Economic Performance Survey (BEEPS), conducted in waves starting in 1999.[10]

Scholars have developed a number of theories to explain and interpret the high incidence of corruption in postcommunist transition countries. Treisman notes the dramatic increase in corruption in the postcommunist countries since 1989 and that "it is true that post-communist countries have unusually corrupt governments" on average. However, he finds that most postcommunist corruption can be explained by these countries' level of economic development and lack of a democratic history, both of which may be attributed to communism.[11] Grzymala-Busse finds that robust political competition reduces corruption and points to the vast difference between corruption perceptions in wealthier, more

TABLE 12.2 Corruption Perceptions

	1996	2000	2005	2010	2015
BALTICS		4.4	5.13	5.27	6.17
Estonia		5.7	6.4	6.5	7
Lithuania		4.1	4.8	5	5.9
Latvia		3.4	4.2	4.3	5.6
VISEGRAD	5.47	4.28	4.25	4.73	5.53
Poland	5.57	4.1	3.4	5.3	6.3
Czechia	5.37	4.3	4.3	4.6	5.6
Hungary		5.2	5	4.7	5.1
Slovakia		3.5	4.3	4.3	5.1
SEE		3.03	3.34	3.84	4.31
Slovenia		5.5	6.1	6.4	6
Croatia		3.7	3.4	4.1	5.1
Romania		2.9	3	3.7	4.6
Montenegro		1.3	2.8	3.7	4.4
Macedonia			2.7	4.1	4.2
Bulgaria		3.5	4	3.6	4.1
Serbia		1.3	2.8	3.5	4
Bosnia-Herzegovina			2.9	3.2	3.8
Albania			2.4	3.3	3.6
Kosovo				2.8	3.3
EUROPEAN FSU	2.58	2.38	2.56	2.67	3.39
Georgia			2.3	3.8	5.2
Armenia		2.5	2.9	2.6	3.5
Moldova		2.6	2.9	2.9	3.3
Belarus		4.1	2.6	2.5	3.2
Azerbaijan		1.5	2.2	2.4	2.9
Russian Federation	2.58	2.1	2.4	2.1	2.9
Ukraine		1.5	2.6	2.4	2.7
CENTRAL ASIA		2.7	2.2	2.04	2.38
Kazakhstan		3	2.6	2.9	2.8
Kyrgyzstan			2.3	2	2.8
Tajikistan			2.1	2.1	2.6
Uzbekistan		2.4	2.2	1.6	1.9
Turkmenistan			1.8	1.6	1.8

Note: On a scale of 0–10, with 0 being the most corrupt and 10 being the least corrupt.
Source: Transparency International Corruption Perceptions Index (2020). In order of low-to-high perceived corruption in 2015.

Western postcommunist countries and poorer Central Asian states.[12] While postcommunist corruption correlates with the lack of democracy and years under communism, the fact that corruption exploded after 1989 makes it hard to say whether communism caused corruption or repressed it. On the one hand, communism, by depressing economic development (at least in some countries) and preventing public feedback mechanisms that might prevent corruption in democratic societies, could have contributed to the burst of corruption after 1989. On the other hand, communism might have functioned to repress corruption below its "normal" level under free market capitalism in this region.

Whatever the case, free markets clearly brought with them a higher level of corruption perceptions and unfairness in the postcommunist countries. The rapid and disorganized way in which capitalism was introduced after 1989 created fertile ground for corrupt practices to take hold in business and politics. As a result, corruption—and the fight against it—has become a central feature of postcommunist public life. In Slovakia, for instance, in 2019, Zuzana Caputova was elected president in a landslide on the basis of an anti-corruption campaign after the murder of a journalist and his fiancée. The murdered journalist, Jan Kuciak, had been investigating connections between the Slovak government and the Italian 'Ndragheta mafia organization. Slovaks reacted angrily to the journalist's murder and Caputova rode a wave of mass protest against corruption and organized crime into office.[13] Many Central and East European governments have won election on an anti-corruption ticket, and heightened perceptions of corruption are one reason that postcommunist governments have seldom won reelection. Scholars Claire Wallace and Rossalina Latcheva find that "trust in public institutions depends to a great extent upon respondents' perception of corruption" and a "belief in the ubiquity of informal relations penetrating public life."[14] Both high-profile and everyday corruption has created a crisis of public trust in postcommunist societies.

Declining Public Trust

Public corruption is one of the reasons, despite growing life satisfaction, that postcommunist countries experienced a decline in general social trust among fellow citizens between 2010 and 2016. During this period, marked by post-crisis recovery and growth, egocentric evaluations of transition increased while, in many countries, sociotropic evaluations fell. When LiT asked the question: "Generally speaking, would you say that most people can be trusted, or that you cannot be too careful in dealing with people?," 34 percent of respondents answered with either "some trust" or "complete trust" in 2010 compared to only 31 percent in

2016, with marked declines noted in Russia and Kazakhstan.[15] In nearly every country, people reported that social trust was higher before 1989 (see Figure 12.1).

In addition, the EBRD's 2016–17 *Transition Report* specifically attributed the decline in public trust to rising inequality. While still celebrating the relative increases in life satisfaction and incomes, the EBRD noted that the region had experienced a dramatic increase in wealth inequality, and the rewards of the transition process had been unevenly distributed. As discussed earlier, younger, urban, more educated, and wealthier men were the disproportionate beneficiaries of the transition process.[16] But the *Transition Report* also noted that children born around the onset of transition in their countries were an average of about one centimeter shorter than their peers in the cohorts immediately before or after them. This is the kind of height difference that you would expect from a war zone, and it means that babies born at this time were subject to both micronutrient deficiency and psychosocial stress.

Underlining the findings on inequality, the 2016–17 report found that income growth had not kept up with levels recorded in the developed G-7 countries for 56 percent of the population in the transition region. Even as postsocialist transition countries caught up with developed countries on average, a majority of the population slipped further behind. The EBRD worried about the growing public anger over inequality:

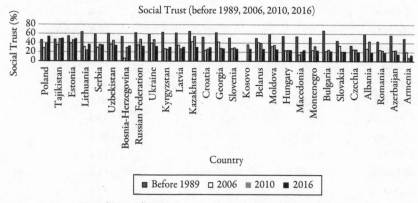

FIGURE 12.1. Social Trust (LiT). Percent who respond with "complete trust" or "some trust" on a 5-point scale for the question, "Generally speaking, would you say that most people can be trusted, or that you can't be too careful in dealing with people?"

Source: Life in Transition Survey (LiTS), European Bank for Reconstruction and Development, 2006, 2010, 2016.

People are overwhelmingly of the view that levels of inequality are high and rising. This may, in part, reflect the legacy of the transition experience. These perceptions may, to some extent, also be a result of the strong concentration of wealth among the very rich, with the region displaying high levels of concentration even relative to other emerging market economies. . . . The fact that wealth is strongly concentrated among the very rich across the region's economies is a source of concern, as it may limit equality of opportunity and undermine confidence in key economic and political institutions, resulting in weaker long-term growth.[17]

While the LiT3 authors suggest that perceptions of inequality are correlated with decreasing support for democracy and free markets, the published report does not openly discuss the overall increase or decrease in support for the changes in the postsocialist countries between 2010 and 2016. Table 12.3 displays the results of International Social Survey Programme (ISSP) surveys conducted in 1992, 1999, and 2009 on perceptions of inequality. ISSP data show that not only did perceptions of inequality increase in several countries from 1992 to 2009, but also substantial majorities in 2009 in Hungary, Croatia, Bulgaria, Latvia, and

TABLE 12.3 Percent that Perceives Society as Highly Unequal

	1992	1999	2009
Slovenia		28.1	26.4
Czechia	27.6	30.3	30.9
Estonia			32.6
Poland	58.5	49.1	37.1
Russia		59.4	40.7
Slovakia	27.6	51.3	43.6
Lithuania			48.8
Hungary	50.3	57	56.6
Croatia			57.4
Bulgaria	58.8	65.1	63.5
Latvia		65.9	68.3
Ukraine			69.1

Note: Respondents were asked to select one of five illustrations of income distribution that best described their society. Table displays percentage of respondents who chose the most unequal version, Type A, a society with "a small elite at the top, very few people in the middle and the great mass of people at the bottom."
Source: International Social Survey Programme (2009, 1999, 1992).

Ukraine indicated that their societies were characterized by "*a small elite at the top, very few people in the middle and the great mass of people at the bottom*," the most unequal choice of five options.

If you dive down into the country-level assessments in the LiT survey, an interesting story emerges about the "success" of the transition process, and it gives you some idea about how frustrated people had become.[18] First, the *average support for the market economy among the 2016 "transition region" was only about 35 percent* compared to 65 percent in Germany and Italy in the same year. Second, the average support for democracy in the "transition region" was about 50 percent compared to 80 percent in Germany and Italy. Third, support for both free markets and democracy was widely variable across the region (see Figures 12.2 and 12.3). Between 2010 and 2016, it increased for both free markets and democracy in Bulgaria, Croatia, Macedonia, Hungary, Latvia, Lithuania, Poland, Romania, Serbia, Slovenia, Ukraine, and Uzbekistan. Enthusiasm decreased for both democracy and free markets in Albania, Armenia, Azerbaijan, Belarus,

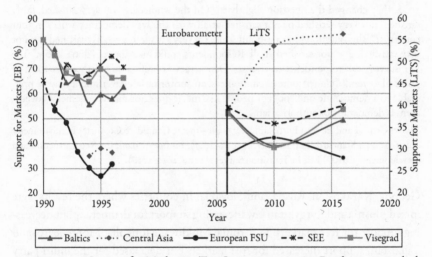

FIGURE 12.2. Support for Markets in Two Surveys, 1990–2016. Eurobarometer asked, "Do you personally feel that the creation of a free market economy, that is one largely free from state control, is right or wrong for [our country's] future?" Respondents could respond "right," "wrong," or "don't know." The LiT surveys ask respondents to choose "A market economy is preferable to any other form of economic system," "Under some circumstances, a planned economy may be preferable to a market economy," and "For people like me, it does not matter whether the economic system is organised as a market economy or as a planned economy."

Source: Central and Eastern Eurobarometer (1990–1997), Candidate Countries Eurobarometer (2002–2004), Standard Eurobarometer (2005–2017), European Bank for Reconstruction and Development (EBRD) Life in Transition Surveys (2006, 2010, 2016).

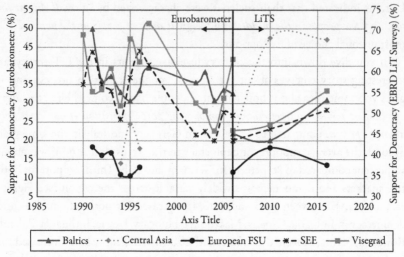

FIGURE 12.3. Support for Democracy in Two Surveys, 1990–2016. Eurobarometer asked, "On the whole, are you very satisfied, fairly satisfied, not very satisfied or not satisfied at all with the way democracy is developing in [our country]?" However, starting in 2002, they changed the question slightly to "On the whole, are you very satisfied, fairly satisfied, not very satisfied or not satisfied at all with the way democracy works in [our country]?" This question is on a 4-point scale: 1 = very satisfied, 2 = fairly satisfied, 3 = not very satisfied, 4 = not satisfied at all. Respondents could also answer "don't know." The LiT surveys ask respondents to choose "Democracy is preferable to any other form of political system," "Under some circumstances, an authoritarian government may be preferable to a democratic one," or "For people like me, it does not matter whether a government is democratic or authoritarian."

Source: Central and Eastern Eurobarometer (1990–1997), Candidate Countries Eurobarometer (2002–2004), Standard Eurobarometer (2005–2017), European Bank for Reconstruction and Development (EBRD) Life in Transition Surveys (2006, 2010, 2016).

Georgia, Kazakhstan, Russia, and Slovakia. In countries where the results were mixed, Bosnia and Kyrgyzstan saw increasing support for democracy but decreasing support for free markets. In Estonia, Moldova, Mongolia, Montenegro, and Tajikistan, support increased for free markets but decreased for the multi-party system, meaning that thirteen countries saw popular falling support for democracy between 2010 and 2016.

Support for a Strong State

Instead, a preference for a strong state endured throughout the region. A 2015–16 Pew Research Center study of religious beliefs and nationalism in the former state socialist countries (and Greece) also included questions about support for democracy.[19] The researchers found that citizens in this region showed lower levels of support for democracy than citizens in both Latin America and sub-Saharan Africa, where the Pew Center also conducted polling. Of the seventeen postsocialist countries surveyed between June 2015 and July 2016 through face-to-face interviews in the local language, majorities who agreed with the statement "democracy is preferable to any other form of government" were only found in Lithuania (64 percent), Georgia (55 percent), Croatia (54 percent), Armenia (53 percent), and Romania (52 percent). In Hungary, Poland, Bosnia, Estonia, Bulgaria, Belarus, Ukraine, Latvia, Russia, Moldova and Serbia, fewer than 50 percent of those surveyed preferred democracy over other forms of government. Russia (31 percent), Moldova (26 percent), and Serbia (25 percent) had the lowest percentages in favor of democracy. Furthermore, 41 percent of Russians and 44 percent of Moldovans agreed that "in some circumstances, a nondemocratic government can be preferable."[20] Despite the higher claims of life satisfaction found in the EBRD's Life in Transition III survey and the reported closing of the happiness gap, support for democracy continued to decline as economic inequality increased. This inequality depressed support for markets and democracy both because more citizens found themselves among the ranks of the "losers" of the transition process *and* because the perceived unfairness contradicted widely held social-market values.

Therefore, in spite of the EBRD's finding of higher levels of life satisfaction, social trust in the region remained in the toilet. When asked, "Generally speaking, would you say that most people can be trusted, or that you can't be too careful in dealing with people?," 50 percent or more believed that they couldn't really trust people, with 93 percent of Bosnians, 89 percent of Bulgarians, 85 percent of Armenians and Serbians, and 83 percent of Croatians suspicious of their fellow citizens.[21] According to the Pew researchers, these appalling low levels of social trust are at least partially responsible for the mixed support for democracy in the region. According to the World Values Survey (WVS), which offers more complete data for social trust that mostly corresponds with Pew findings, in 2017–20, the highest level of trust in fellow citizens was found in dictatorial Belarus (see Table 12.4).

On the upside, except for Ukraine and Moldova, majorities in all other countries agree that "most people are better off in a market economy." At the same time, however, more than 84 percent of people in all countries surveyed believed that the government should do more to help the poor, and in twelve countries, more than 90 percent of the population agreed. This widespread desire for expanded social safety nets derives from an overwhelming pessimism about the economy: "In nearly all countries surveyed, majorities describe their country's economic situation as either "very" bad or "somewhat" bad. Ukrainians nearly universally gave their economies a bad rating (96 percent). In just one country'

TABLE 12.4 Can People Be Trusted?

	1989–92	1995–98	2000–04	2005–09	2010–14	2017–20
Belarus	25	23			32.6	40
Estonia		21.1			39	33.9
Lithuania		21.3				31.7
Hungary		22.5		28.7		27.2
Azerbaijan		19.4			14.8	26.3
Slovenia		15.3		17.5	19.9	25.3
Armenia		23.5			10.9	24.9
Poland	31.3	16.9		18.1	22.2	24.1
Russian Federation	34.7	23.2		24.6	27.8	22.9
Kazakhstan					38.3	22.8
Montenegro		30.4	32.9			21.7
Slovakia	23	25.8				21.4
Czechia	30.2	27.2				21.1
Tajikistan						20.6
Bulgaria		23.7		19.6		17.1
Serbia		28.4	18.3	13.6		16.3
Croatia		22.8				13.6
Kyrgyzstan			16.6		36.3	12.8
Romania		17.9		19.3	7.7	12.1
Bosnia-Herzegovina		26.9	15.6			9.6
Georgia		17.7		17.6	8.8	9
Albania		24.3	23.2			2.8
Ukraine		28.8		24.5	23.1	
Uzbekistan					13.9	
Moldova		21.8	14.1	17.6		
Macedonia		7.5	13.1			
Latvia		23.9				

Note: Percentage agreeing that most people can be trusted.
Source: World Values Survey (2020). From high-to-low trust in 2017–2020.

surveyed—the Czech Republic—do somewhat more people describe their country's economy as good (53%) than bad (46%)."[22]

Perhaps the most striking finding of the 2015–16 Pew survey was that solid majorities of citizens claimed they were *dissatisfied* with "the way things are going in their country today" (see Table 12.5).[23] Only in the Czech Republic did 52 percent of respondents claim satisfaction with the direction of their nation, in all

TABLE 12.5 Satisfaction with How Things Are Going in Country

	2002	2009	2015–16	2019
Czechia	36	28	52	54
Slovakia	11	37		54
Belarus			47	
Russian Federation	20	34	46	43
Estonia			46	
Lithuania		7	42	52
Poland	9	36	34	65
Hungary		6	34	41
Latvia			31	
Serbia			27	
Romania			24	
Armenia			21	
Bulgaria	4	18	21	22
Croatia			17	
Georgia			17	
Bosnia			12	
Moldova			11	
Ukraine	9	7	2	23

Note: Percentage who are satisfied with the way things are going in their country today.
Source: Pew (2009, 2011, 2017, 2019). From high-to-low satisfaction in 2015–16.

other countries this figure was below 50 percent, and in eight of those, satisfaction was below 25 percent.[24] This means that although people were reporting increases in satisfaction with their own personal lives, they were also reporting dissatisfaction with the direction of their countries, and much of this had to do with unhappiness with the continued social costs attributed to the transition to free markets. In most countries, solid majorities also believed that unemployment and income inequality were "big problems."[25] Perhaps not surprisingly, then, a separate poll conducted in Poland, Hungary, the Czech Republic, and Slovakia by the Center for Insights in Survey Research of the International Republican Institute confirmed that only a majority of Czechs (53 percent) thought their country was heading in the "right direction."[26] In Slovakia, 59 percent believed their country was headed in the "wrong direction," as did 57 percent of Poles. When asked if "today's generation of young people" had a good future in their country, 57 percent of Czechs, 67 percent of Slovaks, 74 percent of Hungarians, and 75 percent of Poles said "no." That is an awful lot of pessimism in four of the

countries that performed the best economically since the demise of state socialism in 1989. It sets the stage for understanding the strong performance of populist
parties.

By 2019, thirty years after the fall of the Berlin Wall, the Pew Global Attitudes
Survey presented a better perspective for at least some countries.[27] A majority of
the population in four counries now expressed satisfaction in the overall direction of their country: Poland, Czechia, Slovakia, and Lithuania (see Table 12.5).
In addition, perspectives on the economic situation improved dramatically since
2009 (the peak of the global financial crisis), with a majority of the population in
Poland and the Czech Republic now saying that the economic situation was better than under communism. Other Central Europe and Baltic countries were just
behind, in the 40s. Hungary had shot up from 8 percent to 47 percent between
2009 and 2019, during the time that populist prime minister Viktor Orbán was
in office. But still, Russia, Ukraine, and Bulgaria hovered around 25 percent.
Only one-quarter of those surveyed believed that the economic situation in their
country was better in 2019 than under communism. Russia was the only country
where evaluations declined, probably due to sanctions imposed after its invasion
of Crimea in 2014. Most postcommunist countries were not included in the 2019
survey, and it is likely that Southeast European and former Soviet republics were
closer to Bulgaria and Russia than to Poland and the Czech Republic, the relative
winners.[28]

Growth without a Social Contract

In 2019, the World Bank published a watershed report, "Toward a New Social
Contract: Taking on Distributional Tensions in Europe and Central Asia." The
report found that the postcommunist region remained one of the most *equal* in
the world in measured income equality. Greater income equality reflected the
institutional and attitudinal legacy of communism, but also cultural preferences
of Europeans, shared with Western Europe. Most of the world's most equal countries are in Europe and Central Asia. This is reinforced by social norms that support social cohesion and a strong government role in redistribution, providing
jobs and social guarantees. For instance, an analysis of World Values Survey data
shows that about 70 percent of people in the United States believe the poor can
help themselves to improve their situation. Conversely, in Western Europe, only
40 percent do so. "In Eastern European transition countries, the share drops to
24 percent."[29]

As a result, the report concluded, "Rising income inequality among groups
runs counter to the strong preferences for equity and fairness in the region."[30] In
the postcommunist countries, inequality grew sharply during the transition. The

report shows that the number of billionaires increased dramatically, as did the percentage of national income going to the top 1 percent. Russia now has one of the highest rates of income inequality among the BRICS (Brazil, Russia, India, China, South Africa) countries. The share of total national income going to the top 1 percent of the population nearly quintupled from 4.38 to 20.24 percent in Russia from 1985 to 2014 and tripled from 4.16 to 13.98 percent in Poland (see Table 2.4), more as a share of income than in any West European country during the same time period. The United Kingdom registered a shift of 7.21 percent of national income toward the top 1 percent in the same time period and Germany 2.26 percent.[31]

Perceptions of inequality also matter. Measured inequality, such as the Gini index, may underestimate inequality growth in postcommunist countries, since so much income has been redistributed to the top 1 percent, who are rarely interviewed in the studies that produce income data and because of the rise of the informal economy (see discussion in Part I). But people may also perceive inequality differently. Perceptions of inequality may refer to specific reference groups whose income growth may differ from national trends or to other factors, such as unemployment, or to personal circumstances. Researchers have found that *perceptions* of inequality are just as important as measured inequality in determining demand for redistribution. Therefore, it is important to determine what aspects of inequality bother people most, if one wishes to reconstruct the social contract in low-trust societies.

The 2019 World Bank report reflected an urgent concern with voting for extreme parties across Europe, decline in trust in social institutions, and other indicators that the social contract was fraying. Part of the problem was labor market trends, such as non-traditional and part-time employment, which provide less income security than people want, as well as regional disparities within countries, and the fact that young people of the region had been hit particularly hard by increasing income insecurity. In the postcommunist countries, a growing number of people believed that one needs connections to get jobs, particularly secure jobs in the public sector. At the same time, public policies have not adequately adjusted to new conditions or provided the levels of security the population demanded. The report advocated changing social policies to allay new labor market realities and emphasized universal social policies—such as family policies, universal basic income, and guaranteed minimum income or conditional cash transfer programs—to take the sting out of growing labor market inequality. It pointed out that some recent policy changes, such as the introduction of a flat tax in many postcommunist countries, had worsened inequality by reducing rates paid by the top earners.

Overall, the report was notable as a shift in World Bank thinking about the transition region. One chapter of the report relied on public opinion surveys to explore dissatisfaction that did not accord with the J-curve narrative. Benchmarking the postcommunist region with Western Europe, rather than poorer developing countries, "Toward a New Social Contract" concerned itself with the political reaction to liberalism and advocated more ambitious and universal social policies. All of a sudden, after populist reactions, we observe a new attention to what people think.

Conclusions

Based on public opinion surveys, including those conducted by the EBRD and the World Bank, we find that inequality reduced support for market reforms and democracy in the postcommunist societies by two routes, one egocentric and the other sociotropic. On the one hand, inequality reduced the number of people who benefited from transition, leading to lower evaluations. On the other, rapid increases in inequality jarred widely shared sensibilities about fairness and justice. Of course, we observe substantial sub-regional variation: while Central and East European populations remained more positive about market reforms throughout the 1990s, Russian support for market reforms hit rock bottom. Yet throughout the postcommunist region, by the mid-2000s, only a significant minority of the population remained enthusiastic supporters of markets and democracy. In most countries, support for alternatives such as central planning outpaced support for liberal markets. Red nostalgia grew as strong majorities believed that transition had led to advantages for often corrupt elites while not delivering much for average earners and "ordinary people." While economic growth lifted many boats and poverty declined precipitously after 1999, only a significant minority of the post-socialist population experienced high life satisfaction in 2016.

For many people, postcommunist transitions precipitated massive negative repercussions, in some countries lasting a few years, in others a few decades. Where one found oneself in the distribution of costs and benefits determined, to a large extent, whether one expressed support for markets and democracy or reported high life satisfaction. But ours is not only a story of winners and losers. For people socialized under communism, the new inequality of income and wealth offended their sensibilities about justice and fairness and the role of government in society.[32] Only a minority of the postcommunist population accepted the new social contract, which seemed to be based on little more than raw greed, exercised under conditions of limited legal restraint. Red nostalgia grew and support for markets plunged—below a majority of the population in most countries. Some public opinion data clearly support the disaster capitalism narrative, but others provide strong support for the J-curve narrative. Once again, we find a Janus-faced story about the transition; successes and failures co-exist.

The greatest success of the postcommunist transitions was that the peoples of Eastern Europe now enjoy much greater *political freedoms* than they had under communism. Public opinion polls reveal that most people recognize this as a key difference between market democracy and communism and appreciate it by wide margins. Whereas heavy-handed communist leaders forced people to work, prevented them from traveling, and tried to limit their alcohol consumption, the postsocialist era brought a new world of personal liberty. Whereas communist citizens were once trapped in societies they could not change, postcommunist citizens were free to leave and seek their fortunes elsewhere. Men and women can now make autonomous decisions about the fate of their own lives and futures. Certainly, this was an improvement over the infantilizing politics of a massive and repressive state. These are major achievements, not to be ignored or dismissed.

At the same time, however, the transition shattered confidence in state institutions, creating the potential for political changes that might undermine these cherished freedoms. Decline in public trust reached extreme levels in many countries. Higher life satisfaction under capitalism coupled with nostalgia for the communist past. Enhanced political freedoms coupled with diminishing trust in public institutions. These contradictions define the postcommunist transitions and can be explained, in part, by recognizing the enormous differences in outcomes that accrued to the winners and losers of reform. Growth alone cannot reestablish a social contract. As with the economic and demographic data, public opinion data also reveal a story of two worlds: a successful postcommunist transition for some and a long recession leading to disillusionment for many more after thirty years of transition.

PART IV

The Ethnographic Evidence

13

Portraits of Desperation

SO FAR IN this book we have been telling a largely quantitative story about the social impacts of transition, using various measures to understand the vast diversity of experiences of people living in the postsocialist world. The scale of our questions about the effects of the transition process have been regional, sub-regional, and national, but the data we collected makes it clear that there is a lot of diversity within each national context. Not only is there a large and growing gap between the rich and the poor, the educated and the uneducated, the young and the old, and men and women, but there are also important geographic divides between the urban and rural areas and between sub-national regions that are either closer to or farther away from Western Europe or Russia (for instance, the distinct east and west parts of Ukraine or Estonia).

One of the shortcomings of looking at aggregate statistics is that we can lose sight of the individuals living through these momentous changes. Each unique data point, each population unit calculated in the GDP per capita, is someone's mother or father, daughter or son, husband or wife. We can look at poverty rates or changes in Gini coefficients without engaging with the men and women who are now rich or poor or who find themselves in the top or bottom deciles of the income distribution. Economics can be a very impersonal discipline, dealing in abstractions about what is good for the economy as a whole without ever dealing with the very personal experiences of living in a certain moment in history. It may well be that for policymakers and politicians, individual stories are mere distractions, narratives that complicate the hard decisions that must be made in the name of overall growth and macroeconomic stability. And it also may be that building free and open societies in Eastern Europe required a necessary amount of collateral human damage—that some people just weren't prepared to take control of their own lives in newly liberalized labor markets. But this shouldn't make their suffering less real or more easily dismissible.

This part of the book dives down to the level of local communities and explores how they coped with the massive upheavals that followed the fall of the Berlin Wall and the implosion of the Soviet Union. Relying on the work of ethnographers, we examined the individual subjective experiences of the transition on the lives of ordinary men and women struggling to get by in a world where all of the old rules had been changed overnight. Our hope here is to breathe some more human life into the data that we have thus far presented in this book. The numbers show us that there were both winners and losers of the transition process, and the ethnographic scholarship allows us to switch the scale of our analysis from the macro to the micro to provide a more robust, nuanced, and personal picture of the social impacts of transition.

What Is Ethnography?

Alfred Kroeber, one of the early fathers of American cultural anthropology, is reported to have said, "Anthropology is the most humanistic of the sciences and the most scientific of the humanities."[1] This means that ethnography, the methodological tool most often used by cultural anthropologists, is often derided by other, "harder" social scientists as not being "scientific" enough. Unlike other social scientific methods based on modeling, experimentation, or random sampling, ethnography requires a deep submersion among a subject population for an extended period of time. Ethnographers—whether they are from anthropology, sociology, geography, media studies, education, or a host of other disciplines that have embraced the value of this qualitative method—must learn local languages and blend in as participant-observers to understand the worldviews of the people being studied as well as the fabric of their day-to-day experiences and the meanings attached to them. It's not enough just to watch a cockfight with the locals; ethnographers use the experience of the cockfight to understand the unique cultural values and priorities of those participating in the event on their own terms.

Because of the highly individualized nature of doing this kind of research, evidentiary standards in ethnography differ from those in other social science disciplines. The messy nature of snowball samples and the subjective point of view of the research make ethnographic studies almost impossible to replicate, and as a result, they are of limited value for producing generalizable knowledge. But ethnographers are not looking for "Truth" with a capital "T." Where quantitative data allow for breadth, these qualitative data provide depth, giving voice to the individual men and women whose lives have been radically transformed by larger geopolitical processes. For example, the public opinion surveys may reveal that many East Europeans are nostalgic for the socialist past, but the narratives of *why* those who long for the one-party system and the planned economy do so are fully accessible only by talking to men and women after building a relationship of trust with them over an extended period of time.

To take another example, demographers recognize that increased alcohol consumption accounted for much of the decrease in male life expectancy in Russia. But whether the transition process *caused* the increased alcohol consumption is harder to establish through an analysis of morbidity and mortality rates alone. It is only in reading an ethnographic study about treatment for Russian alcoholics in the postsocialist context that we begin to understand the devastating social consequences of unemployment on individual men as an underlying cause of that alcoholism. In Eugene Raikhel's 2016 book, *Governing Habits: Treating Alcoholism in the Post-Soviet Clinic*, the ethnographer spent over a year doing research in various alcoholic treatment facilities around St. Petersburg. After getting to know a middle-aged alcoholic named Sasha, Raikhel heard about the despair and hopelessness that many Russian men felt. Sasha told him:

> I think that people like me, or people close to me in spirit, we are not needed, not by the state, not by the police, not by anyone. We're thrown-away people [*my vyibroshennye liudi*]. So I think that all of these [alcohol] stores which are open twenty-four hours a day, are especially there for people of my generation—of the 1950s and '60s—which grew up on port wine—just to drown us in drink [*chtoby nas prosto spoit'*] so that we'll just die off. I think that way, and no one can convince me otherwise. Because all of my good friends have died—starting when they were thirty-eight years old, forty, forty-two—all of my friends. Some died from vodka, others died in the camps—in the camps they all died from vodka. One died from a heart attack, but he also drank. As though it was all on purpose. . . . Here [*u nas*] the state's policies [*politika*] toward my generation are to drown us in drink so that we'll all die off.[2]

A similar narrative could be found in postsocialist Romania. The ethnographer Bruce O'Neil spent over a year living with homeless populations in Bucharest and recorded their deep disillusionment with the promises of democracy. One of his informants, a man he calls Costel, explains to O'Neill, "We are the sacrificed generation—those born in the fifties and sixties. . . . We did alright until communism ended in '89–'90. . . . Now we wait at churches and nongovernmental organizations for a plate of food. And that's all the help we get. We cannot speak of social aid from the state."[3] In Lithuania, the anthropologist Neringa Klumbytė conducted ethnographic research among rural inhabitants who spoke of "feeling isolated, unneeded, and worthless." One 50-year-old former collective farm worker told Klumbytė, "We lived well then [in Soviet times], we had jobs. Everyone was needed somewhere. For example, I was the administrator [of a warehouse]. I worked for three years. I started to understand my job and I was needed. Now you're trash, not a human. If you don't work, who considers you a person?"[4] Reflecting these same sentiments, Lothar de Maizière, the last GDR prime minister, told the *New York Times* in 2015, "I always said there was a 10/10 generation—10 years too long in East Germany to really make a fresh start, and 10 years too young to retire. And that is tragic, because they were the people who for 40 years effectively carried East Germany. And then they were told we don't need you anymore."[5]

This idea of "thrown away people," "the 10/10 generation," and the "sacrificed generation" are powerful metaphors for the experience of the transition from state socialism to democracy and free markets. Of the hundreds of ethnographic studies conducted in the former Soviet Union and across Eastern Europe since 1989, a great many of them focus on these "thrown away people" of the region, those who have been left behind and forgotten. And like Sasha the alcoholic, many of them increasingly believe that this was "done on purpose" by the West, by corrupt elites, by a shadowy international network of secret bankers controlling the world, or by whomever they can pin the blame on. Understanding the alienation and marginalization of the transition process gives us a much richer context within which to understand the quantitative data that have been presented in this book thus far.

Although there have been calls for "studying up,"[6] ethnographers tend to conduct their research among more marginalized groups in society: ethnic or religious minorities, the urban or rural poor, the elderly, the ill, the homeless, drug users, alcoholics—and the ethnographic studies of Eastern Europe and the former Soviet Union prove no exception. Part of the explanation is a question of access; political, economic, and cultural elites are less likely to let some random foreigner just hang out with them (although there are some notable exceptions). This disciplinary proclivity to side with the point of view of the powerless is a reaction to the earlier complicity of ethnographic knowledge producers with the colonial projects of Great Britain and the United States in the Global South. Perhaps the best argument for the value of ethnographic knowledge is that governments and private corporations have found it extremely useful when they have a vested interest in politically or economically dominating a society or community, and this pattern replicated itself in the 1990s when the US government generously dispensed funds to promote the fieldwork of anthropologists and qualitative sociologists in the postsocialist countries of Eastern Europe.[7] During the Cold War, few East European governments allowed American scholars to conduct extended research in their countries, and when this was allowed, the scholars in question were often seen as spies or saboteurs.[8] But after 1991, postsocialist countries opened up and Western scholars rushed in, fueled by federal grants and fellowships for both language study and international research. This produced an explosion of new scholarship.

Because so much scholarship has been produced—books, articles, essays, reports, films, blogs—it is impossible to review it all in one chapter. A full overview of the ethnographic work on the transformations across Central and Eastern Europe and the former Soviet Union after 1989 would require a book of its own, particularly if we were to include the non-English language scholarship. Instead, we will present a relevant selection of the ethnographic studies that directly reflect on or further elucidate the core themes that we have already discussed in this book, particularly the affective experience of growing inequality and loss of social solidarity. The qualitative data here help us better understand how and why there is so much variation across regions and sub-regions and to explore the lived experience of the social impacts of transition. These ethnographic studies also confirm that there is not one story to tell about transition; while it was good for those in a position to take advantage of the new opportunities brought by the coming of democracy and free markets, many others found themselves unmoored in their new societies, struggling to make sense of a world with new rules.

A Breakdown in Social Trust

The key finding of these ethnographic chapters is that the economic, mortality, and out-migration crises in many postsocialist countries contributed to a cultural shift from a kind of collective identity—a shared suffering perhaps—but a unique form of socialist sociality that is difficult to measure but which everyone who grew up under socialism can speak about. Many citizens believe that this collective identity or shared poverty was replaced by a crass and crude form of selfish individualism that was orthogonal to the values that they grew up with. If you remember back to the public opinion chapters, when asked "Generally speaking, would you say that most people can be trusted, or that you can't be too careful in dealing with people?," majorities in all postsocialist countries surveyed believed that they couldn't really trust their fellow citizens. These numbers were particularly abysmal in the Balkans, with 93 percent of Bosnians, 89 percent of Bulgarians, 85 percent of Serbians, and 83 percent of Croatians stating that they felt wary of others.[9]

Perhaps the best-known chronicler of the transition in the Soviet Union is Caroline Humphrey, who started her research in the USSR in the mid-1960s. The Soviet government gave Humphrey permission to conduct ethnographic fieldwork in 1966, and she was among the first Western anthropologists allowed to do so. She lived among the Buryat people of Siberia, and her award-winning book,

The Karl Marx Collective: Economy, Society, and Religion in a Siberian Collective Farm (1983), was an intimate look at daily life in the Soviet Far East. After the collapse of the Soviet Union in 1991, Humphrey returned to Siberia and republished an updated version of her book called, *Marx Went Away, but Karl Stayed Behind*, a detailed portrait of the upheavals of the transition. In her time in the field, Humphrey reports speaking with a Buryat economist who told her:

> The collective farmers under socialism were subject to administrative serfdom. Today they are subject to economic serfdom. Their plots are too small to produce a surplus, and even if they succeeded there is no public transport now and they cannot take produce to market on their backs. They have to rely on the collective farm to plough the land as they have no machines. That means they have no alternative but to bow to the farm leadership, to give their labor at any rate the boss will offer. The vast majority cannot even escape to the city—they don't have the money to pay to get there. What is that but serfdom?[10]

In a 2002 collection of essays, *The Unmaking of Soviet Life: Everyday Economies after Socialism*, Humphrey took a worm's eye view of the transition process in Russia and found widespread misery and despair where people had hoped for freedom and prosperity:

> The collapse of party rule, the ending of full employment, massive inflation after decades of stable prices, a labyrinth of new, widely disobeyed laws, and the chasm of unbelief opened after the rejection of Soviet ideology all combined to cast people into a state of radical uncertainty. As the years passed, it became evident that the promised "transition" to prosperous market democracy was not going to happen in the near future, if at all. Accustomed institutions were disintegrating and decaying, and it seemed that only "wild" moneymaking and big-man politics were taking their place. Russians were used to inequality of status, but now suddenly miserable poverty came to exist alongside soaring, inexplicable wealth.[11]

In Romania, Maria Bucur and Mihaela Miroiu found evidence of similarly dramatic breakdowns in social trust. In 2009 and 2010, they interviewed a snowball sample of 101 women in Hunedoara County. They divided their interview subjects into three distinct generations depending on how long they had lived under Romanian communism: the "communist generation," the "transition generation," and the "democracy generation." Both the communist and transition generations commented openly on the changes in the quality of human relationships before and after the coming of democracy. In their chapter on "Communities," Bucur and Miroiu report a pervasive sense that social relations had deteriorated since 1989. "Our interviewees attributed this to the development of a free market—pursuing wealth or survival in a capitalist system of competition."[12] One woman commented that "in a relatively status- and income-homogenous society, people had greater consideration for one another and cheated less."[13]

Later in the book, the authors returned to this theme and suggested that the experience of an economy of shortage forged a stronger feeling of solidarity among people struggling against a common enemy: the communist state. "Our respondents contrasted the value placed on and the quality of human relationships during periods of shortage to 'the selfishness and loneliness of nowadays.'"[14] Another interviewee reported, "Nobody does anything anymore without a reward. People are no longer as good or kind. Everybody seems stressed out, nervous. They do not have the strength to work with one another, as they barely solve their own issues. The richer one gets, the worse, more selfish, and greedier one becomes."[15]

In rural Uzbekistan, Tommaso Trevisani found a similar breakdown in social relations among rural elites with regard to the transformation of the Soviet-era cotton cooperatives.[16] Older forms of patronage where local bosses looked after agricultural workers in a joint effort to resist, undermine, or subvert the designs of Soviet central planners to increase the well-being of rural Uzbeks gave way to a new class of predatory elites who now enriched themselves at the expense of their poorer compatriots. Where there had once been solidarity on the *kolkhoz*, a sort of Robin Hood mentality where local elites stole from the rich (the Soviet state) to give to the poor (kolkhoz workers), there was now only self-interest and greed, which ruptured social bonds and turned neighbor against neighbor. To Western observers, enterprising local businessmen were "entrepreneurs," but to ordinary citizens they were bandits stealing the once collective wealth for themselves.

In 2009, the Bulgarian historian Maria Todorova reflected back on the first two decades of the transition and argued that the nostalgia for the state socialist past did not mean wishing the old system back. Instead, she recognized that there were some positive aspects to the predictable rhythms of the planned economy: "Post-communist nostalgia is not only the longing for security, stability and prosperity but also the feeling of loss for a specific form of sociability," she wrote in *The Guardian*.[17] According to Todorova, who herself grew up under communism, something important was lost in 1989, a feeling of community and belonging that had been devastated by the cutthroat competition of the free market economy. Many former citizens of state socialist regimes felt that a profound moral shift had occurred across the region.

East Germans also mourned the loss of a particular form of socialist sociality. The anthropologist Daphne Berdahl lived in the village of Kella in East

Germany, so close to the border with West Germany that she could see the barbed wire fence dividing the countries every day. There was no road sign to Kella, and the village was full of stories of the people who crossed the border or tried to cross and failed. But when the Wall fell in 1989, the villagers of Kella were completely unprepared for the disaster and disorientation that would devastate their local solidarities. In one chapter, Berdahl discusses the fate of the Kella women who had worked in two local factories making suspender clips and toys. Both of the factories closed just eighteen months after the Wall came down, throwing almost all of the village's women out of work in one fell swoop. Since many of them were over forty, they could not find new jobs to replace the ones they lost and were forced to stay home. In her conversations with the women, Berdahl found that the thing they missed the most was the sociality of their former lives. She wrote:

> Apart from close friends and relatives, women largely stopped seeing each other except for occasional encounters at Sunday mass or the village Konsum [store]. Feelings of superfluousness and financial insecurity, as well as the loss of a worker identity inculcated through forty years of state ideology and physical labor, contributed to many women's confusion and depression. "My friend Sylvia," one woman told me, "she just sits at home and cries." Another woman in her midforties, who often shared with me her feelings of depression and isolation, explained sadly: "This idea that a woman should stay at home and only do her housework came all at once. It happened overnight, too quickly.[18]

Berdahl also discusses the humiliation that the East Germans felt during the reunification process. The *Wessis* treated them as half-people, permanently damaged by their lives under what the West Germans considered the twentieth-century's second totalitarianism.[19] The *Ossis* were seen as dupes of the regime, subjugated masses with no will of their own, a subjective position that most East Germans rejected. Berdahl tells a wonderful anecdote about a "tree of unity" which is planted in Kella to symbolize reunification. It died within a year of being planted. The villagers of Kella planted a second tree and surrounded it with a piece of the old barbed wire fence that used to separate the East and West. One of the villagers noted with some irony that the tree thrived when the fence went back up, giving voice to the growing feeling of *Ostalgie*, or nostalgia for the East. The roots of the ongoing East German resentment of Western Germans found fertile soil in the harsh upheavals of the early transition process, and continue to resonate to this day, even after three decades.

There is no question that life has been more individualistic since the end of state socialism, and in many respects, this is what the revolutions of 1989 set out to achieve; to increase individual opportunities for citizens whose lives were circumscribed by heavy-handed centralized state authorities who severely limited personal freedom. But many Central and East European and former Soviet citizens rejected this stark individualism and look back fondly on a vision of the past, which promoted cooperation over competition. In the 1990s, Western advisors and economic elites considered this penchant for the collective a weakness born of socialist brainwashing and theorized that it would soon be replaced by a healthy and "natural" self-interest that would help fuel the capitalist economy. And indeed, for young, urban, and educated people who were the main beneficiaries of the increased economic opportunities available in the new market economy, the loss of this particular form of sociality was more than made up for by their newfound freedom and mobility, including the ability to move to Western Europe in search of better jobs and better lives.

New cosmopolitan political, cultural, and economic elites also found greater satisfaction in their international networks. They could travel abroad and had access to goods and services their parents and grandparents only dreamed of. Many newly wealthy entrepreneurs bought properties in London, Paris, and New York, and sent their children to elite Western schools and universities. But for those left behind, the profound value shift from an old grudging communalism to the new savage individualism was one of the biggest disappointments of the postsocialist era. Like Sasha the alcoholic in Raikhel's study, many men and women felt like they had been thrown away, just as their previous value systems and moral compasses had been delegitimized in the sudden rush to get rich quick.

We find evidence of these attitudinal shifts clearly in the work of anthropologists who studied the same communities both before and after 1989. For example, Gerald Creed lived and worked on a collective farm in the Bulgarian village of Zamfirovo on and off for a decade between 1987 and 1997. Creed's book, *Domesticating Revolution*, is unique because it viewed the transition process as it unfolded from a rural location far from the center of decision-making in Sofia. Creed established his relationships with the cooperative farmers in Zamfirovo before the fall of the Berlin Wall, and he learned that the villagers had enjoyed a relatively egalitarian social structure even before the advent of collectivization. Like the Uzbeks, the members of the collective farm in Zamfirovo had found ways to make the socialist system work for them. They were the beneficiaries of rural industrialization projects that helped equalize the living standards across the population of Bulgaria. To his surprise, Creed found that the rural Bulgarians he studied maintained a deep commitment to equality, and that "no potential change disturbed villagers more than the specter of inequality."[20]

From the front lines of the transition process, Creed reported:

In 1992, some villagers clearly saw the transition as a referendum on equality. When I asked one woman worker in the cooperative farm for her opinion of the changes, I got a defense of equality instead: "Why do we have to be rich and poor? Why can't everybody have a little bit? What's wrong with that? That mother-fucking Gorbachev is to blame for this mess." Other villagers were visibly tormented by emerging inequality: "I can't face the idea of telling my kid that he cannot have something when other children have it. We are used to everybody being the same and having the same things. I simply can't tell him that we are too poor. It doesn't make sense. These are the same friends he played with before as equals.[21]

Another informant told Creed the advent of privatization and free markets had improved the lives of only a few villagers. "They are a handful, that's all. For everybody else it's worse than before. Is this democracy, for life to get worse for the 99 percent so 1 percent can do better?"[22]

As the Bulgarian government moved to break up the collective farms, Creed found that the villagers actively resisted de-communalization because they did not want to return to a long-defunct system of peasant farming without machine equipment, and indeed Creed found that the process of decollectivization seriously eroded the living standards of the former co-op members. Even if they received titles to small plots of land, they were unable to get credit from banks to make the land more productive. Many returned to subsistence agriculture and left the modern economy, a process Creed called "re-peasantization." This resulted in a massive loss of social status for the rural population, and an exodus to the big cities. The privatization or liquidation of the cooperative farms was disastrous; it was done too fast and resulted in a total collapse of agricultural productivity, and Bulgaria soon became an importer of many agricultural products once grown domestically. Today, formerly thriving rural cities and villages are ghost towns, and unsurprisingly, the villagers who remain look back on the socialist period as a golden era.

The sociologist Michael Burowoy and the anthropologist Katherine Verdery also conducted fieldwork in Eastern Europe before and after 1989. Burowoy worked in Hungary and Verdery in neighboring Romania, and in 1999 the two co-edited a collection of essays that tracked the difficulties and widespread despair experienced by ordinary people during the long recession that followed the revolutions of 1989.[23] The chapters reveal in careful detail the disenfranchisement of rural populations and the urban poor, and there were plenty of warning signs that the new market economy was tearing communities apart. While the local political elites and Western advisors promised that the suffering was necessary and would only last a few years, ethnographers identified deep structural issues—fuzzy property rights, lack of real estate cadasters, the rise of barter and demonetization, the increase in crime and violence—that seemed to suggest that the transition process would take much longer than anticipated. They were ignored.

A second collection edited by Daphne Berdahl, Matti Bunzl, and Martha Lampland also investigated how ordinary people experienced the emotional dislocations of the transformation of their daily lives.[24] The critical essays revealed a growing sense that East Europeans felt like second-class citizens compared to the rapacious West Europeans flooding into their countries looking for good investment opportunities[25] and cheap gay sex.[26] Both edited collections exposed widespread human suffering, and the ethnographers warned that societies built on such unpredictable, uneven, and violent transformations would be unstable in the long run. Too many people would remember the upheavals of the 1990s and the problematic basis on which markets were created.

In Central Asia, the anthropologist Mathijs Pelkmans studied the social and economic upheaval that led to Kyrgyzstan's Tulip Revolution in 2005. Unlike other former Soviet Republics, Kyrgyzstan was an avid follower of Western economic and political advice and was widely lauded for the speed of its transitional reforms. Western observers and officials in the World Bank and the IMF celebrated the country as the "Switzerland of Central Asia" because it embraced the tough but necessary medicine of shock therapy and neoliberal austerity. But the speed and totality of the reform failed to improve the lives of ordinary people, and in many respects it exacerbated the pain of the transition in Kyrgyzstan, especially when compared to the country's more autocratic and resource-rich Central Asian neighbors. According to Pelkmans,

> The tragedy was, however, that although these policies were internationally applauded, attracted numerous economic advisers, and resulted in the highest per capita "transition aid" in the region, they did not attract major investment nor result in sustainable economic growth. . . . International experts had predicted "transitional" difficulties, but it turned out that when the pace of change slowed down, production levels of industry and agriculture remained "stable" on levels far below those of the Soviet period. These difficulties had profound effects on everyday life. Throughout the 1990s the percentage of people living below the poverty line increased, while unemployment and underemployment became rampant.

These were not the expected results of embracing Western reforms.

14

Resistance Is Futile

PERHAPS ONE OF the most perplexing questions about the postsocialist transition is why more men and women in the region didn't fight against the corruption, greed, and criminality infecting their everyday lives after 1989–91. After all, in many of these countries, people risked their lives to oppose and/or escape from authoritarian regimes, so why wasn't there more citizen participation in the building of functioning democracies? As mentioned earlier, the political scientist Pieter Vanhuysse has argued that Central European governments strategically crafted specific social policies (i.e., early retirements) to dampen resistance to reform.[1] But this is also the question that many ethnographers have grappled with over the last three decades.

Several key factors prevented collective resistance to the social and economic chaos of the 1990s. In the first place, and as discussed previously, many men and women lacked a basic understanding of what capitalism was and how it worked. To the extent that they had heard stories about unemployment, homelessness, or boom and bust cycles, they often believed this to be anti-capitalist propaganda used to justify the cruelties of actually existing socialism.[2] Second, postsocialist populations failed to understand that while the advent of free markets would bring new and exciting consumer goods, those same markets would precipitate drastic price increases for goods and services previously subsidized by the socialist state. Price liberalization forced a desperate scramble to meet basic needs: food, heat, electricity, and medicine. As people struggled to earn the money necessary to pay for the utilities, goods, and services they once took for granted, they had precious little time for activism. And even if they had the time, they were often too cold, hungry, and sick to participate in public protests. Third, as Katherine Verdery, Robert Hayden, and many other ethnographers argued beginning in the mid-1990s, the postsocialist rise of nationalism across the region made it difficult for people to articulate grievances against new local elites with whom they shared an ethnic or religious affiliation. This was especially true in Central Asia in the republics with new titular majorities. The fantasy that domestic elites would be more just than foreigners lured many into embracing the myth that ethnic self-determination would mean greater prosperity for all. Perhaps more than any other region of the former Soviet Union, the five new Central Asian republics saw an unprecedented outflow of non-titular ethnic populations in the 1990s. According to the anthropologist Serguei Abashin, "The new states fashioned out of the former Soviet republics based their legitimacy on a national narrative of the rebirth and liberation of the titular ethnic group. An inevitable consequence of this ideological shift was the large-scale resettlement of people in the countries that they considered 'their own': ethnic Russians (and also Tatars, Chechens, and Ingush) left for Russia, Ukrainians (and also Crimean Tatars) for Ukraine, ethnic Germans for Germany, and Jews (even Bukharan Jews) for Israel."[3] Although many non-titular ethnic populations began leaving Kyrgyzstan, Kazakhstan, Uzbekistan, Tajikistan, and Turkmenistan in the 1970s and 1980s, the outflow in the 1990s was both sudden and massive, profoundly changing urban landscapes and local social dynamics.

The early dreams of independence and economically viable ethnic states in Central Asia were crushed by the realities of crony capitalism and the continuation of authoritarianism with an ethnic face. Those disaffected with the failed reforms in their own ethnic states soon emigrated to Russia after the ascendancy of Putin and the post-1998 stabilization of the Russian economy. By the fall of 2013, about 4.5 million Central Asian citizens lived in Russia, and roughly 4 million of them belonged to "titular" ethnic groups. As Abashin explains, "The sharp, almost catastrophic drop in living standards, uncertain life prospects, and periodic political cataclysms inevitably produced an outflow of people seeking new well-being and new stability outside their own country. Unemployment and paltry wage rates and pensions propelled people into new labor markets where even low—by local standards—incomes were much higher than those that could be earned back home."[4] But based on his extensive fieldwork in the region, Abashin also argued that the massive out-migration of Central Asians had as much to do with seeking better economic prospects as with extricating the migrants from societies where old social relations, hierarchies, and shared ideals had broken down. Why stay and fight for change when you can just leave and start over in a better place?

Many anthropologists, sociologists, and cultural geographers have documented the push and pull factors that led to massive out-migration from the former socialist countries after 1989–91.[5] Many young and educated Central and East European or former Soviets relocated after the collapse of socialism gutted opportunities for local resistance, not to mention local economic development.

In Moldova, Leyla Keough followed "worker-mothers" in their circular migration to work as domestics and live-in elder care providers in Istanbul.[6] The
anthropologist Madeline Reeves also conducted nineteen months of fieldwork
in the Batken region of Kyrgyzstan and showed how a "season" of labor in Russia
became almost a rite of passage for Kyrgyz men, a way of proving that they were
eligible for marriage, particularly their ability to pay ever-growing bride prices.[7]
But economics definitely exacerbated the sociocultural factors. According to
Reeves, an unskilled laborer in Moscow could hope to earn the ruble equivalent of about $320 per month in 2005, whereas a teacher with twenty-five years
of experience (in the highest rank) was earning about $56 per month. One of
Reeves's informants, a university student named Jengish, shared the following
joke: "What does the student who used to get 'twos' [i.e., failing grades] now
have? A car and an apartment. What does the student who used to get 'threes'
[poor grades] now have? A car, an apartment, and a *dacha!* And what does the
student who used to get 'fives' [*otlichnik*—i.e., excellent grades] now have? Debts,
fines, fears, illness, and hopelessness." Not surprisingly, Jengish soon abandoned
his university studies for illegal work in Russia.[8] In Central and Eastern Europe,
another important aspect of the transition process that undermined possibilities
for concerted social activism against the unchecked spread of neoliberalism was
the new possibility for out-migration to the West, particularly after the accession
of many former socialist countries to the European Union in 2004 and 2007.[9]
As discussed in the demographic chapters, the rapid shrinking of the population
across Eastern Europe is one of the most drastic impacts of the transition process.

But perhaps the most important reason that men and women in the region
embraced the sudden appearance of markets is that they were told (and they truly
believed) that capitalism was a superior economic system and that their lives
would improve once it was firmly established. As discussed in the economic chapters, both domestic and international elites asserted that in the short term there
would be a lot of pain, but in the long term it would all be worth it. This is the
J-curve narrative, and it was repeated over and over again throughout the 1990s.

Ordinary people did their best to cultivate the correct attitudes and behaviors
they thought necessary to thrive in a market economy. For instance, Elizabeth
Dunn's book, *Privatizing Poland*, documents the ethnographer's experiences
working on an assembly line with women in a baby food factory that was privatized by the American company Gerber Foods. She tracks the changes in social
habitus necessary for workers to accommodate themselves to the new capitalist
expectations and management techniques and shows that some Poles were better able to make the psychological transition than others. Dunn explores how
ordinary Poles attempted to reshape their personhood and began to internalize
new free market perspectives. For those young and flexible enough to do so, these

market attitudes could be cultivated over time. But as many Poles soon found out, having the right attitude did not guarantee success despite their continued belief that capitalism would make work more efficient and ultimately provide greater avenues for social mobility.

Perhaps one of the most poignant studies of this belief in the ultimate triumph of the free market is sociologist Elaine Weiner's 2007 book, *Market Dreams*. Weiner lived in Prague and conducted formal and informal interviews with women between 1999 and 2000. In total, she spoke with seventy-four Czech women who had grown up and spent some part of their adult lives under socialism. Weiner was particularly interested in the narratives that women told themselves about the hardships and struggles of the transition period and her sample included twenty-six women who worked as managers and considered themselves "winners" of the transition period. The remaining forty-eight women were factory workers whose social circumstances either stayed the same or worsened after 1989. But rather than being critical of the new system, Weiner found that the workers believed that they were sacrificing themselves for the future of their children, and that things would be better for the next generation.

Weiner's case study examines the power of the neoliberal meta-discourses that circulated throughout Central Europe in the 1990s. She argues that in the Czech Republic, a darling of Western investors, postsocialist domestic and international elites, and in particular Vaclav Klaus, mounted a sustained ideological campaign to convince people that the social and economic inequalities of the transition period either did not exist or that they were the fault of individuals not working hard enough because they were "spoiled" or "ruined" by the previous ease of ordinary life under the socialist system. To supplement her interviews, Weiner did an extensive discourse analysis of speeches, newspaper articles, and reports circulating among Czechs in the 1990s, a ceaseless barrage of pro-market rhetoric used to forestall critiques of the emerging inequalities in society. This pro-market rhetoric convinced the women Weiner interviewed to remain passive and hope for the best, despite their eroding living standards.

Weiner's interviews with the "losers" of transition reveal that they believed their leaders, and especially Klaus, who told them that the hardships would be temporary and that their situations would improve once the market economy got up and running. But after a decade of transition in the Czech Republic, the factory workers' real wages were still below their pre-1989 levels, prices had skyrocketed, much needed welfare programs had been dismantled, and women faced discrimination in newly competitive labor markets. As they watched the state shred the social safety net, they didn't direct their anger toward capitalism but rather turned inward and blamed themselves. They internalized the rhetoric that their declining standards of living resulted from their own personal inability to adapt to the new rules of competition. They clung to the hope, reinforced by the popular pro-market rhetoric of the 1990s, that even if they suffered, future generations of Czechs would benefit. They retreated from politics and focused their attentions on surviving in a world with previously unknown deprivations.

This "every man for himself" spirit of the 1990s also deeply impacted the personal subjective experiences of Muscovites who found themselves unmoored in a time of massive social, political, and economic upheaval. Sociologist Olga Shevchenko's 2009 book, *Crisis and the Everyday in Postsocialist Moscow*, provides an intimate ethnographic exploration of the experience of crisis among men and women in their everyday lives. Through extended interviews and participant-observation, Shevchenko reveals how Russians constructed and deployed the discourse of crisis within their most quotidian moments. She argues that the imagination of the crisis was just as important as the crisis itself, and that individual reactions to personal hardships reinforced and deepened the larger societal crisis, further undermining social trust.

In a particularly astute chapter on the new atomization of social experience after socialism, Shevchenko explores how people built (or attempted to build) new regimes of autonomy and self-sufficiency. She argues that Muscovites internalized a particular brand of postmodern individualism and walled themselves off both from the state and from each other. As with other ethnographies of the postsocialist era, Shevchenko's study points to a change in the way people related to each other, to a loss of shared goals and camaraderie, and to a moral shift in the way people valued themselves and each other in a market economy. Human worth increasingly centered around money and material goods, and capitalism was seen as a zero-sum game: one person's gain was another's loss. Although there were certainly negative behaviors encouraged by the deprivation, stagnation, and widespread apathy of late socialism, an era that produced the fabled *Homo Sovieticus*, socialist states once offered a basic level of stability and security, which many people had come to take for granted even if it was economically unsustainable in the long run. The cutthroat competition and unchecked greed and ostentation that characterized the 1990s came as a profound shock even to those who had once sneered at the bankruptcy of the Marxist-Leninist system.

Down in Central Asia, David Abramson conducted extended fieldwork in Kokand and also reported widespread dissatisfaction with life in newly independent Uzbekistan. Abramson found that Uzbeks, suffering from the loss of old ideals, morals, and communities, were also confused by the greater purposelessness of the market economy whose only goal seemed to be producing wealth for a select few. He writes: "People talked of loss in countless ways: loss of interest in life's prospects, loss of friends and relatives to emigration, loss of jobs and economic security, and loss of 'city life.' They expressed the belief, despite hardships, oppression, and humiliation, that everything that existed and took place during the Soviet period in Central Asia was meaningful, because it was leading somewhere, that is progressing, developing, civilizing."[10]

Once again, Abramson also identifies a certain loss of an egalitarian sociality unique to state socialism, which, in the case of Central Asia, often meant the loss of multiculturalism as ethnic Russians abandoned countries to their titular majorities. Once cosmopolitan cities also lost masses of people to out-migration, especially among the young and educated who idealized the global metropoles of Moscow and St. Petersburg. One 29-year-old unmarried Uzbek woman, who had been educated in an Uzbek school and spoke Uzbek at home with her family, told Abrahamson that she mourned the loss of her Russian-speaking friends and neighbors, and she described the people of Kokand as having lost their values and "sense of community." She explained: "In the past, there was a fun, multinational spirit on our street. We used to all know one another and meet out in the street and talk. We always socialized together. Now a lot of new people, mostly Uzbek, have moved in and there is no longer a sense of community. They are always rushing around making money. Children are much more class-conscious and materialistic, distinguishing wealthier kids from poorer ones. These are the groups in which they socialize now."[11]

Across Central Asia, anthropologists have examined how the sudden breakup of the USSR fueled the rise of regional nationalisms and interethnic tensions as well as local insecurities about what it meant to be "modern" in the wake of previously heavy-handed and often culturally insensitive Soviet modernization projects (e.g., Mostowlansky in Tajikistan,[12] Laszczkowski in Kazakhstan,[13] Schröder in Kyrgyzstan,[14] Megoran on the Kyrgyzstani-Uzbekistani border[15]). Morgan Liu wrote an eloquent ethnography of the daily trials and tribulations of the Uzbek community in the southern Kyrgyz city of Osh before the ethnic violence that erupted there in 2010.[16] Liu spoke Uzbek, Kyrgyz, Russian, and Mandarin, and his multifaceted exploration of ethnic identity formation after 1991 revealed that the Uzbeks continued to hold on to their old "Soviet" ways of thinking, particularly with regard to having a strong centralized state. The Uzbeks valued production over trade and believed that their new independent government had a responsibility to provide for its citizens through work guarantees, generous subsidies to agriculture, and strong regulation of markets. Given that Kyrgyzstan was such an early and enthusiastic adopter of neoliberal reforms and that its residents were not members of the titular majority but a geographic remnant of the ever-fading Soviet past, the Osh Uzbeks struggled to navigate the new postsocialist realities. Uzbek and Kyrgyz families who had shared a city for decades suddenly found themselves in a struggle for control of the economy, particularly the newly privatized collective farms. The vortex of ethnic tensions and political instability led to the clashes in 2010, in which over 400 Uzbeks were killed and another 80,000 displaced. Liu found that as a result, many former Soviet citizens longed for the stability and security of the socialist past.

Julie McBrien further reports that disillusionment with capitalism fueled a turn toward more orthodox forms of Islam.[17] McBrien spent two years as a Peace Corps volunteer in Kyrgyzstan, learning both Kyrgyz and Uzbek, and returned to the region for fourteen months of fieldwork in 2003 and 2004. In an ethnographic investigation of the shifting place of secularism and religiosity, McBrien introduces us to Mukadas, a young woman who decided to start veiling herself as a reaction to the social changes around her, explaining, "When Mukadas contemplated veiling, she perceived herself as fully modern, even as she watched the modernity of her society crumble. The economic and social decay of the post-Soviet period precluded the institutional enactment of either Soviet norms or the new capitalist, consumption-orientated vision of modernity."[18] Because frustration with and disdain for the perceived amorality of both capitalism and democracy coincided with the breakdown of old and familiar socialist ways of being, McBrien also discovered that many Kyrgyz citizens sought solace in the religion of their forefathers. Targeted by Islamic aid and missionaries from the wider Muslim *ummah*, the resurgence in Islam across the Balkans and Central Asia emerged directly from the ideological vacuum and profound sense of loss and unfairness that followed the sudden embrace of free markets and multi-party elections. McBrien explains:

> [Mukadas's] actual encounter with the realities of post-socialist life provoked more disillusionment and disappointment than celebration. Dreams and values nurtured in the Soviet period were accompanied by institutional arrangements that provided for their possible fruition. Socialist ideals of modernity had been possible to enact, even if they were never fully attainable.... There was a sense that some dreams could be reached—for example, the education and employment of women, along with their full participation in society—and that the system could be changed to make the implementation of these ideals more complete. However, when these same dreams and values were set in the radically new context that we may loosely term 'capitalist', the possibility of their fulfilment was largely curtailed. A deficit of jobs, absence of child care, lack of money, and limited access to 'quality goods' meant Mukadas was constantly frustrated by the mismatch of her dreams and realities.[19]

The postsocialist era proved particularly difficult for many women raised in Eastern Europe or the Soviet Union, where they expected a certain level of public support for their roles as both workers and mothers. The collapse of socialism meant not only the end of a political and economic system but also the sudden shift in norms, values, and expectations about how ordinary people were supposed to live their lives: whether to go to university, to get married, to have children, to stay home or emigrate abroad. What had made sense under one system became unfeasible under the other, and many postsocialist citizens mourned these changes.

15

Return to the Past

ANOTHER COMMON EXPERIENCE of postsocialism for ordinary people was the feeling of going back in time. In Lithuania, anthropologist Neringa Klumbytė conducted participant observation and over 150 interviews with ordinary Lithuanians in three villages and in the city of Kaunas between 2001 and 2008. She deliberately targeted people over 35, who had personal memories of life in the Soviet Union, trying to understand the roots of the growing sense of longing for socialism. Klumbytė paints a picture of rural life steeped in nostalgia for the material comforts of the socialist past, and she documents how the slow return to pre-modernity was felt as a profound existential loss. "For the villagers," Klumbytė explains, "abandoning the [collective] farms, letting the forest take over the former rye fields, turning to subsistence farming and temporary employment, and suppressing their identities as farmers is viewed as an experience of post-Soviet decline and proof of their own marginalization."[1] Klumbytė spoke with one woman in her late 30s who had moved to the village after becoming unable to support herself in town: "Then [in Soviet times], neither I, nor my children lacked anything. I myself could afford everything that I wanted. We used to go with my husband to a restaurant or a bar. We could take a vacation with the children. We used to go to a resort by the sea every summer. And now? Now I have no money to go to the city for the allowance for children. When I have to take a child to the doctor we ride a horse."[2] For this Lithuanian woman, living in a member state of the European Union, the image of herself, a former urban-dwelling, educated Soviet citizen taking her child to see the doctor on horseback represented everything that had gone wrong with the postsocialist transition.

In Ghodsee's 2005–07 fieldwork in the Bulgarian city of Madan, she also encountered whole families forced back into subsistence agriculture in order to survive.[3] One resident lamented that the villages around Madan were "going back to the 19th century," as the few young men who stayed behind had no job options and became shepherds in the Rhodope Mountains. In one case, an extended family of nine people subsisted off the land or through their domestic animals. The one state pension paid to the grandmother was used to buy bread and cooking oil, the only two commodities not produced by the household. Children who would have once been in school spent days harvesting wild mushrooms and berries in the woods, while the women grew tobacco and vegetables on the land around the house. For heat in the winter, they illegally collected firewood for a stove; for light at night, they burned candles made from wax collected from beehives.

Other anthropologists documented the slide into past strategies for survival. In postsocialist Russia, for instance, Nancy Ries used the potato as a metaphor for the hardships of transition. Former professionals and urban-dwellers from across the country returned to the private cultivation of potatoes, which became a core tool for survival in uncertain times as it had been even before the Bolshevik revolution.[4] Also in Russia, Doug Rogers explored how homemade moonshine became a type of currency after the price liberalizations of the 1990s. Rather than embracing the new free markets, many men and women left the formal economy altogether and conducted their lives through barter exchanges.[5] In Bulgaria, Gerald Creed and Janine Wedel found that the potato became a form of currency that people used to survive when the country was wracked with hyperinflation following the 1996 banking collapse.[6] Indeed, across the postsocialist region, private gardens and distilleries guaranteed survival in a world turned upside-down, and for many people this felt like returning to a pre-modern past.

Nowhere was this expulsion from the formal economy more profound than in the case of those who became unemployed and/or homeless in the wake of the political transition from socialism to capitalism. As discussed in the demographic chapters, many "thrown away people" turned to alcohol to drown their sorrows. Tova Höjdestrand's 2009 book, *Needed by Nobody: Homelessness and Humanness in Postsocialist Russia*, is a rich ethnographic study of the human detritus of the 1990s.[7] Höjdestrand grapples with the perennial chicken or egg question that haunts studies of social marginalization: are homeless people substance abusers because they are homeless or are they homeless because they are substance abusers? In the case of Russia in the 1990s, Höjdestrand spends time with alcoholics and shows that many of them were orphans without kinship networks to help them through the transition process. Whereas the socialist state once provided shelter and care for chronic alcoholics (even if this meant forced incarceration in special profilactoriums),[8] the liberalization of the postsocialist era set them loose into society with little or no way to survive. In Höjdestrand's view, it was the cruelty and brutality of homeless life in Russia that led them to drink to excess. It was the only way to dull the pain of being a thrown-away person.

For his book, *Getting by in Postsocialist Romania*, anthropologist David Kideckel spent many years working among the miners of the Jiu Valley, exploring the traumas and dislocations of the transition to capitalism. Once lionized as the most valuable and masculine workers of the Romanian economy, the miners of the Jiu Valley endured disappointment after disappointment in the years following 1989, watching the steady decline of their living standards in the wake of mine privatization and liquidation. As an American anthropologist with many years of fieldwork in Romania, Kideckel examined the depression, despair, and nihilism of the miners, writing:

> Workers' terror that their bodies are falling apart is, after all, correct, though the decline is less the product of improper health practices, failing institutions, or even increased disease vectors than of daily stress. As workers observe shuttered factories, closed mine galleries, media distortions, the luxury cars and villas of the moneyed classes, and the outstretched hand of the family physician, they raise a number of pointed questions. If factories don't hire and mines will close, why have children? If our legitimate demands are met only with truncheons or broken promises, why stand up and make them? If my spouse's efforts to secure a small income are negated at a whim, why work harder? If our children's attempts to secure an education are made irrelevant by others' bribes, why learn? And if our attention to our health and bodies is rendered useless by defective plumbing, heating, housing, and diet, why stay sober, why stay clean, why struggle? Why, indeed![9]

Following in the footsteps of David Kideckel, anthropologist Bruce O'Neill spent over a year living among Bucharest's vast homeless population to understand the conditions that have created extreme social marginalization in a society that once guaranteed full employment. Unlike Höjdestrand and Kideckel, who often focused on men driven to drink, O'Neill encountered many ordinary people who once enjoyed stable, productive lives under socialism. Reflecting on his fieldwork, O'Neill argues that whereas state socialism actively persecuted those deemed undesirable in society, capitalism just pushes people to the margins and lets them die. Socialist violence was active; postsocialist violence is passive, but no less devastating to those who find that they no longer have a role to play in society. O'Neill explains, "This affective suffering is not inflicted by spectacular trauma but was wrought through the mundane (yet persistent) grind of life without work, without home, and without the ability to participate in a social world that increasingly unfolds through practices of consumption. Importantly, the brutality of 'letting die' is not a state of exception set apart from society. It is part of the everyday logic of globalization, where heightened market pressures discard the redundant."[10]

But even those who have kept their homes are not spared from the violence of these everyday logics of globalization. When free markets came to Romania, there were more workers than there were jobs in the new private economy, and many people found themselves marginalized by the competitive labor markets that favored the young, urban, and educated population. When even the young could not find jobs, they emigrated en masse out of Eastern Europe in search of better fortunes abroad. This further impoverished people's sense of community and affective ties to family, friends, and former colleagues who scattered to the four winds. The psychological effects of the transition devastated many men and women ill equipped to weather the storms of political upheaval. Speaking of his ethnographic subjects in Romania, Kideckel reports that

> the onslaught of postsocialist forces atomizes and commodifies them at their workplaces (when they are lucky enough to have a job). The restructuring of society neutralizes and anathematizes their political identities and practices. Their families and communities are wracked by massive emigration, deterioration of their housing and diet, and the unraveling of networks, and these processes are spurred on by the lash of new consumption demands, which they are ill able to meet. Their identities and practices as men and women are buffeted, and must be intensively reworked if they are to survive. Their bodies, health, and emotional strength and stability paradoxically suffer from too much anger and too much apathy. Struggling in every sector of their lives, workers look back to and fictionalize the heyday of socialism as a model of the good life, which further dampens their ability to plan for, act on, and achieve their desires.[11]

The great irony is that while the objective material declines in their standards of living after 1989 make them nostalgic for the past, it is their nostalgia that gets blamed for their increasing social marginalization. Just as Klumbytė found in Lithuania and Höjdestrand in Russia, in Romania the media and popular discourses blame the poor and elderly for their inability to compete in the market economy. The young, urban, and educated view the rural poor as backward and lazy, drowning in alcoholism. Their deteriorating living conditions are seen as their own fault and therefore not worthy of state intervention. Moreover, stereotypes about the rural poor make it difficult for them to find jobs in the cities, since employers discriminate against them. Is it any wonder that these "thrownaway" people have turned to alcohol to drown their growing despair? This debate about the role of alcoholism in the postsocialist mortality crisis hinges on the idea that some people were just incapable of making the transition to free markets. It is not necessarily mass privatization that is to blame for the excess deaths in the early 1990s but rather the inability of people to cope with new expectations and their heavy reliance on alcohol when they fail.

But who or what is really to blame for this situation? Is rampant alcoholism the reason that rural populations have suffered disproportionately from the economic transition? Or are widespread alcoholism and deteriorating mental health just two of the negative externalities caused by the rapid economic transition from state socialism to capitalism in the region? Or is it a bit of both? The Romanian dictator, Nicolae Ceaușescu, was probably one of the worst East European leaders before 1989, and most Romanians celebrated his summary execution on Christmas Day 1989. But no one anticipated the hardships and chaos of the 1990s and today many Romanians pine for their lives before 1989, united only in their shared sense of dislocation and injustice.

16

The Patriotism of Despair

ANTHROPOLOGIST SERGUEI OUSHAKINE found post-Soviet misery so pervasive during his extended fieldwork in Barnaul, Siberia, that he wondered if Russians might form a new collective identity around it. Many Russians reflected on the chaos of the 1990s as a trauma they survived, and they called themselves "people cut in half," referring to the temporal bifurcation of their lives. Collective trauma became the main way that ordinary people articulated their experiences of the transition. Shared rituals and stories about loss and suffering allowed Russians to re-forge the collective bonds that had been shredded by the sudden collapse of the USSR. Oushakine relates a wonderful narrative about his experience of moving back to Barnaul, the Soviet town where he grew up. When he arrived, the neighborhood where he was living was plunged into a two-year public blackout. The copper and aluminum wires had been stolen by bandits, and the local municipality had no funds to replace the wiring. This was a part of Barnaul with about 20,000 residents, several schools, and a large hospital, but they had no streetlamps. In the very long, dark Siberian nights, men, women, and children now navigated their city in pitch blackness. To add insult to injury, the municipality then proceeded to reduce the number of public buses, making it very difficult for residents without private cars to travel within or outside of the neighborhood. Oushakine's neighbors felt utterly abandoned by the state—isolated and living in almost perpetual darkness.[1]

Through formal and informal interviews, as well as discourse analysis of Russian newspapers and scholarly publications, Oushakine argues that the liberalizing elites that led Russia's post-Soviet transformation focused almost exclusively on the political and economic aspects of change but failed to create a new system of social symbols and positive values that could replace the old socialist slogans and egalitarian discourses of the Soviet Union. The post-modern, almost nihilistic individualism that followed the breakdown of ideology left people without a basis for optimism or hope. As old social networks fell apart under the weight of the new marketization of everything and the vacuum of postmodernity (so well documented by Humphrey in *The Unmaking of Soviet Life* and Shevchenko in *Crisis and the Everyday in Postsocialist Moscow*), Oushakine argued that the only shared bond left between ordinary Russians was their collective sense of loss and trauma. He asserts that the shared negative experience of the transition became the basis for a new collective identity, what he calls the "patriotism of despair."

Oushakine also shows that Russians seemed keen to reassert a basis for a collective national identity that was not linked to the market. For seven decades, access to goods and services was determined not by money, but by connections and one's place in a vast web of social networks. Social relationships were forged and nurtured over lifetimes, and many of these connections disintegrated after 1991. By embracing a national identity based on loss and trauma, Oushakine suggests that Russians tried to forge a new non-market collective sense of themselves, something that could not be bought or sold. They strove for a particular form of sociality that characterized state socialism, which the advent of capitalism had destroyed.

For these Russians, then, their collective trauma became something positive, a way to create a new sense of collectivity steeped in an almost messianic idea of Russian exceptionalism. Shared suffering became a virtue, and ritual displays of mourning and loss allowed men and women to embody and enact a new sense of Russianness liberated from the old Marxist tropes of the USSR. This patriotism of despair is thus the basis for a resurgent Russian nationalism, one that views the Russian "ethnos" as historically victimized and persecuted. Politicians soon seized on this sense of shared victimhood, and, for Oushakine, the patriotism of despair became the new meta-narrative for belonging in the Russian Federation.

This loss of a sense of belonging and the collective embrace of a shared national victimhood has similarly influenced the dominant political discourses of Bulgaria, Hungary, and Poland, and may go a long way to explain the turn to more nativist politics across the region, which we will discuss further in the conclusion. The sense of shared victimhood in many countries in Central and Eastern Europe may have also been challenged by the fear of immigration, particularly from the Middle East and North Africa after 2015. In countries that appear to be facing an irreversible demographic death spiral and where conspiracy theories about a Western-led genocide against Eastern Europe spread, the threat of immigration feels particularly acute.

Indeed, in Eastern Europe, as in the former Soviet Union, nationalism has swept in to fill the void left by socialist ideologies. The sudden dismantling of local industrial capacity in Eastern Europe was felt as a deep blow to the shared national pride in many postsocialist countries whose citizens were told for over forty years to celebrate the strength of their national industries. Katherine Verdery has argued that it was the particular form of capitalism in 1989–91 that made it so hard for former planned economies to adapt to the demands of globalization.[2] She argues that East European countries had industrialized using the old Fordist model of mass producing similar products to achieve economies of scale and bring down unit costs. When they entered the global economy in the early 1990s, the capitalist world had already embraced the production model called "flexible specialization," which meant fluid supply chains that could adapt to the changing needs of the market. Production was less homogenized and more tailorable to micro-fluctuations in consumer preferences or demand, making the products of East European industry boring, uniform, or hopelessly out of date.

An excellent example of this phenomenon comes from Judd Stitzel's case study of the East German fashion industry. When polyester fabric was introduced in the West, socialist planners marveled at its durability. The East German government invested heavily in imported Western machines for the production of polyester fabrics, but by the time the factories were up and running, Western fashion houses had moved on and embraced a new preference for natural fibers like cotton, wool, silk, and linen. The East German industry was not flexible enough to move away from polyester, and so East Germany mass produced polyester ready-to-wear for years after it had gone out of favor in the West.[3] Nevertheless, in the decades following reunification, many East Germans became nostalgic for their old fashion industry because it was their own. Across the region, everyday objects once produced by socialist-era industries have achieved cult status as symbols of prior national greatness. The same is true for socialist-era films and television, as well as foods and drinks. In a globalized world, where almost all industrial and cultural products come from China or the West, the deep desire for domestically produced goods and cultural content takes on a uniquely nationalist flavor.

Furthermore, in the West in 1989, the dominant cultural framework was a kind of individualistic cultural relativism or late-capitalist postmodernism. The sudden insertion of East Europeans into this quasi-nihilistic worldview produced a particularly difficult moral vacuum for postsocialist citizens raised in societies with strong ideological coherence, even if these ideologies were rejected in practice. In Bulgaria, Ghodsee found that previously secular Muslim minorities started to embrace a more orthodox form of Islam in order to resist the breakdown in social norms and moral values that followed the introduction of free markets into the country.[4] For those unable or unwilling to make money the measure of all human worth, religion offered an alternative narrative and had the added benefit of reinforcing national or ethnic identities. Across Eastern Europe, the coming of free markets was accompanied by a construction boom for new churches, cathedrals, and mosques, as many postsocialist populations rejected communist ideology by replacing it with ethno-national religious belief.

Resisting the centralized authority of the state had also become a kind of shared experience during the state socialist era, because there was a clear face of power in the Party apparatus and the communist leaders. Whether they were Soviet hippies,[5] religious dissidents, or Czechoslovak or Slovenian punk rockers,[6] East Europeans forged intimate communities of resistance to create pockets of freedom in their lives. After 1989, power and authority were far more diffuse, and it was harder to identify who was in charge of the transition process or who was to blame for its failures. Previously countercultural identities became commercialized and lost their oppositional meaning. Against the forces of globalization and the perceived cosmopolitanism of new economic elites, many East Europeans embraced nativism and nationalism as avenues to express deep discontent with the inequality of the transition process. The electoral success of rightwing parties in Poland, Hungary, Bulgaria, Russia and in the states of former East Germany results from the bitterness and discontent we find in the public opinion surveys.

Finally, Hilary Appel and Mitchell Orenstein have argued that the nationalist turn in Eastern Europe is also related to the local disillusionment with democracy.[7] For many years, East Europeans had actually voted for politicians promising to resist neoliberalism, but had been subjected to neoliberalism nonetheless. After losing faith in the mainstream parties who had almost without fail kowtowed to the demands of the European Union, the World Bank, and the International Monetary Fund, voters perhaps understandably chose to vote for more extreme parties, particularly those that position themselves as anti-Western. More than three decades have passed since the fall of the Berlin Wall in November 1989, and the reverberations of that event and the social hardships of transition still have profound effects on politics in the region.

Conclusion

TOWARD AN INCLUSIVE PROSPERITY

BACK IN 2017, we got inspired to start doing the research for this book because of a disagreement over Branko Milanović's November 3, 2014, blog post, "For Whom the Wall Fell? A Balance Sheet of Transition to Capitalism."[1] In his short essay, Milanović, a former World Bank economist, looked at GDP, Gini coefficients, and an independent measure for the consolidation of democracy, and argued that the transition from communism to capitalism had been a relative failure for most East European citizens. He wrote:

> Most people's expectations on November 9, 1989 were that the newly-brought capitalism will result in economic convergence with the rest of Europe, moderate increase in inequality, and consolidated democracy. They are fulfilled most likely in only one country (Poland), and at the very most in another, rather small, two. Their total populations are 42 million, or some 10% of all former Communist countries. Thus, 1 out of 10 people living in "transition" countries could be said to have "transitioned" to the capitalism that was promised by the ideologues who waxed about the triumph of liberal democracy and free markets. . . .
>
> So, what is the balance-sheet of transition? Only three or at most five or six countries could be said to be on the road to becoming a part of the rich and (relatively) stable capitalist world. Many are falling behind, and some are so far behind that they cannot aspire to go back to the point where they were when the Wall fell for several decades. Despite philosophers of "universal harmonies" such as Francis Fukuyama, Timothy Garton Ash, Vaclav Havel, Bernard Henry Lévy, and scores of international "economic advisors" to Boris Yeltsin, who all phantasized about democracy and prosperity, neither really arrived for most people in eastern Europe and the former Soviet Union. The Wall fell only for some.[2]

Milanović's blog post made the rounds of our shared scholarly circles, and even David Brooks wrote a column commenting on it in the opinion pages of the *New York Times*.[3] While many economists contested Milanović's findings, Brooks accepted them but argued that the fault for the lack of progress in the former communist world lay with the legacies of their communist past rather than with the way democracy and free markets were imported into the region. Ghodsee, who had conducted much of her research in the Balkans or East Germany among women and ethnic minorities, believed that Milanović's findings were essentially correct but were most likely underestimating the negative impacts of transition by focusing only on GDP, inequality, and democratic consolidation. Orenstein, on the other hand, whose early career was spent conducting research on the transition processes in Poland and the Czech Republic, believed that Milanović's findings were overly pessimistic. Poland had done spectacularly well and living standards had increased in many countries. We realized that although we had both been working in Eastern Europe for over twenty-five years, our disciplinary backgrounds and our geographic foci produced two very different perspectives on the transition.

The process of writing this book together has been an ongoing discussion and debate about how best to measure the social impacts of transition given the data available to us. Through many conversations and email exchanges, we wrestled with the sometimes contradictory findings and sent our tireless research assistant, Nicholas Emery, back into the data to crunch ever more numbers. Each time we studied the data, we both found evidence for our different positions. We realized that answering a simple question like "was the transition a success?" was complicated by how you interpreted the word "success" and which populations you happened to be studying. There is no doubt that people suffered, but the J-curve narrative posited that the suffering was all worth it in the end. For some men and women, this was definitely true, and many of these people were our own academic colleagues and friends in Eastern Europe. Their personal and professional opportunities exploded after 1989, particularly those who spoke Western languages (especially German, French, and English) and who had cultivated wide international networks.

But when Milanović proposed that the suffering had produced few results for 90 percent of the former socialist population, a series of larger political questions presented themselves. How much suffering was necessary for these countries to break with their communist past? Could it have been avoided with a different set of policies? How much inequality and poverty does a dynamic and productive capitalist economy need? If free societies require some level of inequality in order to promote innovation and diligence, how much is too much? Can social protections be implemented without the repression of communist regimes? Could a

Marshall Plan for the postsocialist countries have worked? And do East Europeans have a right to be angry and resentful about the recent past? Or should they be grateful that the West freed them from the horrors and inefficiencies of their former autocratic states and planned economies? Finally, where can we go from here?

As we wrote this conclusion, we knew that many of our colleagues believed we should no longer be talking about the postsocialist transition.[4] As far as they were concerned, the transition process was over, and continuing to focus on the history of the last three decades not only perpetuated "Orientalizing" knowledge production but also constrained political futures. So much has occurred since 1989–91 that it was stubborn to insist on a narrative of rupture over one of continuity. But when Ghodsee visited the former East German state of Brandenburg in the summer of 2019 as we were writing this book, she noticed that the right-wing Alternative for Germany party (AfD) based its campaign strategy on rousing pent-up anger over the transition process. Using the slogans *"Wende 2.0"* and *"1989–2019, Vollende die Wende"* ("The Change 2.0" and "1989–2019, Complete the Change") (see Figure 17.1) as well as *"Der Osten steht auf!"* (The East Rises Up), and the resurrection of the 1989 protest slogan *"Wir sind das Volk"* ("We are the people"), AfD politicians made it abundantly clear that for many men and women in the former states of East Germany the transition process was far from over.

FIGURE 17.1. "The East Rises Up"—2019 campaign poster in Potsdam [*left*]; "Take your land back!" and "We are the people"—2019 campaign posters in Potsdam [*right*]

As part of the work of writing this book, we also organized a conference on the thirtieth anniversary of the fall of the Berlin Wall, held at the University of Pennsylvania in November 2019. Bringing together a wide variety of scholars, representatives from the World Bank, and transition economic advisors, we spent two days reviewing literature and perspectives on the social impacts of transition. We realized that, despite the many protestations to stop talking about transition already, East Europeans may never stop. Why? Because the postsocialist transition was a shared experience that drastically reshaped millions of lives and may have become the basis for new nationalist identities—such as Serguei Oushakine's idea of a "patriotism of despair." In the sheer magnitude of its impact on individual lives, it can be compared to the other major events of the last century in Europe: the First World War, the Russian Revolution, the Great Depression, the Second World War, and perhaps the 2019 coronavirus pandemic. Just as the Great Depression lives in our collective memory in the United States nearly 100 years later and shapes economic policy to this day, so too will the memory of the postsocialist transition recessions linger in the affected countries. It will not be forgotten. For many, it will not be overcome. In this brief conclusion, we take the opportunity to step back and reflect on the data we have collected and the contemporary legacies of the postsocialist transitions, with an eye to informing better policymaking in the future.

The Collapse of Empire

To fully understand the social impacts of transition, we need to go back in time to the last decade of the Cold War. By the 1980s, East European socialism was in trouble. Socialist economies were stagnating and falling further behind the West. Life expectancy, which had risen sharply, particularly in less developed countries, after the imposition of socialism, had begun to plateau and even decline. Some countries, like Hungary and Poland, sought to address these crises by borrowing heavily on international capital markets and ended up deeply in debt, sparking inflation and social unrest. Socialist leaders found that overt political repression was no longer sufficient to motivate citizens to participate in what was widely perceived as a bankrupt and broken system. Visiting Prague in 1987, Orenstein recalls sitting in a pub at two in the afternoon with a man in military uniform who was decrying the inefficiency of communism, pointing out that the pub shouldn't be so crowded, since everyone was supposed to be working at that time of the day. Nationalist sentiments (particularly in the Baltics) began to threaten Soviet territorial integrity. And across the socialist world, citizens began to demand more political freedoms. Something had to be done.

The last Soviet premier, Mikhail Gorbachev, recognized the structural problems the USSR faced and the growing resistance to Soviet domination in the Warsaw Pact states of Eastern Europe. In an attempt at internal reform, Gorbachev instituted the twin policies of *perestroika* and *glasnost* in the mid-1980s. Like Alexander Dubček in Czechoslovakia in the 1960s, Gorbachev wanted to create a socialism with a more human face. However, Gorbachev's reforms were too little, too late. The world had moved on. Led by US president Ronald Reagan and UK prime minister Margaret Thatcher, the international community was committed to free markets and democratization worldwide. Perestroika (literally: restructuring) brought limited market reforms to the Soviet economy to increase efficiency and improve the ability of the system of central planning to meet material needs. The goal was never to abandon socialism but rather to improve productivity and flexibility. Similarly, glasnost (literally: openness) attempted to invite public debates about the necessity for reforms, to encourage a collective conversation about possible solutions and begin a slow expansion of liberal political freedoms. Gorbachev never intended to precipitate the demise of the Soviet Union. Rather, he hoped to strengthen the socialist system from the inside. However, these limited reforms encouraged ever more radical demands for change. Gorbachev lost control of the process and decided not to intervene in similar reform processes in Eastern Europe, which led to the peaceful revolutions of 1989, causing enterprising Soviet politicians and managers to grab new opportunities for power. Hardliners reacted with a coup that led to the collapse of the Soviet Union, initiating a period of chaos.

Within the space of two years, the Cold War suddenly ended, not with a nuclear war but with millions of jubilant East Europeans waving flags in the streets. Both of us were in the region in the summer of 1990, marveling at the remarkable changes occurring in these countries once sealed off behind the Iron Curtain. (Orenstein drove from Berlin to Istanbul via Prague, Budapest, Timisoara, Nis, and Sofia and back to Prague; Ghodsee rode trains for three months from Istanbul to Belgrade [through Bulgaria] and then from Belgrade to Bucharest, Cluj, Budapest, Prague, and to East Berlin). Hopes for a shared future of peace and prosperity were high, but so was social need, and not everyone agreed on what exactly needed to be done. (Orenstein recalls passing hundreds of Roma children in Romania begging on the sides of a state highway as cars roared past at fifty miles per hour, older women fighting in raucous bread lines in Bulgarian villages, and people selling household items in impromptu flea markets on the streets of Moscow; Ghodsee shared a train compartment with shuttle traders smuggling Heinz ketchup from Turkey into Yugoslavia, fled Bucharest when the miners descended to terrorize the urban population after student demonstrations, and celebrated the "reunification" of the two German currencies on an Alexanderplatz heaving with revelers on June 30, 1990.)

At that time there were many questions. Should the former Warsaw Pact states embrace capitalism and strive to become carbon copies of the capitalist West? Or should they strike out on their own and strive to create some kind of third way between socialism and capitalism? In the case of East Germany, the popular vote that approved a rapid reunification under the West German constitution dashed any hopes of finding a way to democratize and reform the socialist system. On October 3, 1990, less than a year after the opening of the Berlin Wall, East Germany ceased to exist as a state, and its population was thrown headlong into a capitalist system. Other countries still faced a choice, but one that was rapidly discredited by local elites as well as Western advisors hoping to assist the coming reform process. Writing in *The Economist* in 1990, Jeffery Sachs argued:

> The eastern countries must reject any lingering ideas about a "third way", such as a chimerical "market socialism" based on public ownership or worker self-management, and go straight for a western-style market economy. . . . Eastern Europe will still argue over the ends: for example, whether to aim for Swedish-style social democracy or Thatcherite liberalism. But that can wait. Sweden and Britain alike have nearly complete private ownership, private financial markets and active labour markets. Eastern Europe today has none of these institutions; for it, the alternative models of Western Europe are almost identical.[5]

Reformer Vaclav Klaus stated, "The third way is the fastest way to the third world." Only unbridled capitalism, he believed, would enable the fast growth postsocialist countries needed to catch up with the developed West.

Writing retrospectively about the decision to abandon hopes for a Third Way, Ivan Krastev and Stephen Holmes argued that "1989 heralded the onset of a thirty-year Age of Imitation" and "the replacement of communist orthodoxy by liberal orthodoxy." Most East European countries lacked real choices about their futures because "the Western-dominated unipolar order made liberalism seem unchallenged in the realm of moral ideals."[6] Krastev and Holmes also decried the fundamentally non-democratic way in which the political and economic reforms were implemented in Eastern Europe after the collapse of communism, recognizing that

> even for the inhabitants of economically successful countries such as Poland, the project of adopting a Western model under Western supervision feels like a confession of having failed to escape Central Europe's historical vassalage to foreign instructors and inquisitors. . . . A feeling of

being treated disrespectfully was also fomented by what can be reasonably identified as the central irony of post-communist democracy-promotion in the context of European integration: the Central and East European countries ostensibly being democratized were compelled, in order to meet the conditions for EU membership, to enact policies formulated by unelected bureaucrats from Brussels and international lending organizations. Poles and Hungarians were told what laws and policies to enact, and simultaneously instructed to pretend that they were governing themselves.[7]

While Krastev and Holmes focus on the countries of Central and Eastern Europe, deep anger about the injustice of the transition can be found throughout the postcommunist world, particularly in Russia, Ukraine, and many of the other successor states of the Soviet Union. Yet, in many respects, a significant percentage of people in this region of the world are living measurably better lives, not only in terms of their political freedoms and newfound ability to travel and partake of a cornucopia of desirable Western consumer goods but also in terms of their own self-reported life satisfaction. Twentieth-century state socialism was a flawed system that its own people could see was outcompeted by Western capitalism. The peaceful revolutions of 1989 brought clear upsides: new personal freedoms and opportunities, ranging from the mundane—not being afraid to discuss politics with friends at home or in a pub—to the transformative, such as increased opportunities to study, travel, or work where you want. These positives are very real, and we do not seek to erase them. Many people have put the drab housing, repression, and conformity of the socialist era behind them to live freely in better houses; to study, work, and vacation all over the world; and to lead the world in their chosen fields. But focusing only on the positive story (as so many Western accounts have tended to do) ignores many negative aspects of the decision to uncritically accept Western reforms. As Krastev and Holmes opine: "After the fall of the Wall, across-the-board imitation of the West was widely accepted as the most effective way to democratize previously non-democratic societies. Largely because of the moral asymmetry it implies, this conceit has now become a pre-eminent target of populist rage."[8]

The length and depth of the various transition crises documented in this book profoundly darkened popular views about the transition process. Despite widely shared gains in terms of political freedoms and the increase in economic opportunities and life satisfaction, the social impacts of transition and the feeling of being bullied by the West has poisoned the long-term prospects for democracy and free markets in the region. But is this "populist rage" based on real or imagined grievances? Was there an alternative?

Collateral Damage

For those who see the transition as a rupture, a period of "creative destruction," to use Schumpeter's term once again, the transition to capitalism was always going to entail significant social pain. Western economists expected this. Although China and Vietnam proved able to reform socialism and create capitalism in a period of unbroken economic growth, this may not have been possible in a post-Gorbachev Eastern Europe and Eurasia. Dynamic growth in China and Vietnam was premised on continued communist party control of the economy, forcibly deployed, as well as rural migration to cities. In Eastern Europe and Eurasia, socialism had always been measured against the brightly shining lights of an elusive Western model of democratic capitalism. This was especially true in Eastern Germany, where people could see what was going on in the West on their televisions, and in other countries with relative media freedom, or at least limited access to Western culture, as in Yugoslavia or Hungary. In these countries, the end of socialism meant the start of democratic capitalism. And that meant tantalizing opportunities and freedoms, along with trauma and failure as millions of people and institutions groped their way toward an entirely new way of ordering their societies.

Yet one cannot ignore the policies of transition. Our review of the economic, demographic, public opinion, and ethnographic evidence shows that the economic reform programs implemented in Eastern Europe proved to be deeply insensitive to the human costs of transition. In line with Western economic theories, the transition process seemed to treat people as rational economic actors making decisions to maximize their personal utility; but not only did it do grievous harm to their utility in many cases, it also paid insufficient attention to their beliefs, expectations, and desires. It treated those brought up under communism as bearers of harmful and outmoded socialist ideas. It overestimated their willingness to endure economic pain for a promised bright capitalist future and the proportion who would benefit from it. By implementing policies previously field tested in Latin America, the international financial institutions failed to account for the local East European context, failed to prevent widespread poverty, and ignored cultural expectations of what transition would bring. Most important, reformers in the region ignored or downplayed the severity of the pain inflicted on helpless populations who had been promised a rapid transition to freedom and prosperity.

The social impacts of transition were severe, despite frequent attempts documented earlier to deny this. They were so severe, in fact, that scholars often have a hard time comprehending the depth of their severity. This cognitive dissonance that beguiles transition studies has been further exacerbated because the damaging impacts of transition occurred at the same time that a substantial minority of the postsocialist population—the more visible, educated, and urban part—experienced growing prosperity and life satisfaction. It is one thing to be suddenly thrust into deep poverty for the first time in your life. It is quite another thing to be thrust into poverty when some of the people around you are enjoying previously inconceivable levels of personal wealth. It proved hard for participants and analysts alike to comprehend. Yet, the sudden onset of poverty together with enormous prosperity has left deep scars of the collective psyche of postsocialist populations.

While it is certainly true that the most advanced postsocialist countries got through transition with an economic downturn that was somewhat milder in depth and duration than the Great Depression of the 1930s in the United States, it is worth repeating here that the median postsocialist country endured an economic trauma that was between *two to six times as great*. For the countries affected most deeply, the extent of the collapse depends on whether one considers the depth (twice as deep in the worst affected countries), duration (two to three times as long in the worst affected countries), or the total loss of consumption (the area under the status quo line in Figure 2.2 is approximately six times greater in the worst affected countries). Long-term economic growth data collected by the Maddison Project show postsocialist transition to have resulted in the largest and most enduring economic collapse to affect any world region in modern history from 1870 to 2016.[9] In contrast to the Great Depression of the 1930s, many postsocialist countries had not fully recovered in terms of GDP per capita nearly thirty years later, as Milanović pointed out in 2014.

It is also worth remembering here that in 1929, leading businessmen and capitalists fatally threw themselves off roofs at the same time as millions went hungry. Everyone suffered together. In 1989, however, some people enjoyed rapid progress toward Western-style prosperity while many others found their life prospects crushed by the economic collapse. The overarching narrative of the transition after 1989–91 was that the future was bright and that the suffering would be worth it. And there is no doubt that it was worth it for those who came out on top. The scholarly literature is littered with studies providing evidence for success. But the other part of this story has been largely ignored, in part because of the concerted effort of postsocialist elites to dismiss the human collateral damage, perhaps believing the old French proverb: "Ne saurait faire d'omelette sans casser des œufs."

The socioeconomic collapse was definitely not a mirage, as some have claimed,[10] nor was it over in the blink of an eye, as many continue to believe. In some countries, whole generations of people perceived themselves as "thrown away" or cast off, as discussed in the ethnographic literature reviewed in Part

IV. Countries that had previously provided a wide range of social benefits and civic belonging—through guaranteed jobs, income, housing, health care, and the sociability that accompanied it—suddenly eliminated many of those lifestyle privileges for hundreds of millions of people. Those cast off experienced the transition as a *betrayal* of everything they knew and believed in, a theft of their way of life. Unfortunately, neoliberal policies sought to "stay the course" and did not respond to these traumas, believing them to be an unfortunate consequence of communism. Yet the negative ramifications continued for decades. In no world is decades the same as "the blink of an eye."

As detailed throughout this book, the transition process combined dramatic new freedoms and opportunities for some and increased poverty and misery for others. High rates of mortality, low rates of fertility, and a veritable exodus of young migrants out of most transition countries has darkened the long-term prospects for some postcommunist states. For many, transition turned out to be a biblical struggle, seven—or seventeen—lean years.[11] Indeed, the length of time of transition is now approaching that of the Mosaic journey through the desert, and not all people will see the promised land. Soon, a number of countries will have spent more time in transition than they did living under communism, without quite achieving the prosperity they were promised, a sobering thought.

Unprepared for Cutthroat Capitalism

There is a wonderful joke told in many East European countries about citizens' first experiences of crisis, unemployment, and poverty. Referring to their previously mandatory courses on Marxism-Leninism, East Europeans after 1989 realized that "everything they told us about communism was a lie, but everything they told us about capitalism was true." Without an accompanying welfare state in which social programs funded by a progressive income tax redistribute from the rich to the poor, capitalism can be a deeply unfair system where a small, well-connected elite captures a majority of the wealth and power, and not necessarily through meritocratic processes. In the absence of a frontier, individualist, pull-yourself-up-by-the bootstraps mentality (often cultivated through years of anti-communist propaganda) free markets need to be combined with significant social safety nets in order to gain the consent of those subjected to its inevitable boom and bust cycles. Yet local attitudes about fairness were discounted in the transition process, and the resulting breakdown in social trust proved toxic to support for free markets. The tragedy many East Europeans are living today is that the failings of transition now have imperiled the democratic reforms that produce freedom and opportunity. As we discussed in Parts I and III, perceptions of inequality and fairness are just as important, if not more important, than measured inequality, and postsocialist citizens show a particular aversion to vast disparities of income and wealth.

In 1982, the German economists Werner Güth, Rolf Schmittberger, and Bernd Schwarze developed "the ultimatum game," which tested individual propensities toward self-interested, economistic thinking and social perceptions of fairness.[12] The game works by giving one player, called the "proposer," a certain amount of money. The proposer is then asked to split the money with a second player, the "responder," where the proposer and the responder are not allowed to communicate, collude, or negotiate: thus, the name of the game. The proposer proposes a percentage split of the money, and the responder may either accept or reject the proposal. If the responder accepts the proposed split, the money is allocated to the two players according to the percentages proposed. But if the responder rejects the proposed percentage split, neither player gets to keep any of the money at all. Both players walk away with nothing. The proposer and responder know the rules of the game and the consequences of a responder rejection of the split before they are asked to make their proposals and responses.

Obviously, from a rational economic point of view, the responder should accept any proposed split since some money is always better than no money. If Mitchell has $100 and offers to give Kristen $10, she should accept the offer because even if Mitchell gets to keep $90, she still walks away with ten dollars that she didn't have before. But multiple iterations of this test have shown a propensity for fairness among players. Responders offered less than what they think is a fair percentage of the money will reject the proposed split. Perceptions of fairness, and perhaps deep-seated feelings of pride or social justice, result in many responders rejecting offers that are not perceived as fair, leading to a surprising propensity for offers under 30 percent to be rejected. Furthermore, proposers understand that responders will not think in rational economic terms and that fairness is expected, particularly if both proposer and responder share an identity. Players of the same ethnicity or religious affiliation, for instance, expect more fairness of each other than they do of strangers.

It turns out that East Europeans may have an even greater propensity for fairness. In 2006, Bahry and Wilson published a paper in the *Journal of Economic Behavior & Organization* examining the results of the ultimatum game played in two postcommunist, multi-ethnic Russian republics: Tatarstan and Sakha. In both republics, the authors found an interesting divergence between the way the game was played between younger, urban, and wealthier populations and older, rural, and poorer populations, with the latter more committed to equitable outcomes. Despite the differences between different sub-populations, however, the researchers also found an unusually high level of what they called "hyper-fair" outcomes compared to other cultural contexts, with responders rejecting both low and *high* offers. Almost two-thirds of the subjects in Tatarstan and almost three-quarters of those in Sakha made 50/50 split offers, leading the authors to conclude that "in this sense [the players in Tatarstan and Sakha] appear to have a strong commitment to a norm of fairness defined as an equal split of the pie. We think that this norm is a residual from the Soviet era for a certain segment of the population, but its impact seems to extend beyond that segment, by leading other people to egalitarian behavior as well."[13]

It should not be a surprise, therefore, that postsocialist citizens have found it difficult to accept inequality. Under socialism, citizens enjoyed many social benefits that became scarce after 1989: subsidized housing, universal free health care, subsidized public transport, free day care and university education, pension benefits, price-controlled foodstuffs, guaranteed jobs, and other services. Unlike in most countries of the Global South, where these services were never provided for the entire population, state socialism brought modernity to many East European populations (as evidenced by the rapid gains in life expectancy in some countries during the socialist era discussed in Part II). It is worth remembering that most citizens of the Soviet Union did not have access to electricity until after the Bolshevik revolution, and that electrification was seen as a gift of the Soviet government to its people. Before 1989, certain utilities and services were seen as basic *rights* of citizenship, and a portion of the shared redistributed product was theoretically the reward for allowing the state to operate the economy on behalf of the workers.[14]

After 1989, when the "Age of Imitation" required the sudden dismantling of guarantees, standards of living collapsed for those at the low end of the income distribution, for those in economically struggling regions, for those with lower education and job qualifications, and for those too old to adapt to or thrive in newly competitive labor markets. Means-tested or targeted social safety nets failed. The transition process planted seeds of deep discontent that sprouted into populist anger[15] as citizens blamed their governments for failing to build the required institutions or to cultivate the attitudes and ideals necessary for people to accept the inevitable inequalities produced by free market systems. We recognize that culture, geography, and religion provided some protection from the worst effects of shock therapy—with social cohesion and religious faith providing bulwarks against the nihilism and despair produced by the social and economic upheavals. Similarly, opportunities for outmigration created a pressure valve for discontented youth to strike out for their fortunes abroad rather than staying home to protest corruption and injustice. Overall, we find a pattern of anger and resentment rooted in a collective memory of the negative social impacts of transition. When the AfD Party in Brandenburg encourages the East to "rise up" and to "take back their land," it seeks to mobilize this frustration to win political power.

Could It Have Been Avoided?

Many former socialist citizens, as well as political leaders like Vladimir Putin, believe that the chaos and pain of the transition process was deliberately inflicted by the West on its former enemies, as punishment for the East's long defiance of liberal democratic norms and market freedoms. Implicit in this critique is the idea that the transition could have been done differently, with less human suffering, and without the imposition of liberal fundamentalism that drove the reform process. So, was there another way? In Poland, the political scientist David Ost has argued that many of the worst effects of transition could have been avoided, but Western advisors and local elites did not make the necessary efforts.[16] Indeed, the rejection of the "third way" in favor of neoliberal reform policies may have exacerbated the social impacts of transition, but the only way to consider how things might have been different is to delve into the precarious realm of the counterfactual. What if glasnost and perestroika had worked to reform the USSR from within? What if East European countries had been allowed to pursue a "third way"? What if socialism had been reformed gradually and under state control rather than all at once and without consideration for local social and cultural contexts? Unfortunately, we cannot rewind the clock and rerun the experiments to see how things might have turned out differently. But we can examine other comparable cases, and consider what a more gradual, controlled model might have looked like.

By the 1980s, both China and Vietnam had stagnating planned economies that were falling behind the West, poorer, but otherwise not dissimilar to those of the former Eastern Bloc. But leaders in China and Vietnam decided to reform communism more slowly, ushering in a period of dynamic growth and prosperity without deep transitional recessions such as those caused by shock therapy in Eastern Europe, as we discussed in Part I.[17] Geopolitically, the West may have been less keen on promoting this option in Eastern Europe, perhaps first, because Soviet communism was considered the main ideological enemy of the West; second, because Eastern Europe was closer to the West both geographically and culturally; and third, because Western political and economic elites were eager to open up previously closed markets for Western manufactures. In a keynote address that Jeffery Sachs delivered to our November 10, 2019, conference at the University of Pennsylvania, he made it clear that, at least in his opinion, US and West German foreign policy considerations far outweighed economic arguments about the best way to achieve reform in Eastern Europe.

As we also discussed in Part I, reformers and their advisors all understood that there would be an initial period of deep economic pain, but they argued that this period of recession was necessary because "you cannot cross a chasm in two jumps."[18] But by letting this metaphor dictate the terms of reality, advocates of the shock therapy assumed no other pathway forward was possible. In any event, policymakers believed that since economic gains would come quickly (after a few years at most), they would wipe away the necessary (but temporary) pain. Despite the Chinese and Vietnamese examples, few reformers working in Eastern Europe in the 1990s considered the Asian model a viable alternative. Chinese and Vietnamese reforms allowed for the creation and dynamic growth of a new private economy alongside a diminishing state sector. Rather than shutting down or privatizing the entire state sector at once, China and Vietnam sought to restructure, privatize gradually, and eventually phase out the state-owned enterprises over a period of several decades, to minimize the social impacts on their respective populations.

Many have argued that this option was not available to reformers in Eastern Europe and the successor republics of the Soviet Union, because Western advisors and local leaders wished to throw off authoritarianism and feared that their countries might backslide into communism and leave populations even worse off.[19] Yet, in the case of East Germany, reunification required that the ownership of state-owned industries be handed over to the Treuhandanstalt for a rapid privatization process that destroyed the East German industrial base almost overnight. Skyrocketing unemployment rates in the East required massive transfers of wealth from West German taxpayers, the Solidarity Tax, which then fueled decades of East-West resentment. A different approach could have been tried if politicians had prioritized a softening of the social impacts and the avoidance of long-term resentments. In the mortality belt of the European former Soviet Union, an aggressive health policy intervention might have prevented tens of thousands of excess deaths, or at least generated a different perception of Western intentions.

Instead, Western self-congratulatory triumphalism, the political priority to irreversibly destroy the communist system, and the desire to integrate East European economies into the capitalist world at any cost took precedence. In the early 1990s, many international organizations and Western economists believed in the primacy of market solutions and saw the end of the Cold War as definitive proof that the capitalist economic system had won. Overall, having undergone the grand experiment of communism, East European countries decided to rejoin the capitalist West in order to enjoy its perceived freedom and prosperity. For historical, cultural, and geographic reasons, Asian economies were less inclined to supplicate their societies to the neoliberal fundamentalisms coming out of the West and chose a path that gave them dynamic flexible economies with fewer human costs and less long-term resentment (albeit, in the Chinese case, without attempting to embrace even the façade of democracy). Pundits like

David Brooks might blame the communist legacy for the failures of transition in Eastern Europe, but the examples of Vietnam and China show us that the fault may lie in the transition policies themselves (see Figure 4.1). A liberal orthodoxy was largely imposed on Eastern Europe by Western advisors and local elites in many cases without the consent of those subjected to the economic changes even as these same economic advisors were promoting the ideals of liberal democracy, whereby citizens would have a say about their future through the organization of free and fair multi-party elections. But as Krastev and Holmes have argued, economic policies were geared toward creating capitalism and not necessarily toward lifting the economic prospects of a majority of the population, no matter how many times electorates chose anti-reform parties. Thus, the irony is that the transition to liberal democracy and free markets was largely achieved through undemocratic means and failed to quickly generate widespread prosperity.

Targeted versus Universal Benefits

A large part of this failure arose from the inadequacy of social protections in the transition. Nearly all transition economists knew that some form of transitional recession was unavoidable and recommended some form of social benefits for people whose lives were destroyed by the sudden changes. Yet, as companies privatized, shed labor, and shut down, these countries entered transitional recessions. Tax bases shrank and postsocialist states found themselves with insufficient funds to replace the generous social programs provided directly through socialist enterprises, municipalities, or the central government. Budget restraints made it necessary to spend whatever money states did have as efficiently as possible. The World Bank led the way in advocating specifically targeted social benefits by the states for the poor or very poor. Whereas socialist-era programs provided universal benefits to all citizens—regardless of income or need—experts in the international financial institutions regarded this as wasteful, channeling scarce funds to people who might not need it. The most efficient solution, they thought, would be to replace universal benefits with cheaper targeted benefits.

But targeted social policies did not achieve their objectives. For example, IFIs advised countries to eliminate rent controls and privatize housing while at the same time providing poor people with some sort of compensation that they could use to find housing in the market. In theory, this sort of reform would enable private investment in housing and encourage a growing private market that could more closely meet most people's needs. But these targeted payments never reached their intended recipients in many cases. Advocates of targeted benefits expected people to file claims with newly created institutions—a bureaucratic nightmare because under socialism, there had been no unemployment or housing checks. Even in the bureaucratically advanced United States, unemployment insurance systems collapsed under the weight of a surge in claims during the 2020 coronavirus pandemic.

Whereas socialist governments created relatively simple mechanisms for providing benefits to all, finding and channeling scarce social payments to the poorest of the poor required a very specific and complex bureaucracy. In many cases, the agencies responsible for targeting the meager benefits in the chaotic transition environment failed to do their jobs adequately. One study of housing subsidies in Russia, for example, found that targeted benefits often failed to reach recipients. As many as one-fourth to one-fifth of all legitimately needy families were refused access to government benefits because of the bureaucratic (and sometimes corrupt) nature of targeting programs. Many poor people were not informed of their eligibility. Others failed to sign up. Still others were excluded for some technical reason. Some localities had sufficient funds to support targeting; others did not. Often, the poorest regions provided the lowest benefits, exacerbating inequalities. IFIs expected postsocialist states to manage these targeting programs fairly and efficiently. But states that were collapsing in legitimacy and where wages were low faced dramatically growing needs and proved unable to manage needs-based targeting.[20] Western experts were either too optimistic or chose to ignore these problems, hoping that a return to economic growth would quickly relieve them.

But in many cases, targeting was really just a thin cover for the reality that benefits had been cut extensively or effectively eliminated. Privatization of housing, for instance, caused new investment in housing for economically successful people but no improvements to the extant housing stock and little investment in new affordable housing. Today, many postsocialist citizens still live in their socialist era housing blocs. Likewise, health care reforms and privatization exacerbated the increase in mortality and higher rates of disease.[21] Socialist countries had provided universal health care to everyone. Even if care was less than perfect, it was free and universally accessible. Now, patients were expected to pay fees for service, often informal fees or bribes. Rural hospitals and clinics were closed while new for-profit, private hospitals appeared, where only the wealthy could afford treatment. The closure of subsidized child care facilities forced many women out of the workplace at a time when two incomes were more necessary than ever. Fear of rendering oneself undesirable on newly competitive labor markets encouraged many young women to delay or forgo childbearing altogether, leading to a steep decline in fertility rates. The rapid removal of food subsidies forced many postsocialist citizens (in some countries a majority) back to the land to grow their own food. Making housing and health care a privilege for the newly rich, forcing professional women to stay home with their children, and pushing urbanites back into the villages to scratch out a meager existence from the land was bound to be seen as a massive regression. How could advisors and policymakers not consider the long-term effects of these new realities?

We believe that social safety nets should have been strengthened during the transition rather than destroyed and that benefits should have remained universal. Even if it meant allowing socialist states to hold on to enterprises for a while longer, these state-owned enterprises could have been used to support employment and universal welfare programs until transitional recessions had passed, tax revenues had increased, and functioning new bureaucracies were established to help citizens in need. Subsidies for utilities, housing, child care, and basic foodstuffs could have been phased out more gradually without damaging new business opportunities. Instead, a handful of well-connected elites enriched themselves as the prices of daily necessities skyrocketed for ordinary people. In their rush to destroy socialism, the power of "red" directors, and the planned economy, reformers created a manifestly unjust society and killed growth. Social spending and growth could have gone hand in hand, as they did in the Visegrad countries, which spent more on social policies and redistribution and experienced less dramatic economic declines and better demographic outcomes.

If leaving profitable enterprises under public ownership offended the pro-market sensibilities of Western leaders, then a massive program of foreign aid—like the Marshall Plan following World War II—could have been implemented to shore up social safety nets until the former socialist economies recovered. Indeed, when the Russian people decisively rejected Boris Yeltsin's policies for rapid economic reform in the 1993 parliamentary elections, the Clinton administration briefly considered abandoning its support for shock therapy.[22] Strobe Talbot, Clinton's top Russia specialist, worried that Clinton had overemphasized the creation of free markets and underestimated the deleterious social impacts on the daily lives of ordinary Russians. As we quoted earlier, Talbot suggested that the US government needed to support "less shock and more therapy for the Russian people."[23] Jeffery Sachs also insisted that the United States needed to provide more aid to support Russia's faltering social safety net, but the Clinton administration refused to loosen the purse strings.[24] Instead, Clinton pressured the International Monetary Fund to grant Russia a $10.2 billion loan in the run up to the 1996 presidential elections, much of which might have been stolen by corrupt elites.[25] Rather than acknowledging the eroding effects of social upheaval on the prospects for democracy, the United States dispatched campaign advisors who "rescued" Yeltsin's leadership to keep Russia on the path of radical economic reform.[26]

One might be tempted to speculate about why American leaders supported a Marshall Plan for the defeated Nazi Germany but not for the former Soviet Union, but it is clear that some form of economic aid from the West could have staved off the worst social consequences of the transition process. There are surely many arguments to be made about why and how these programs could have been paid for, but the bottom line is that under the international financial institutions' preferred strategy of shock therapy and targeted social benefits, *191 million people in the postsocialist region fell into poverty*, more than half the current population of the United States. While many excuses have been made, it is hard to conclude that targeting proved to be an effective poverty prevention strategy. Provision of universal benefits, such as universal health care and family policies, can allow the poor to maintain income while also spurring growth. This is a lesson that should not be forgotten in the wake of the global economic contractions that have followed the coronavirus pandemic.

Political Reactions

Failure to provide social security for the majority of the postsocialist population eventually translated into a political liability. As the majority of people became disillusioned with markets and public institutions (discussed in Part III), the politics of market reform slowly began to change. Earlier in some countries (such as Russia) or later in others (such as Poland and Hungary), voters began to turn toward authoritarian nationalist parties that promised a new social contract based on the kinds of social benefit schemes that we believe should have been implemented in the early 1990s. These nationalist social policies are quite diverse but appear to share some central themes: (1) attention to the growing demographic problems of population decline, low fertility, and out-migration; (2) a turn toward universalism over targeting in social benefits, and (3) provision directed not to the poorest of the poor but rather toward various categories of the "deserving" poor, such as those who work or provide social care in traditional families.[27] Right-wing populist parties have reintroduced policies and programs similar to those once associated with the previous state socialist regimes, albeit under the guise of nationalism.

For example, under President Vladimir Putin, Russia pioneered the use of child subsidies to incentivize family formation and childbearing to reverse population decline. In 2007, Russia increased child subsidy payments, doubling them for the second child. The government provided women with 40 percent of their prior income for time off during pregnancy, birth, and early child care. The government also reintroduced pre-school education subsidies, increasing with each child, to help women get back into the labor force. Most significantly, women who gave birth to a second child were given a 250 thousand ruble "maternity capital" payment (around $4,000 in 2019) that could be used for any purpose, often to put a down payment on a house or apartment.[28] Partially as a result of these policies as well as the improving economic situation because of high oil prices, Russia's fertility rate increased from 1.4 to 1.7 between 2007 and 2017, although it had hovered around 2.0 between 1970 and 1990. In the future, Russians may see the expansion of high-quality, subsidized public child care facilities, which seem to be the most effective policy available for encouraging higher birth rates.[29]

Other nationalist governments in Central and Eastern Europe adopted policies patterned on Russia's pro-natalist initiatives. In 2015, Poland's Law and Justice (PiS) government launched the Family 500+ program, which provides universal benefits to families with children (on top of a strict abortion ban). To qualify, there is no income test. Families apply at the start of the school year and every family receives 500 zlotys per month ($130 in 2019) for each child. Poland's fertility rate edged up slightly from 1.32 in 2015 to 1.39 in 2017, but there was no evidence of a dramatic increase in fertility rates in 2019. Child poverty, however, dropped by 80 percent, the most significant achievement of this program.[30] One study found that "as the most expensive and wide-scale redistribution policy in post-1989 Poland, Family 500 plus has been met with a positive response from the society . . . most significantly by socially disenfranchised groups," benefiting the ruling party.[31] Hungary's prime minister Viktor Orbán announced new pronatalist policies in 2019 that included more subsidized day care spaces, loans for women who marry and have children, a subsidy for the purchase of a larger family car, and the eligibility of grandparents for family benefits.

Liberals and feminists have criticized these pro-natalist policies on a variety of different grounds. Liberals contend that they are too expensive and disincentivize paid work. Some feminists contend that these reforms repress women and intend to keep them at home, economically dependent on men.[32] However, these criticisms ignore the extent to which socialist-era welfare state guarantees benefiting women and families have been dismantled by previous liberal governments since 1989. One way of looking at these policies is as compensation for the unpaid labor and care work that many women would be doing anyway. They do not require women to have children (though they are often accompanied by public relations campaigns to encourage family formation), and some nationalist governments also wish to restrict women's reproductive rights. If having children is a service to society, then society should help compensate women for the financial burdens they take on when they start families. Done correctly, these types of policies to support women can mobilize female labor by providing day care, paid parental leaves, and other forms of support that enable women to work while having a family. They can be geared toward creating a better home-life balance for women by subsidizing work that falls predominantly on women for cultural reasons.

Furthermore, these policies represent a departure from the previous neoliberal orthodoxy by reintroducing elements of universalism once common in the former socialist states. Most of these new nationalist benefits are provided on the basis of citizenship. All citizens (in certain categories, such as females) are eligible by virtue of their belonging to the national community, without an income test. In Poland, for instance, Family 500+ benefits are available to any family that contains children, regardless of race, religion, ethnicity, or sexual orientation (for now). These types of benefits may foster a sense of collective belonging that can increase public trust. They may also have better outcomes—for instance, in preventing poverty.[33]

Another characteristic of these policies, besides the lack of targeting, is their generosity. To make a difference in the lives of the average person means paying benefits at a higher level. It should come as no surprise that more generous benefits are better at fighting poverty. While liberals have often argued that robust welfare state policies would bankrupt governments, this has not proven to be the case. Generous universal benefits can provide a useful stimulus for the economy, since most beneficiaries are needy and spend their benefits in full, increasing economic growth, particularly in poorer regions. In Poland, for example, these benefits are particularly popular in smaller towns and rural areas, where incomes are lower, and may reduce regional disparities as well as undergird continued political support for the governments that create them. As Western countries consider future forms of universal basic income (UBI) or citizens' dividends to protect their populations from the economic disruptions of pandemics, automation, or other "black swan" events, the experiences of Eastern Europe should be instructive.

The data presented in this book have shown how different social scientific disciplines have measured the social impacts of transition. By bringing together these diverse perspectives, our goal has been to show that while many people today live happier, healthier, and more liberated lives, with many more personal and professional opportunities to consume, to travel, and to make autonomous choices about what to believe, where to reside, and whether or not to start a family, millions also suffered. On some level, we recognize that this is a reality of contemporary global capitalism: inequality and competition are seen as necessary to fuel productivity and innovation. Proponents of the free market argue that too much social and economic security depresses dynamism and growth.

The process of jump-starting markets after decades of planned economies was bound to cause massive disruption and it was perhaps naive to think that the process could be achieved in a few years without long-term negative consequences. In countries where two or more generations of citizens grew up with job guarantees and access to generous social safety nets, much attention was paid to breaking this addiction. In other words, the actual attitudes and beliefs of people were not taken seriously. If it is true that former socialist citizens value equality and fairness more highly than people in the West or the Global South, then the brutal and often corrupt way that capitalism took root in Eastern Europe and the former Soviet Republics was bound to create problems. We believe the growing popular discontent among voters in the region today, the rejection of liberalism, and the growing anti-Western sentiment flowed directly from the ideological, culturally, and socially insensitive way transition was pursued. So, what can we learn from the experience of transition in Eastern Europe? In these final pages we offer just a few specific suggestions for policies that might have worked better in the past and that may still be pursued in the future.

Looking to the Future

Social and economic policy after socialism has been far too ideological, based on liberal, individualist reactions to socialist collectivism. Yet both individualist and collectivist logics have a place in modern socioeconomic policy, despite the sharply divided ideological rhetoric of political leaders. Every society demands a mix of individualist and collectivist institutions to protect the interests of a *majority* of citizens. In addition, the question of which economic model works best is also a political query—who gets the benefits? The fundamental problem of the liberal policies advocated worldwide by the international financial institutions beginning in the 1980s was (and remains) a simplistic belief that economic growth will lift all boats and that growth is always a good thing, even if it creates vast societal inequalities. If the results of studies based on the Ultimatum Game discussed earlier should teach us anything, it is that many people have a deep and profound psychological aversion to inequality and injustice. A well-functioning democratic society must be established on the basis of an economic model that is widely perceived to be both fair and effective. Otherwise it will break.

This insight is beginning to make inroads into the World Bank itself, the international financial institution that most identifies itself with social progress and a "world free from poverty."[34] In a 2018 report on the "social contract" in post-communist countries, World Bank researchers explored the conundrum: despite positive growth, a majority of people in the postcommunist countries are disenchanted with the economic system and have limited trust in government. The World Bank researchers find that discontent is related to inequality but not to increases in the Gini coefficient, a measure of income inequality as explored in Part I. Instead, demand for greater social provision rises based on *perceptions* of inequality. These could arise from perceived differences between regions in a country, a sense of precariousness due to limited labor protections, or rapid economic changes. Perceptions matter, and as we have shown in the previous chapters, there is a widespread perception that the transition to capitalism was a *deeply flawed and unfair process*.

The World Bank authors conclude that no economic system can exist, particularly in a democracy, without the consent of the people in the form of a basic social contract. Even if transition policies appear to be working in some sense economically, they have failed to galvanize the consent of the people. Therefore, as a start, international financial institutions should seek to help the postsocialist countries to develop a social consensus on economic policy. In particular, the report states that the World Bank should move beyond the liberal targeting approach that has characterized its social policy advice since 1989. Since this strategy did not prevent poverty and goes against the social values of the citizens of the postsocialist countries, the report advocates a social policy strategy that (1) emphasizes greater labor protections for all categories of contracts to fight a sense of precarious employment and lack of well-being, (2) moves from targeting to universality in the provision of social assistance, social insurance, and basic quality services, (3) makes income taxes more progressive (after two decades of experiments with flat tax regimes), and (4) taxes wealth in addition to income. These are the kinds of policies that, had they been implemented in the 1990s, would have softened the blow of the transition recession and transformed the lives of a good portion of the 191 million people who became poor. These are also the kinds of insights that can help Western political leaders prevent new social and economic upheavals in their own countries.

Obviously, these recommendations are very far from the Washington consensus policies that the international financial institutions advocated in the 1990s. They indicate the extent to which the Washington Consensus on development has broken down in the IFIs and the postsocialist region. There is a growing realization that, as Polish finance minister Grzegorz Kolodko wrote ten years after the start of transition, "the belief that a market economy can be introduced by 'shock therapy' has proven wrong. . . . The erroneous assumption that emerging market forces can quickly substitute for the government in its role in setting up new institutions, in investing in human capital, and in developing infrastructure has caused severe contraction and growing social stress in transition countries."[35]

Going forward, policymakers, scholars, and politicians must acknowledge the bifurcated experiences of transition—dynamic growth and higher life satisfaction accompanied by mass impoverishment, mass out-migration, and mass distrust in public institutions. And they must develop policies that balance the individualism that inspires innovation and accomplishment with the collectivism that enables people to live peacefully with one another in just and equitable societies. Socialist countries experimented with extremes: an extreme form of socialism that wiped out individual ownership, accountability, responsibility, and freedom of thought, movement, and association and an extreme form of capitalism that erased most forms of collective life, destroying social norms, families, cultural centers, taken-for-granted social services, and shared social meaning. Today, post-socialist societies aim for a new balance between individualism and collectivism and a mixed economy that will generate the economic growth needed for prosperity while at the same time creating forms of collective meaning, belonging, and responsibility that support human flourishing.

The former socialist countries are not the only part of the world where a new balance should be sought. As we face economic upheavals caused by pandemics, natural disasters, and climate change, as well as rapid advances in algorithms and automation and the rise in extreme inequality, Western leaders and policymakers need to embrace policies for the future that balance personal liberties for the strong with social safety nets for the weak, enabling all citizens to develop their capacities to the fullest. Like socialism, postsocialism has been a grand experiment whose results hold lessons for the rest of the world. Together, these experiments have shown that attempts to exclude markets or states from economic life lead to disaster. Both are needed. Ultimately, it is down to the nature of our humanity itself. We, as people, all have moments of great strength and great weakness—moments of independence and moments of dependence. Economic systems must work to promote overall human happiness and flourishing. As the citizens in the nations of Central and Eastern Europe and Eurasia have experienced twice in the last century, ideologically driven policies that willfully downplay or ignore the social consequences of their state-led or market-driven imperatives will inevitably fail in the long run. To better serve the needs of humanity, a proper balance must be found.

APPENDIX

Data Sources

For this project, we collected data on the twenty-nine transition countries. See www.socialimpactsoftransition.com for the full dataset. A majority of the economic and demographic data is available from the World Bank and United Nations, although we chose to use data from the US Department of Agriculture's Economic Research Service for gross domestic product (GDP) and GDP per capita because this service interpolates missing values in 1989 for a number of countries that are lacking in World Bank and UN data. We also used Maddison Project GDP growth data when making historical comparisons. As there is a lack of consensus in the literature about how to measure the unofficial economy, we select the MIMIC (Multiple Indicators, Multiple Causes) approach from Medina and Schneider, "Shadow Economies around the World," due to the completeness of their dataset. The correlation between the MIMIC dataset and the NIPA (National Income and Product Account) dataset employed by Feige and Urban, "Measuring Underground (Unobserved, Non-Observed, Unrecorded) Economies," is 0.99. Democraphic data come largely from the UN and World Bank. Public opinion survey data are more limited and are collected from a variety of sources, including various Eurobarometer surveys, the Russian Longitudinal Monitoring Survey, the World Happiness Report, and the European Bank for Recovery and Development (EBRD) Life in Transition Reports. Although each of these surveys has limitations, together they provide a fairly comprehensive picture of public attitudes in the transition region, with the possible exception of Central Asia, where survey coverage is relatively sparser.

In general, we calculated the percent change since 1989 for each variable of interest in order to highlight growth paths since the start of transition. As well, when we grouped countries, we decided to rank them by duration and intensity of the decline since 1989. Top ten countries are the ten best performers, bottom ten countries are the ten worst performers, and median countries are the remaining nine. This allowed us to clearly and simply differentiate between the widely disparate effects of transition. We used figures to show change over time and maps to highlight whether geography had an effect on the best and worst performers on various indicators.

Bolt, Jutta, Robert Inklaar, Herman de Jong, and Jan Luiten van Zanden. "Rebasing 'Maddison': New Income Comparisons and the Shape of Long-Run Economic Development." Maddison Project Working paper 10. *Maddison Project Database, version 2018.* 2018. https://www.rug.nl/ggdc/historicaldevelopment/maddison/releases/maddison-project-database-2018.

Center for Insights in Survey Research. *Public Opinion in Hungary, Poland, Czech Republic and Slovakia.* Washington, DC: Center for Insights in Survey Research, 2017. https://www.iri.org/sites/default/files/four_country_full_presentation_may_24_2017.pdf.

Ekman, Joakim, and Jonas Linde. "Communist Nostalgia and the Consolidation of Democracy in Central and Eastern Europe." *Journal of Communist Studies and Transition Politics* 21, no. 3 (2005): 354–374, doi: 10.1080/13523270500183512.

EU Open Data Portal. *Standard Eurobarometer 62–88.* 2018. https://data.europa.eu/euodp/en/data/dataset?q=standard+eurobarometer&ext_boolean=all&sort=.

European Bank for Reconstruction and Development. *Life in Transition Survey I.* 2006. https://www.ebrd.com/news/publications/special-reports/life-in-transition-survey-i.html.

European Bank for Reconstruction and Development. *Life in Transition Survey II.* 2010. https://www.ebrd.com/what-we-do/economic-research-and-data/data/lits.html.

European Bank for Reconstruction and Development. *Life in Transition Survey III.* 2016. https://www.ebrd.com/what-we-do/economic-research-and-data/data/lits.html.

European Bank for Reconstruction and Development. *Life Satisfaction in the Transition Region.* 2018. http://litsonline-ebrd.com/life-satisfaction/.

European Bank for Reconstruction and Development. *Transition Indicators (1989–2014).* 2020. https://www.ebrd.com/economic-research-and-data/transition-qualities-asses.html.

European Bank for Reconstruction and Development. *Transition Report 2016–17.* 2017. https://www.ebrd.com/news/publications/transition-report/transition-report-201617.html.

European Commission. "Life Satisfaction." In *Eurobarometer Interactive.* European Commission Directorate General of Communications. Accessed on June 5, 2020. https://ec.europa.eu/commfrontoffice/publicopinion/index.cfm/Chart/index.

Eurostat. "European Demography: EU25 Population Up by 0.5% in 2004." 136/3005. October 25, 2005. http://epp.eurostat.ec.europa.eu/pls/portal/docs/PAGE/PGP_PRD_CAT_PREREL/PGE_CAT_PREREL_YEAR_2005/PGE_CAT_PREREL_YEAR_2005_MONTH_10/3-25102005-EN-AP.PDF.

Feige, Edgar L., and Ivica Urban. "Measuring Underground (Unobserved, Non-Observed, Unrecorded) Economies in Transition Countries: Can We Trust GDP?" 2008. *Journal of Comparative Economics*. Retrieved from https://www.sciencedirect.com/science/article/pii/S0147596708000152.

Gapminder. *Life Expectancy (years)*. 2020. https://www.gapminder.org/data/.

GESIS. *Applicant and Candidate Countries Eurobarometer*. 2016. https://www.gesis.org/eurobarometer-data-service/survey-series/candidate-countries-eb/.

GESIS. *Central and Eastern Eurobarometer 1–8*. 2004. https://www.gesis.org/eurobarometer-data-service/survey-series/central-eastern-eb/.

Helliwell, John, Richard Layard, and Jeffrey Sachs. *World Happiness Report*. New York: United Nations, 2012, 2013, 2018. https://worldhappiness.report/ed/2012/; https://worldhappiness.report/ed/2013/; https://worldhappiness.report/ed/2018/.

International Monetary Fund. *Expenditure by Functions of Government (COFOG)*. 2020. https://data.imf.org/?sk=5804C5E1-0502-4672-BDCD-671BCDC565A9.

Macrotrends. "Hungary Fertility Rate 1950–2020." 2010–2020 Macrotrends LLC, Data from United Nations—World Population Prospects. https://www.macrotrends.net/countries/HUN/hungary/fertility-rate.

Maddison Project Database, version 2018. Jutta Bolt, Robert Inklaar, Herman de Jong, and Jan Luiten van Zanden. "Rebasing 'Maddison': New Income Comparisons and the Shape of Long-Run Economic Development." Maddison Project Working Paper no. 10, 2018. https://www.rug.nl/ggdc/historicaldevelopment/maddison/releases/maddison-project-database-2018?lang=en.

Medina, Leandro, and Friedrich Schneider. "Shadow Economies around the World: New Results for 158 Countries over 1991–2015." *CESifo Working Paper Series No. 6430*, 2015. Retrieved from https://papers.ssrn.com/sol3/papers.cfm?abstract_id=2965972.

Pew Research Center. *European Public Opinion Three Decades after the Fall of Communism*. Washington, DC: Pew Research Center, 2019. https://www.pewresearch.org/global/wp-content/uploads/sites/2/2019/10/Pew-Research-Center-Value-of-Europe-report-FINAL-UPDATED.pdf

Pew Research Center. *Religious Belief and National Belonging in Central and Eastern Europe*. Washington, DC: Pew Research Center, 2017. https://www.pewforum.org/2017/05/10/religious-belief-and-national-belonging-in-central-and-eastern-europe/.

Pew Research Center. *Twenty Years Later: Confidence in Democracy Wanes in Former Soviet Union*. Washington, DC: Pew Research Center, 2011. https://www.pewresearch.org/global/2011/12/05/confidence-in-democracy-and-capitalism-wanes-in-former-soviet-union/.

Pew Research Center. *Two Decades after the Wall's Fall: End of Communism Cheered but Now with More Reservations*. Washington, DC: Pew Research Center, 2009. http://assets.pewresearch.org/wp-content/uploads/sites/2/2009/11/Pew-Global-Attitudes-2009-Pulse-of-Europe-Report-Nov-2-1030am-NOT-EMBARGOED.pdf.

Popkin, Barry. *RLMS-HSE Household and Individual Data.* 2015. https://dataverse.
    unc.edu/dataset.xhtml?persistentId=hdl:1902.29/11735.

Public Opinion Research Center (CBOS) "Polish Public Opinion: Assessment of
    Systemic Transformation." June 5, 2019. https://www.cbos.pl/PL/publikacje/pub-
    lic_opinion/2019/05_06_2019.pdf.

Rose, Richard, and Christian Haerpfer. *New Baltic Barometer I, II, III, IV, and V.*
    Glasgow: CSPP Publications, 1993, 1995, 1996, 2000, 2001, 2004.

Rose, Richard, and Christian Haerpfer. *New Democracies Barometer I, II, III, IV, and V*
    Glasgow: CSPP Publications, 1991, 1992, 1993, 1994, 1995.

Rose, Richard, and Christian Haerpfer. *New Russia Barometer IX, XIV, and XVIII.*
    Glasgow: CSPP Publications, 2000, 2005, 2009.

Solt, Frederick. "Measuring Income Inequality across Countries and over Time: The
    Standardized World Income Inequality Database." *Social Science Quarterly* 101, no. 3
    (2020): 1183–1199. https://fsolt.org/swiid/.

Statista, Aaron O'Neill. "Number of Passenger Cars Produced in Select European
    Countries"; "Infant Mortality in Bulgaria 1895–2020"; "Infant Mortality in Russia
    1870–2020"; "Life Expectancy in Albania from 1920 to 2020"; "Life Expectancy in
    Bulgaria 1800–2020"; "Life Expectancy in France, 1765–2020"; "Life Expectancy
    in Germany, 1875–2020"; "Life Expectancy in Russia, 1845–2020"; "Total Fertility
    Rate of Bulgaria, 1875–2020"; and "Total Fertility Rate of Russia, 1840–2020," all
    from www.statista.com.

Transparency International. "Corruption Perceptions Index." Transparency
    International, 2020. https://www.transparency.org/en/.

UN Data. *Net Migration Rate (per 1,000 population).* 2018. http://data.un.org/Data.asp
    x?q=Net+migration+rate&d=PopDiv&f=variableID%3a85.

UN Development Programme. *Human Development Index (HDI).* 2018. http://hdr.
    undp.org/en/content/human-development-index-hdi.

UN Office on Drugs and Crime. *Victims of Intentional Homicide, 1990–2018.* 2020.
    https://dataunodc.un.org/content/data/homicide/homicide-rate.

United States Department of Agriculture Economic Research Service. *Real GDP (2010
    dollars) Historical.* 2018. https://www.ers.usda.gov/data-products/international-
    macroeconomic-data-set/international-macroeconomic-data-set/#Historical%20
    Data%20Files.

Wegener, Bernd, and David Mason. "International Social Justice Project, 1991 and
    1996." *ICPSR.* 2010. Retrieved from https://www.icpsr.umich.edu/web/ICPSR/
    studies/6705.

World Bank. "Life Expectancy at Birth, Total (Years)." World Bank, 2018.

World Bank. "Population, Total." World Bank, 2018. https://data.worldbank.org/indi-
    cator/SP.POP.TOTL.

World Bank. "GDP (constant 2010 USD)." World Bank Group. Accessed August 19, 2019.
    https://data.worldbank.org/indicator/NY.GDP.MKTP.KD?locations=CN-RU.

World Bank. *Death Rate, Crude (per 1,000 people)*. 2018. https://data.worldbank.org/ indicator/SP.DYN.CDRT.IN.

World Bank. *Fertility Rate, Total (births per woman)*. 2020. https://data.worldbank. org/indicator/SP.DYN.TFRT.IN.

World Bank. *GDP (constant 2010 US$)*. 2018. https://data.worldbank.org/indicator/ NY.GDP.MKTP.KD.

World Bank. *Households and NPISHs Final Consumption Expenditure (constant 2010 US$)*. 2018. https://data.worldbank.org/indicator/NE.CON.PRVT.KD.

World Bank. *Income Share Held by Highest 10%*. 2020. https://data.worldbank.org/ indicator/SI.DST.10TH.10.

World Bank. *Life Expectancy at Birth, Total (years)*. 2018. https://data.worldbank.org/ indicator/SP.DYN.LE00.IN.

World Bank. *Population, Total*. 2018. https://data.worldbank.org/indicator/SP.POP. TOTL.

World Bank. *Poverty Headcount Ratio at $5.50 a Day (2011 PPP) (% of population)*. 2018. https://data.worldbank.org/indicator/SI.POV.DDAY.

World Happiness Report. *World Happiness Report 2020*. 2020. https://worldhappiness. report/ed/2020/.

World Health Organization. "Mortality Database." UN, 2020. https://apps.who.int/ healthinfo/statistics/mortality/whodpms/.

World Health Organization. "World Health Statistics Data Visualizations Dashboard: Harmful Use of Alcohol." World Health Organization, 2016. https:// apps.who.int/gho/data/node.sdg.3-5-viz?lang=en.

World Inequality Database. "Percent of National Income Flowing to the Top 1% before Taxes and Transfers." *World Inequality Database*, 2020. https://wid.world/.

World Values Survey. *World Values Survey Waves 1–7*. 2020. http://www.worldvalues-survey.org/WVSOnline.jsp.

Notes

AUTHORS' NOTE ON TERMINOLOGY

1. Sharad Chari and Katherine Verdery, "Thinking between the Posts: Postcolonialism, Postsocialism, and Ethnography after the Cold War," *Comparative Studies in Society and History* 51, no. 1 (2009): 6–34, http://www.jstor.org/stable/27563729.

INTRODUCTION

1. See "Authors' Note on Terminology" at the front of the book.
2. James Roaf, Ruben Atoyen, Bikas Joshi, and Krzysztof Krogulski, *25 Years of Transition: Post-Communist Europe and the IMF* (Washington, DC: IMF, 2014); Marcin Piatkowski, *Europe's Growth Champion: Insights from the Economic Rise of Poland* (New York: Oxford University Press, 2018); Marcin Piatkowski, *Poland's New Golden Age: Shifting from Europe's Periphery to Its Center* (Washington, DC: World Bank, 2013). Anders Åslund, *How Capitalism Was Built: The Transformation of Central Europe, Russia, the Caucasus, and Central Asia* (New York: Cambridge University Press, 2013); Oleh Havrylyshyn, *Present at the Transition: An Inside Look at the Role of History, Politics, and Personalities in Post-Communist Countries* (New York: Cambridge University Press, 2020).
3. Michael Burawoy and Katherine Verdery, eds., *Uncertain Transition: Ethnographies of Change in the Postsocialist World* (Lanham, MD: Rowman and Littlefield, 2000); Janine R. Wedel, *Collision and Collusion: The Strange Case of Western Aid to Eastern Europe* (New York: St. Martin's Press, 2015); Peter Gowan, "Neoliberal Theory and Practice for Eastern Europe," *New Left Review* 213 (1995): 3–60; Dimiter Philipov and Jürgen Dorbritz, *Demographic Consequences of Economic Transition in Countries of Central and Eastern Europe* (Strasbourg: Council of Europe, 2003).

4. Svetlana Alexievich, *Secondhand Time: The Last of the Soviets* (New York: Random House, 2016).

5. Adam Przeworski, *Democracy and the Market: Economic Reforms in Eastern Europe and Latin America* (Cambridge: Cambridge University Press, 1991).

6. Andrei Shleifer and Daniel Treisman, "Normal Countries: The East 25 Years after Communism," *Foreign Affairs*, November/December 2014, https://www.foreignaffairs.com/articles/russia-fsu/2014-10-20/normal-countries.

7. Piatkowski, *Poland's New Golden Age*, 2.

8. Joseph A. Schumpeter, *Capitalism, Socialism, and Democracy*, 3rd ed. (New York: Harper & Row, 1950).

9. Minsoo Lee and Moon Joong Tcha, "The Color of Money: The Effects of Foreign Direct Investment on Economic Growth in Transition Economies," *Review of World Economics* 140, no. 2 (2004): 211–229.

10. Havrylyshyn, *Present at the Transition*.

11. "Wage Bargaining in Kecskemet (Hungary) Plant of Mercedes Benz—2 Years Wage Agreement, 2019–2020," Marmol Social Research Budapest, January 8, 2019, http://www.socialresearch.hu/2019/01/08/wage-bargaining-in-kecskemet-hungary-plant-of-mercedes-benz-2-years-wage-agreement-2019-2020/.

12. Valerie Hopkins, "Hungary Ties Growth to Bumper of German Carmakers," *Financial Times*, November 21, 2018, https://www.ft.com/content/d5f4115e-e8bb-11e8-8a85-04b8afea6ea3; Automotive Industry in Hungary, Hungarian Investment Promotion Agency, Automotive Industry in Hungary (September 2018), Budapest, https://hipa.hu/images/publications/hipa-automotive-industry-in-hungary_2018_09_20.pdf.

13. Wim Naudé, Aleksander Surdej, and Martin Cameron, "Ready for Industry 4.0? The Case of Central and Eastern Europe," in *Industry 4.0 and Engineering for a Sustainable Future* (Cham, Switzerland: Springer, 2019), 153–175.

14. John Feffer, *Aftershock: A Journey into Eastern Europe's Broken Dreams* (London: ZED, 2017), 8

15. Feffer, *Aftershock*, 10.

16. John Salt and Jane Millar, "Foreign Labour in the United Kingdom: Current Patterns and Trends," *Labour Market Trends* 114, no. 10 (2006): 335–355; John Salt and Jane Millar, "International Migration in Interesting Times: The Case of the UK," *People and Place* 14, no. 2 (2006): 14; Sara Lemos and Jonathan Portes, "New Labour? The Impact of Migration from Central and Eastern European countries on the UK Labour Market," 2008, https://www.econstor.eu/bitstream/10419/35467/1/582911966.pdf.

17. Alan Travis, "80% of Britain's 1.4m Eastern European Residents Are in Work," *The Guardian*, July 10, 2017, https://www.theguardian.com/world/2017/jul/10/majority-of-britain-eastern-european-residents-are-in-work.

18. Kevin Rawlinson, "Polish Is Second Most Spoken Language in England, as Census Reveals 140,000 Residents Cannot Speak English at All," *The Independent*, January 30, 2013, https://www.independent.co.uk/news/uk/home-news/polish-is-second-most-spoken-language-in-england-as-census-reveals-140000-residents-cannot-speak-8472447.html.

19. Naomi Klein, *The Shock Doctrine: The Rise of Disaster Capitalism* (New York: Picador, 2008).

20. Giovanni Andrea Cornia, "Poverty, Inequality and Policy Affecting Vulnerable Groups in Moldova," UN, Innocenti Research Center. Innocenti Working Paper 2006–5 (2006), 13.

21. William D. O'Neill, *The Great Depression in Facts and Figures*, 2009, http://www.analysis.williamdoneil.com/Depression_Facts.pdf.

22. Cornia, "Poverty, Inequality, and Policy," 52.

23. Johannes Linn, "Ten Years of Transition in Central Europe and the Former Soviet Union: The Good News and the Not-So-Good News," in *Transition: The First Decade*, ed. Mario I. Bléjer and Marko Skreb, 15–44 (Cambridge, MA: MIT Press, 2001)..

24. Jeffrey D. Sachs, "Shock Therapy in Poland: Perspectives of Five Years," *Tanner Lectures on Human Values* (1995): 265–290; Havrylyshyn, *Present at the Transition*.

25. Yoshiko M. Herrera, *Mirrors of the Economy: National Accounts and International Norms in Russia and Beyond* (Ithaca, NY: Cornell University Press, 2010).

26. Owen Dyer, "US Life Expectancy Falls for Third Year in a Row," *British Medical Journal* 363, no. k5118 (2018): doi: 10.1136/bmj.k5118; Olga Khazan, "Americans Are Dying Even Younger: Drug Overdoses and Suicides Are Causing American Life Expectancy to Drop," *The Atlantic*, November 29, 2018, https://www.theatlantic.com/health/archive/2018/11/us-life-expectancy-keeps-falling/576664/.

27. Ruben Atoyan, Lone Engbo Christiansen, Allan Dizioli, Christian Ebeke, Nadeem Ilahi, Anna Ilyina, Gil Mehrez, Haonan Qu, and Faezeh Raei, *Emigration and Its Economic Impact on Eastern Europe* (Washington, DC: IMF Staff Discussion Note, 2016), https://www.imf.org/external/pubs/ft/sdn/2016/sdn1607.pdf.

28. "Bhutan's Gross National Happiness Index," Oxford Poverty & Human Development Initiative (OPHI), https://ophi.org.uk/policy/national-policy/gross-national-happiness-index/.

29. The dataset we relied on for tables, charts, figures, and analyses for this book is available online at http://www.takingstockofshock.com.

30. Alpa Shah, "Ethnography? Participant Observation, a Potentially Revolutionary Praxis," *HAU: Journal of Ethnographic Theory* 7, no. 1 (Spring 2017): 45–59, doi: 10.14318/hau7.1.008.

31. Anne Case and Angus Deaton, *Deaths of Despair and the Future of Capitalism* (Princeton, NJ: Princeton University Press, 2020).

32. Janine R. Wedel, *Collision and Collusion*.

33. Krzysztof Jasiewicz, "The New Populism in Poland: The Usual Suspects?" *Problems of Post-Communism* 55, no. 3 (2008), 7–25, 13.

34. Simeon Djankov, *Russia's Economy under Putin: From Crony Capitalism to State Capitalism*, No. PB15-18 (Washington, DC: Peterson Institute for International Economics, 2015).

35. Ivan Krastev and Stephen Holmes, *The Light That Failed: A Reckoning* (London: Penguin Books, 2019).

CHAPTER 1

1. Olivier Blanchard et al., *Reform in Eastern Europe* (Cambridge, MA: MIT Press, 1991), xvi.

2. Caroline Humphrey, introduction to *The Unmaking of Soviet Life: Everyday Economies after Socialism* (Ithaca, NY: Cornell University Press, 2002).

3. Giovanni Andrea Cornia, "Transition, Structural Divergence, and Performance: Eastern Europe and the Former Soviet Union over 2000-2007," No. 2010/32, WIDER Working Paper (2010), 13.

4. The minutes of many of these meetings are now available, as the international institutions impose a twenty-year wall of secrecy on their deliberations before releasing them to the public. Today, most of the discussions of the 1990s have been revealed and are searchable on the IMF and World Bank websites. See Hilary Appel and Mitchell A. Orenstein, *From Triumph to Crisis: Neoliberal Economic Reform in Postcommunist Countries*, chap. 1 (Cambridge: Cambridge University Press, 2018).

5. Blanchard et al., *Reform in Eastern Europe*.

6. John Williamson, "What Washington Means by Policy Reform," in *Latin American Adjustment: How Much Has Happened?*, ed. John Williamson (Washington, DC: Peterson Institute, 1990), 90–120.

7. Blanchard et al., *Reform in Eastern Europe*, 1.

8. Dani Rodrik argues that ignorance of local context has been a downfall of economic advice under neoliberalism. Even application of the same principles in different contexts can and should produce surprisingly different policies. He argues against the cookie cutter policies advised by the IFIs. See Dani Rodrik, *The Globalization Paradox: Democracy and the Future of the World Economy* (New York: Norton, 2011).

9. Blanchard et al., *Reform in Eastern Europe*, xii.

10. Blanchard et al., *Reform in Eastern Europe*, 8.

11. Blanchard et al., *Reform in Eastern Europe*, 13.

12. Mario I. Blejer and Alan H. Gelb, "The Contraction of Eastern Europe's Economies: Introduction to the Conference," in *Eastern Europe in Transition: From Recession to Growth?*, ed. Mario I. Blejer et al. (Washington, DC: World Bank, 1993), 3. The authors argue that there were no clear models for estimating the effects of transition.

13. Blanchard et al., *Reform in Eastern Europe*, xiii.

14. Blanchard et al., *Reform in Eastern Europe*, xiii.

15. John Cassidy, "Always with Us? Jeffery Sachs's Plan to Eradicate World Poverty," *New Yorker*, April 3, 2005, https://www.newyorker.com/magazine/2005/04/11/always-with-us.

16. Blanchard et al., *Reform in Eastern Europe*, xiv.

17. Katherine Verdery, *The Vanishing Hectare: Property and Value in Postsocialist Transylvania* (Ithaca, NY: Cornell University Press, 2003), 3.

18. Joseph A. Schumpeter, *Capitalism, Socialism, and Democracy*, 3rd ed. (New York: Harper & Row, 1950).

19. Blanchard et al., *Reform in Eastern Europe*, xvi.

20. Pavel Žufan and Jiří Erbes, "Key Driving Forces in the Czech Brewing Industry," *Agricultural Economics* 48, no. 7 (2002): 311–314.

21. Kristen Ghodsee, *The Red Riviera: Gender, Tourism, and Postsocialism on the Black Sea* (Durham, NC: Duke University Press, 2005), and Kristen Ghodsee, *Muslim Lives in Eastern Europe* (Princeton, NJ: Princeton University Press, 2010).

22. Blanchard et al., *Reform in Eastern Europe*, xviii.

23. Blanchard et al., *Reform in Eastern* Europe, xxi–xxii.

CHAPTER 2

1. Blejer and Gelb, "The Contraction," 3.

2. Verdery, *The Vanishing Hectare*, 4.

3. Karla Brom and Mitchell Orenstein, "The Privatised Sector in the Czech Republic: Government and Bank Control in a Transitional Economy," *Europe-Asia Studies* 46, no. 6 (1994): 893–928.

4. Vadim Volkov, *Violent Entrepreneurs: The Use of Force in the Making of Russian Capitalism* (Ithaca, NY: Cornell University Press, 2002).

5. Susanne Karstedt, "Legacies of a Culture of Inequality: The Janus Face of Crime in Postcommunist Countries," *Crime, Law and Social Change* 40, no. 2–3 (2003): 295–320;Leslie Holmes, "Corruption and the Crisis of the Post-communist State," *Crime, Law and Social Change* 27, no. 3–4 (1997): 275–297.

6. Vadim Volkov, *Violent Entrepreneurs*, 33.

7. Vadim Volkov, *Violent Entrepreneurs*, 149.

8. As quoted in Verdery, *The Vanishing Hectare*, 1.

9. David S. Altshuler, "Tunneling Towards Capitalism in the Czech Republic," *Ethnography* 2, no. 1 (2001): 115–138.

10. Jan Fidrmuc, "Economic Reform, Democracy, and Growth during Post-Communist Transition," *European Journal of Political Economy* 19, no. 3 (2003): 585, doi: 10.1016/S0176-2680(03)00010-7.

11. Dominik Paprotny, "Measuring Central and Eastern Europe's Economic Development Using Time Lags," *Social Indicators Research* 127, no. 3 (2016): 939–957.

12. Jutta Bolt, Robert Inklaar, Herman de Jong, Jan Luiten van Zanden, "Rebasing 'Maddison': The Shape of Long-Run Economic Development," VoxEU, January25, 2018, figure 2, https://voxeu.org/article/rebasing-maddison; Jutta Bolt, Robert Inklaar, Herman de Jong, and Jan Luiten van Zanden, "Rebasing 'Maddison': New Income Comparisons and the Shape of Long-Run Economic Development," Maddison Project Working Paper 10, figure 1, https://www.rug.nl/ggdc/html_publications/memorandum/gd174.pdf.

13. Sachs, "Shock Therapy in Poland," 265–290.

14. J. Barkley Rosser Jr., Marina V. Rosser, and Ehsan Ahmed, "Income Inequality and the Informal Economy in Transition Economies," *Journal of Comparative Economics* 28, no. 1 (2000): 156–171.

15. Friedrich Schneider, "Shadow Economies around the World: What Do We Really Know?," *European Journal of Political Economy* 21, no. 3 (2005): 598–642.

16. Mária Lackó, *Do Power Consumption Data Tell the Story? Electricity Intensity and Hidden Economy in Post-Socialist Countries*, No. BWP-1999/2 (Budapest Working Papers on the Labour Market, 1999), 2, https://www.econstor.eu/handle/10419/108393.

17. Richard Rose, *Understanding Post-Communist Transformation: A Bottom Up Approach* (London: Routledge, 2009), 56–58.

18. Rose, *Understanding Post-Communist Transformation*, 81–82.

19. Rosser, Rosser, and Ahmed, "Income Inequality and the Informal Economy."

20. Stephan Haggard and Robert R. Kaufman, *The Political Economy of Democratic Transitions* (Princeton, NJ: Princeton University Press, 2018).

21. Bukowski, Pawel, and Filip Novokmet, "CEP Discussion Paper No 1628 June 2019 between Communism and Capitalism: Long-Term Inequality in Poland, 1892–2015" (2019). See also Michal Brzezinski, Barbara Jancewicz, and Natalia Letki, "The Rise of Inequalities in Poland and Their Impacts: When Politicians Don't Care but Citizens Do," in *Changing Inequalities and Societal Impacts in Rich Countries: Thirty Countries' Experiences*, vol. 2 (Oxford: Oxford University Press, 2014), 488–513.

22. Brian Nolan, Max Roser, and Stefan Thewissen, *GDP per Capita versus Median Household Income: What Gives Rise to Divergence over Time?* (No. 672. LIS Working Paper Series, 2016).

23. Bukowski and Novokmet, "CEP Discussion Paper No 1628, 2019," 44.

24. "Polish Public Opinion: Assessment of Systemic Transformation," Public Opinion Research Center (CBOS), June 5, 2019, https://www.cbos.pl/PL/publikacje/public_opinion/2019/05_06_2019.pdf.

25. Ewa Ruminska-Zimny, *Human Poverty in Transition Economies: Regional Overview for HDR 1997* (New York: Human Development Report Office, United Nations Development Programme, 1997).

26. Ruminska-Zimny, *Human Poverty in Transition Economies*.

27. "The Face of Poverty in Europe and Central Asia," *World Bank*, February 10, 2014, https://www.worldbank.org/en/news/feature/2014/02/10/face-of-poverty-in-europe-and-central-asia.

28. Some of the key works in the significant literature on postcommunist social policy are Nicholas Barr, ed., *Labor Markets and Social Policy in Central and Eastern Europe: The Accession and Beyond* (Washington, DC: World Bank, 2005); Alfio Cerami and Pieter Vanhuysse, *Post-Communist Welfare Pathways: Theorizing Social Policy Transformations in Central and Eastern Europe* (Basingstoke: Palgrave Macmillan, 2009); Bob Deacon and Michelle Hulse, "The Making of Post-Communist Social Policy: The Role of International Agencies," *Journal of Social Policy* 26, no.1 (1997): 43–62; Noémi Lendvai, "The Weakest Link? EU Accession and Enlargement: Dialoguing EU and Post-Communist Social Policy," *Journal of European Social Policy* 14, no. 3 (2004): 319–333; Mitchell A. Orenstein, *Privatizing Pensions: The Transnational Campaign for Social Security Reform* (Princeton, NJ: Princeton University Press, 2008); Jolanta Aidukaite, "The Formation of Social Insurance Institutions of the Baltic States in the Post-Socialist Era," *Journal of European Social Policy* 16, no. 3 (2006): 259–270; Tomasz Inglot, "Historical Legacies, Institutions, and the Politics of Social Policy in Hungary and Poland, 1989–1999," *Capitalism and Democracy in Central and Eastern Europe* (2003): 210–247; Linda J. Cook, *The Soviet Social Contract and Why It Failed: Welfare Policy and Workers' Politics from Brezhnev to Yeltsin* (Cambridge, MA: Harvard University Press, 1994); Linda J. Cook, Mitchell A. Orenstein, and Marilyn Rueschemeyer, eds., *Left Parties and Social Policy in Post-Communist Europe* (Boulder, CO: Westview Press, 1999); Pieter Vanhuysse, *Divide and Pacify: Strategic Social Policies and Political Protests in Post-Communist Democracies* (Budapest: Central European University Press, 2006).

29. Raymond Struyk and Anastasia Kolodeznikova, "Needs-Based Targeting without Knowing Household Incomes: How Would It Work in Russia?," *Urban Studies* 36, no. 11 (1999): 1885; Christiaan Grootaert and Jeanine Braithwaite, *Poverty Correlates and Indicator-Based Targeting in Eastern Europe and the Former Soviet Union* (Washington, DC: World Bank, 1999).

30. Abel Polese, Jeremy Morris, and Borbála Kovács, "Introduction: The Failure and Future of the Welfare State in Post-Socialism," *Journal of Eurasian Studies* 6, no. 1 (2015), 1–5.

31. Stefan Buzar, *Energy Poverty in Eastern Europe: Hidden Geographies of Deprivation* (Abingdon, UK: Routledge, 2016); Michael Marmot and Martin Bobak, "International Comparators and Poverty and Health in Europe," *British Medical Journal* 321 (2000): 1124–1128, ; Grootaert and Braithwaite, *Poverty Correlates*.

32. Olivier Blanchard, *The Economics of Post-Communist Transition*, chap. 2 (New York: Oxford University Press, 1997).

33. Caroline Humphrey, *The Unmaking of Soviet Life: Everyday Economies after Socialism* (Ithaca, NY: Cornell University Press, 2002), 24.

34. Svetlana Alexievich, *Second Hand Time: The Last of the Soviets*, trans. Bela Shayevich (New York: Random House, 2016).

CHAPTER 3

1. Peter Murrell, "Institutions and Transition," *The New Palgrave Dictionary of Economics*, vol. 2 (London: Palgrave Macmillan, 2006); Bruce Kogut and Andrew Spicer, "Capital Market Development and Mass Privatization Are Logical Contradictions: Lessons from Russia and the Czech Republic," *Industrial and Corporate Change* 11, no. 1 (2002): 1–37.

2. Verdery, *The Vanishing Hectare*.

3. "Carpets for Kilims," in Kristen Ghodsee, *Lost in Transition: Ethnographies of Everyday Life after Communism* (Durham, NC: Duke University Press, 2011).

4. Christopher Jarvis, "The Rise and Fall of Albania's Pyramid Schemes," *Finance & Development* 37, no. 1 (2000): 46.

5. Natasha Tolstikova, "MMM as a Phenomenon of the Russian Consumer Culture," *European Advances in Consumer Research* 4 (1999): 208–215.

6. Jane Perlez, "Pyramid Scheme a Trap for Many Romanians," *New York Times*, November 13, 1993, https://www.nytimes.com/1993/11/13/business/pyramid-scheme-a-trap-for-many-romanians.html. See also Katherine Verdery, *What Was Communism and What Comes Next?* (Princeton, NJ: Princeton University Press, 1996).

7. Gerard Roland, "The Political Economy of Transition," *Journal of Economic Perspectives* 16, no. 1 (2002): 29–50; David Barlow and Roxana Radulescu, "The Sequencing of Reform in Transition Economies," *Journal of Comparative Economics* 33, no. 4 (2005): 835–850; Kenneth J. Arrow, "Economic Transition: Speed and Scope," *Journal of Institutional and Theoretical Economics (JITE)/Zeitschrift für die Gesamte Staatswissenschaft* 156, no. 1 (2000): 9–18.

8. Wedel, *Collision and Collusion*.

9. Jana Hensel, *After the Wall: Confession from an East German Childhood and the Life That Came After*, trans. Jefferson Chase (New York: PublicAffairs, 2004), 93–94.

10. Hensel, *After the* Wall, 113–114.

11. European Bank for Reconstruction and Development, *Annual Report 1996* (London: EBRD, 1996); Jon Elster et al., *Institutional Design in Post-Communist Societies: Rebuilding the Ship at Sea* (Cambridge: Cambridge University Press, 1998).

12. World Bank, *From Plan to Market: World Development Report 1996* (Washington, DC: World Bank, 1996), 14.

13. Appel and Orenstein, *From Triumph to Crisis*, chap. 4.

14. Max Spoor, "Inequality, Poverty and Conflict in Transition Economies," in *Globalisation, Poverty and Conflict* (Dordrecht, the Netherlands: Springer, 2004), 47–65.

15. Petr Pavlínek, Bolesław Domański, and Robert Guzik, "Industrial Upgrading through Foreign Direct Investment in Central European Automotive Manufacturing," *European Urban and Regional Studies* 16, no. 1 (2009): 43–63.

16. Statista, "Number of Passenger Cars Produced in Select European Countries," 2018. https://www.statista.com/statistics/269623/passenger-car-production-in-europe/.

17. Andreas Nölke and Arjan Vliegenthart, "Enlarging the Varieties of Capitalism: The Emergence of Dependent Market Economies in East Central Europe," *World Politics* 61, no. 4 (2009): 670–702.

18. La-Bhus Fah Jirasavetakul and Jesmin Rahman, *Foreign Direct Investment in New Member State of the EU and Western Balkans: Taking Stock and Assessing Prospects* (Washington, DC: International Monetary Fund, 2018).

19. Ichiro Iwasaki and Keiko Suganuma, "Foreign Direct Investment and Regional Economic Development in Russia: An Econometric Assessment," *Economic Change and Restructuring* 48, no. 3–4 (2015): 209–255.

20. Iwasaki and Suganuma, "Foreign Direct Investment."

21. Oleh Havrylyshyn, "Recovery and Growth in Transition: A Decade of Evidence," *IMF Staff Papers* 48, no. 4 (2001): 53–87; Anders Åslund, *Building Capitalism: The Transformation of the Former Soviet Bloc* (Cambridge: Cambridge University Press, 2002); Anders Åslund, *How Capitalism Was Built: The Transformation of Central Europe, Russia, the Caucasus, and Central Asia* (New York: Cambridge University Press, 2013); Jeffrey D. Sachs, "The Transition at Mid Decade," *American Economic Review* 86, no. 2 (May 1996): 128–133.

22. World Bank, *From Plan to Market*.

CHAPTER 4

1. Klein, *The Shock Doctrine*.

2. Anders Åslund, *Russia's Crony Capitalism: The Path from Market Economy to Kleptocracy* (New Haven, CT: Yale University Press, 2019).

3. Verdery, *The Vanishing Hectare*, 4.

4. Jeffrey D. Sachs, "What I Did in Russia," jeffsachs.org, March 14, 2012, http://www.acamedia.info/politics/ukraine/jeffrey_sachs/What_I_did_in_Russia.pdf.

5. Joseph Stiglitz, *Making Globalization Work* (New York: Norton, 2007), 37–39. Stiglitz argued that "the failures of Russia and most of the other countries making the transition from communism to capitalism were far deeper than GDP statistics alone show," and he suggested looking at demographic decline as well. Stiglitz's *Globalization and Its Discontents* (New York: Norton, 2003) gives a more extended critique of Western economists' poor performance in advising Russia.

6. David Stuckler et al., "Mass Privatisation and the Post-Communist Mortality Crisis: A Cross National Analysis," *The Lancet* 373, no. 9961 (2009): 399–407, doi: 10.1016/S0140-6736(09)60005-2.

7. Hilary Appel, "Is It Putin or Is It Oil? Explaining Russia's Fiscal Recovery," *Post-Soviet Affairs* 24, no. 4 (2008): 301–323; Bruno Merlevede et al., "Russia from Bust to Boom and Back: Oil Price, Dutch Disease and Stabilisation Fund," *Comparative Economic Studies* 51, no. 2 (2009): 213–241; Philip Hanson, "Putin and Russia's Economic Transformation," *Eurasian Geography and Economics* 45, no. 6 (2004): 421–428.

8. Frank Schimmelfennig and Ulrich Sedelmeier, "Governance by Conditionality: EU Rule Transfer to the Candidate Countries of Central and Eastern Europe," *Journal of European Public Policy* 11, no. 4 (2004): 661–679; Tim Haughton, "When Does the EU Make a Difference? Conditionality and the Accession Process in Central and Eastern Europe," *Political Studies Review* 5, no. 2 (2007): 233–246; Andrew Moravcsik and Milada A. Vachudova, "National Interests, State Power, and EU Enlargement," *East European Politics and Societies* 17, no. 1 (2003): 42–57.

9. Alya Guseva and Akos Rona-Tas, *Plastic Money: Constructing Markets for Credit Cards in Eight Postcommunist Countries* (Palo Alto, CA: Stanford University Press, 2014).

10. Pradeep Mitra et al., *Turmoil at Twenty: Recession, Recovery and Reform in Central and Eastern Europe and the Former Soviet Union* (Washington, DC: World Bank, 2009).

11. "World Economic Forum 2009: Russia and China Blame West for Economic Crisis," *The Telegraph*, January 29, 2009, https://www.telegraph.co.uk/finance/financetop-ics/davos/4381464/WEF-2009-Russia-and-China-blame-West-for-economic-crisis-Davos.html. See also Youtube: "Putin Lashes Out in Davos," CCTVupload, January 28, 2009, https://www.youtube.com/watch?v=ed2Fok6JAqU.

12. Erik Berglöf et al., "Understanding the Crisis in Emerging Europe," EBRD Working Paper 109 (2009).

13. Appel and Orenstein, *From Triumph to Crisis*, chap. 6.

14. Marcin A. Piasecki, "Was Viktor Orbán's Unorthodox Economic Policy the Right Answer to Hungary's Economic Misfortunes?," *International Journal of Management and Economics* 46 (2015), doi: 10.1515/ijme-2015-0021.

15. János Kornai, "Hungary's U-turn: Retreating from Democracy," *Journal of Democracy* 26, no. 3 (2015): 34–48; Abby Innes, "Hungary's Illiberal Democracy," *Current History* 114, no. 770 (2015): 95; Bojan Bugaric, "Protecting Democracy Inside the EU: On Article 7 TEU and the Hungarian Turn to Authoritarianism," in *Reinforcing Rule of Law Oversight in the European Union*, ed. Carlos Closa and Dimitry Kochenov (Cambridge: Cambridge University Press, 2016): 82–101.

16. Juliet Johnson and Andrew Barnes, "Financial Nationalism and Its International Enablers: The Hungarian Experience," *Review of International Political Economy*

22, no. 3 (2015): 535–569; Piasecki, "Was Viktor Orbán's," 41–71; Simeon Djankov, "Hungary under Orbán: Can Central Planning Revive Its Economy," Peterson Institute for International Economics Policy Brief 15–11 (2015); Ewa Dabrowska et al., "The 'Budapest-Warsaw Express': Conservatism and the Diffusion of Economic Policies in Poland and Hungary," in *New Conservatives in Russia and East Central Europe*, ed. Katharina Bluhm and Mihai Varga, 178–197 (Abingdon, UK: Routledge, 2019; Bojan Bugaric, "The Populist Backlash against Europe: Why Only Alternative Economic and Social Policies Can Stop the Rise of Populism in Europe," in *EU Law in Populist Times: Crises and Prospects*, ed. Francesca Bignami (Cambridge: Cambridge University Press, 2019): 477–504.

17. Kriszta Kovács and Kim Lane Scheppele, "The Fragility of an Independent Judiciary: Lessons from Hungary and Poland—and the European Union," *Communist and Post-Communist Studies* 51, no. 3 (2018): 189–200.

18. Iga Magda et al., "The 'Family 500+' Child Allowance and Female Labour Supply in Poland," OECD Economics Department Working Papers, no. 1481 (2018), 1–18; Stanisława Golinowska and Agnieszka Sowa-Kofta, "Combating Poverty through Family Cash Benefits: On the First Results of the Programme 'Family 500+' in Poland," *Polityka Społeczna* 44, no. 1 (2017): 7–13; Michał Brzeziński and Mateusz Najsztub, "The Impact of 'Family 500+' Programme on Household Incomes, Poverty and Inequality," *Polityka Społeczna* 44, no. 1 (2017): 16–25.

19. Ivan Krastev, "What's Wrong with East-Central Europe? Liberalism's Failure to Deliver," *Journal of Democracy* 27, no. 1 (2016): 35–38.

20. Olivier Blanchard argues that neoliberal policies should not have removed subsidies to the poor because this caused unneeded suffering. Blanchard, *The Economics of Post-Communist Transition*.

21. Branko Milanovic, *Global Inequality: A New Approach for the Age of Globalization* (Cambridge, MA: Harvard University Press, 2016).

22. Some of the prominent works arguing that communism cannot be reformed include János Kornai, *The Socialist System: The Political Economy of Communism* (Princeton, NJ: Princeton University Press, 1992); Jeffrey D. Sachs, *Poland's Jump to the Market Economy* (Cambridge: MIT Press, 1993).

23. Blejer and Gelb, "The Contraction," 3; Kornai. *The Socialist System*.

24. "GDP (constant 2010 USD)," World Bank, accessed August 19, 2019, https://data.worldbank.org/indicator/NY.GDP.MKTP.KD?locations=CN-RU.

25. Alejandro Portes, "Migration and Development: Reconciling Opposite Views," *Ethnic and Racial Studies* 32, no. 1 (2009): 8, doi: 10.1080/01419870802483668; Blejer and Gelb, "The Contraction," 3.

26. Elaine Sciolino, "U.S. Is Abandoning 'Shock Therapy' for the Russians," *New York Times*, December 21, 1993, https://www.nytimes.com/1993/12/21/world/us-is-abandoning-shock-therapy-for-therussians.html.

CHAPTER 5

1. Charles Lane, "Eastern Europe Is Headed toward a Demographic Crisis," *Washington Post*, November 11, 2019, https://www.washingtonpost.com/opinions/global-opinions/the-incredible-shrinking-nations-of-eastern-europe/2019/11/11/fd777326-04a6-11ea-b17d-8b867891d39d_story.html.

2. Aamna Mohdin, "The Fastest Shrinking Countries on Earth Are in Eastern Europe," *Quartz*, January 24, 2018, https://qz.com/1187819/country-ranking-worlds-fastest-shrinking-countries-are-in-eastern-europe/; Dave Lawler, "Eastern Europe Is Shrinking Before Our Eyes," *Axios*, updated July 21, 2018, https://www.axios.com/eastern-europe-is-shrinking-before-our-eyes-1516559604-5b103657-f029-429c-bed8-182cfa43651f.html.

3. Maxim Edwards, "Ukraine's Quiet Depopulation Crisis," *The Atlantic*, March 21, 2020, https://www.theatlantic.com/international/archive/2020/03/ukraine-eastern-europe-depopulation-immigration-crisis/608464/, and "Why Is the Population of Eastern and Central Europe in Freefall?" [television program], *Al Jazeera*, February 4, 2020, https://www.aljazeera.com/programmes/thestream/2020/02/25986-200325175700042.html.

4. Valentina Romei, "Eastern Europe Has the Largest Population Loss in Modern History," *Financial Times*, May 27, 2016, https://www.ft.com/content/70813826-0c64-33d3-8a0c-72059ae1b5e3.

5. Ivan Krastev, "Depopulation Is Eastern Europe's Biggest Problem," *Financial Times*, January 27, 2020, https://www.ft.com/content/c5d3e0ae-36eb-11ea-ac3c-f68c10993b04.

6. United Nations Population Fund EECARO, *Shrinking Populations in Eastern Europe* (United Nations, October 2018), https://eeca.unfpa.org/sites/default/files/pub-pdf/Shrinking%20population_low%20fertility%20QA.pdf.

7. World Bank, "Life Expectancy at Birth, Total (Years)," World Bank Group, 2018. https://data.worldbank.org/indicator/SP.DYN.LE00.IN.

8. Joel Kotkin, "Death Spiral Demographics: The Countries Shrinking the Fastest," *Forbes*, February 1, 2017, https://www.forbes.com/sites/joelkotkin/2017/02/01/death-spiral-demographics-the-countries-shrinking-the-fastest/#6f1cb7e9b83c.

CHAPTER 6

1. Aaron O'Neill, "Life Expectancy in Russia, 1845–2020," Statista, October 1, 2019, https://www.statista.com/statistics/1041395/life-expectancy-russia-all-time/.

2. Aaron O'Neill, "Life Expectancy in Germany, 1875–2020," Statista, September 6, 2019, https://www.statista.com/statistics/1041098/life-expectancy-germany-all-time/.

3. Aaron O'Neill, "Life Expectancy in France, 1765–2020," Statista, September 13, 2019, https://www.statista.com/statistics/1041105/life-expectancy-france-all-time/.

4. Aaron O'Neill, "Infant Mortality in Russia 1870–2020," Statista, October 16, 2019, https://www.statista.com/statistics/1042801/russia-all-time-infant-mortality-rate/.

5. David Stuckler and Sanjay Basu, *The Body Economic: Why Austerity Kills* (New York: Basic Books, 2013), 24.

6. Aaron O'Neill, "Life Expectancy in Bulgaria 1800–2020," Statista, June 4, 2020, https://www.statista.com/statistics/1071016/life-expectancy-bulgaria-1800-2020/.

7. Aaron O'Neill, "Infant Mortality in Bulgaria 1895–2020," Statista, April 9, 2020, https://www.statista.com/statistics/1073127/infant-mortality-rate-bulgaria/.

8. Aaron O'Neill, "Life Expectancy in Albania from 1920 to 2020," Statista, June 4, 2020, https://www.statista.com/statistics/1071003/life-expectancy-albania-1920-2020/.

9. Johan P. Mackenbach, "Political Conditions of Life Expectancy in Europe," *Social Science & Medicine* 82 (2013): 144–145, doi: 10.1016/j.socscimed.2012.12.022.

10. Bernd Rechel, Erica Richardson, and Martin McKee, *Trends in Health Systems in the Former Soviet Countries*, European Observatory on Health Systems and Policies, 2014: 9

11. United Nations Development Programme, *The Human Cost of Transition: Human Security in South East Europe* (United Nations, October 2013), available from http://hdr.undp.org/en/content/human-cost-transition.

12. United Nations Children's Fund Innocenti Research Centre, *A Decade of Transition: Regional Monitoring Report*, no. 8 (Florence: United Nations, 2001), https://www.unicef-irc.org/publications/pdf/monee8/eng/3.pdf.

13. United Nations Development Programme, *Human Development in Eastern Europe and the CIS since 1990: Human Development Report Research Paper* (United Nations, July 2010), http://hdr.undp.org/sites/default/files/hdrp201016.pdf.

14. "World Health Statistics Data Visualizations Dashboard: Harmful Use of Alcohol: Distribution by Country," World Health Organization, 2016, https://apps.who.int/gho/data/node.sdg.3-5-viz?lang=en.

15. Vladimir Shkolnikov, France Meslé, and David A. Leon, "Premature Circulatory Disease Mortality in Russia in Light of Population—and Individual-Level Disease," in *Heart Disease: Environment, Stress and Gender*, ed. G. Weidner, S.M. Kopp, and M. Kristenson (NATO Science Series, Series I: Life and Behavioural Sciences, 2001, 39–68).

16. David Zaridze, Dimitri Maximovitch, Alexander Lazarev, Vladimir Igitov, Alex Boroda, Jillian Boreham, Peter Boyle, Richard Peto, and Paolo Boffetta, "Alcohol Poisoning Is a Main Determinant of Recent Mortality Trends in Russia: Evidence from a Detailed Analysis of Mortality Statistics and Autopsies," *International Journal of Epidemiology* 38 (2009): 143–153.

17. Michel Guillot et al., "Understanding the 'Russian Mortality Paradox' in Central Asia: Evidence from Kyrgyzstan," *Demography* 48, no. 3 (2011): 1081–1104, doi: 10.1007%2Fs13524-011-0036-1.

18. Rechel Bernd et al., *Trends in Health Systems*, chap. 2.

19. Daniel Treisman, "Death and Prices: The Political Economy of Russia's Alcohol Crisis," *Economics of Transition and Institutional Change* 18, no. 2 (April 2010): 281–331.

20. Rechel Bernd et al., *Trends in Health Systems*, chap. 2. See also Treisman, "Death and Prices," 281–331.

21. Stuckler et al., "Mass Privatisation."

22. Elizabeth Brainerd and David M. Cutler, "Autopsy on an Empire: Understanding Mortality in Russia and the Former Soviet Union," *Journal of Economic Perspectives* 19, no. 1 (2005): 127. doi: 10.1257/0895330053147921.

23. Géraldine Duthé et al., "Adult Mortality Patterns in the Former Soviet Union's Southern Tier: Armenia and Georgia in Comparative Perspective," *Demographic Research* 36, no. 19 (2017): 589–608, doi: 10.4054/DemRes.2017.36.19.

24. Regina T. Riphahn and Klaus F. Zimmerman, "The Mortality Crisis in East Germany," *IZA Discussion Papers* no. 6 (1998): 40, http://www.econstor.eu/dspace/bitstream/10419/20852/1/dp6.pdf.

25. William C. Cockerham, Brian P. Hinote, and Pamela Abbott, "Psychological Distress, Gender, and Health Lifestyles in Belarus, Kazakhstan, Russia, and Ukraine," *Social Science & Medicine* 63, no. 9 (2006): 2381–2394, doi: 10.1016/j.socscimed.2006.06.001.

26. Bernd et al., *Trends in Health Systems*, chap. 2.

27. Aytalina Azarova et al., "The Effect of Rapid Privatisation on Mortality in Mono-Industrial Towns in Post-Soviet Russia: A Retrospective Cohort Study," *Lancet Public Health* 2, no. 5 (2017): 231–238, https://dx.doi.org/10.1016%2FS2468-2667(17)30072-5.

28. Azarova et al., "The Effect of Rapid Privatisation," 231–238; Stuckler and Basu, *The Body Economic*.

29. William C. Cockerham et al., "Health Lifestyles in Central Asia: The Case of Kazakhstan and Kyrgyzstan," *Social Science & Medicine* 59, no. 7 (2004): 1409–1421, doi: 10.1016/j.socscimed.2004.01.023; Michel Guillot et al., "Divergent Paths for Adult Mortality in Russia and Central Asia: Evidence from Kyrgyzstan," *PLoS ONE* 8, no. 10 (2013): doi:10.1371/journal.pone.0075314.

30. Cockerham et al., "Health Lifestyles"; Guillot et al., "Divergent Paths."

31. Duthé et al., "Adult Mortality Patterns," 589–608.

32. Brainerd and Cutler, "Autopsy," 114.

33. Cockerham et al., "Health Lifestyles," 1409–1421.

34. Igor Sheiman, "Rocky Road From the Semashko to a New Health Model," interview by Fiona Fleck, *Bulletin of the World Health Organization* 5, no. 91 (2013): 320–321, doi:10.2471/BLT.13.030513.

35. Brainerd and Cutler, "Autopsy," 114.

36. Guillot et al., "Understanding"; Guillot et al., "Divergent Paths."

37. Stuckler et al., "Mass Privatisation," 399–407.

38. John S. Earle and Scott Gehlbach, "Did Mass Privatisation Really Increase Post-Communist Mortality?," *The Lancet* 375, no. 9712 (2010): 372, doi: 10.1016/S0140-6736(10)60159-6.

39. Andrew Jack, "Soviet Sell-Offs Led to Deaths, Says Study," *Financial Times*, January 14, 2009, https://www.ft.com/content/44a495ee-e276-11dd-b1dd-0000779fd2ac.

40. Jay Bhattacharya, Christina Gathmann, and Grant Miller, "The End of the Soviet Union's Anti-alcohol Campaign May Explain a Substantial Share of Russia's 'Mortality Crisis' in the 1990's," *EUROPP* (blog), LSE, October 10, 2013, https://blogs.lse.ac.uk/europpblog/2013/10/10/the-end-of-the-soviet-unions-anti-alcohol-campaign-may-explain-a-substantial-share-of-russias-mortality-crisis-in-the-1990s/; Treisman, "Death and Prices," 281–331.

41. Azarova et al., "The Effect of Rapid Privatisation," 231–238; Stuckler and Basu, *The Body Economic*.

42. Stuckler and Basu, *The Body Economic*; David Stuckler, "The International Monetary Fund's Effects on Global Health: Before and After the 2008 Financial Crisis," *International Journal of Health Services* 39, no. 4 (2009): 771–781, doi: 10.2190%2FHS.39.4.j.

43. Rechel, *Trends in Health Systems*, chap. 2.

44. David Stuckler, Lawrence P. King, and Sanjay Basu, "International Monetary Fund Programs and Tuberculosis Outcomes in Post-Communist Countries," *PLoS Medicine* 5, no. 7 (2008): e143, doi: 10.1371/journal.pmed.0050143; Gary Maynard et al., "IMF Structural Adjustment, Public Health Spending, and Tuberculosis: A Longitudinal Analysis Prevalence Rates in Poor Countries," *International Journal of Sociology* 42, no. 2 (2012): 5–27, doi: 10.2753/IJS0020-7659420201; David Stuckler and Sanjay Basu, "How Austerity Kills," *New York Times*, May 12, 2013, https://www.nytimes.com/2013/05/13/opinion/how-austerity-kills.html.

45. Marina Karanikolos et al., "Financial Crisis, Austerity, and Health in Europe," *The Lancet* 381, April 13, 2013, doi: 10.1016/ S0140-6736(13)60102-6.

46. Cf. Havrylyshyn, *Present at the Transition*.

CHAPTER 7

1. Susan Erikson, "Now It Is Completely the Other Way Around: Political Economies of Fertility in Re-unified Germany," in *Barren States: The Population "Implosion" in Europe*, ed. Carrie B. Douglass (Oxford: Berg, 2005), 49.

2. Steve Crawshaw, "East Germany's Vanishing Babies," *The Independent*, February 9, 1995, https://www.independent.co.uk/news/world/east-germanys-vanishing-babies-1572155.html.

3. Quoted in Kristen Ghodsee and Laura Bernardi, "Starting a Family at Your Parent's House: Multigenerational Households and Below Replacement Fertility in Bulgaria," *Journal of Comparative Family Studies*, Special Issue 43, no. 3 (2012): 439–459.

4. Christoph Conrad, Michael Lechner, and Welf Werner, "East German Fertility after Unification: Crisis or Adaptation?," *Population and Development Review* 22, no. 2 (1996): 331–358.

5. Eurostat, "European Demography: EU25 Population Up by 0.5% in 2004" (136/3005, October 25, 2005), http://epp.eurostat.ec.europa.eu/pls/portal/docs/PAGE/PGP_PRD_CAT_PREREL/PGE_CAT_PREREL_YEAR_2005/PGE_CAT_PREREL_YEAR_2005_MONTH_10/3-25102005-EN-AP.PDF.

6. Brienna Perelli-Harris, "The Path to Lowest-Low Fertility in Ukraine," *Population Studies* 59, no. 1 (2005): 55–70, https://www.tandfonline.com/doi/abs/10.1080/0032472052000332700.

7. Kristen Ghodsee, *Why Women Have Better Sex under Socialism: And Other Arguments for Economic Independence* (New York: Bold Type Books, 2018).

8. Susan Erikson, "Now," 50.

9. Josie McClellan, *Love in the Time of Communism: Intimacy and Sexuality in the GDR* (Cambridge: Cambridge University Press, 2011), 65.

10. Helen Fink, *Women after Communism: The East German Experience* (Lanham, MD: University Press of America, 2001).

11. McClellan, *Love*, 65.

12. Kristen Ghodsee, "Red Nostalgia? Communism, Women's Emancipation, and Economic Transformation in Bulgaria," *L'Homme: Zeitschrift für Feministische Geschichtswissenschaft* (*L'Homme: Journal for Feminist History*) 15, no. 1 (Spring 2004): 23–36..

13. Lynne Haney, *Inventing the Needy: Gender and the Politics of Welfare in Hungary* (Oakland: University of California Press, 2002), 33.

14. Éva Fodor, *Working Difference: Women's Working Lives in Hungary and Austria, 1945–1995* (Durham. NC: Duke University Press, 2003), 171.

15. Haney, *Inventing the Needy*, 38.

16. Erikson, "Now," 66–67.

17. Mieke Meurs and Lisa Giddings, "Decline in Pre-School Use in Post-Socialist Societies: The Case of Bulgaria," *Journal of European Social Policy* 16, no. 2 (2006): 155–166; Raia Staikova-Alexandrova, "Bulgaria: The Present Situation of Women, in: The Impact of Economic and Political Reform on the Status of Women in Eastern Europe" (presentation, proceedings of a United Nations Regional Seminar, 1992).

18. Sergei Zakharov, "Russian Federation: From the First to Second Demographic Transition," *Demographic Research* 19 (2008): 907–972; Inna Leykin, "Population Prescriptions: State, Morality, and Population Politics in Contemporary Russia" (PhD dissertation, Brown University, 2012).

19. G. Mihova, D. Kergoat, M. Nikolova, and D. Donev, *Working Hours, Working Conditions, Demographic Behaviors* (Sofia: Academic Publishing House Marin Drinov, 2007), 225.

20. Mihova et al., *Working Hours*, 225.

21. Mieke Meurs and Lisa Giddings, "Decline in Pre-School Use in Post-Socialist Societies: The Case of Bulgaria," *Journal of European Social Policy* 16, no. 2 (2006): 155–166.

22. Erikson, "Now," 66.

23. Erikson, "Now," 66.

24. Aaron O'Neill, "Total Fertility Rate of Russia, 1840–2020," Statistica, April 23, 2020, https://www.statista.com/statistics/1033851/fertility-rate-russia-1840-2020/.

25. "Hungary Fertility Rate 1950–2020," Macrotrends, https://www.macrotrends.net/countries/HUN/hungary/fertility-rate.

26. Aaron O'Neill, "Total Fertility Rate of Bulgaria, 1875–2020," Statistica, April 9, 2020, https://www.statista.com/statistics/1089850/fertility-rate-bulgaria/.

27. Steven Saxonberg and Tomas Sirovatka, "Failing Family Policy in Post-Communist Central Europe," *Journal of Comparative Policy Analysis* 8, no. 2 (2006): 185–202.

28. Shaun Walker, "'Baby Machines': Eastern Europe's Answer to Depopulation," *The Guardian*, March 4, 2020, https://www.theguardian.com/world/2020/mar/04/baby-bonuses-fit-the-nationalist-agenda-but-do-they-work.

29. Cynthia Gabriel, "Our Nation Is Dying: Interpreting Patterns of Childbearing in Post-Soviet Russia," in *Barren States: The Population "Implosion" in Europe*, ed. Carrie B. Douglass (Oxford: Berg, 2005): 73–92.

30. Rebecca Nash, "The Economy of Birthrates in the Czech Republic," in *Barren States: The Population "Implosion" in Europe*, ed. Carrie B. Douglass (Oxford: Berg, 2005): 93–114.

31. Maria Stoilkova, "A Quest for Belonging: The Bulgarian Demographic Crisis, Emigration, and the Postsocialist Generations," in *Barren States: The Population "Implosion" in Europe*, ed. Carrie B. Douglass (Oxford: Berg, 2005): 115–136.

CHAPTER 8

1. Ivan Krastev, "Depopulation."

2. Andreas Breinbauer, "Brain Drain—Brain Circulation or . . . What Else Happens or Should Happen to the Brains Some Aspects of Qualified Person Mobility/Migration" (FIW Working Paper, No. 4, FIW—Research Centre International Economics, Vienna, 2007).

3. Adrian Favell, "The New Face of East-West Migration in Europe," *Journal of Ethnic and Migration Studies* 34, no. 5 (2008): 701–716, doi: 10.1080/13691830802105947.

4. Dimitru Sandu, "Modernising Romanian Society through Temporary Work Abroad," in *A Continent Moving West? EU Enlargement and Labour Migration from Central and Eastern Europe*, ed. Richard Black et al. (Amsterdam: Amsterdam University Press, 2010), 271.

5. Anne White et al., *The Impact of Migration on Poland: EU Mobility and Social Change* (London: UCL Press, 2018), 5.

6. Alejandro Portes, "Migration and Development: Reconciling Opposite Views," *Ethnic and Racial Studies* 32, no. 1 (2009): 5–22, https://doi.org/10.1080/01419870802483668.

7. White et al., *The Impact of Migration*, 6.

8. Martina Cvajner, *Soviet Signoras: Personal and Collective Transformations in Eastern European Migration* (Chicago: University of Chicago Press, 2019).

9. Cvajner, *Soviet Signoras*.

10. "Romanian Women Suffering from 'Italy Syndrome,'" *BBC*, February 16, 2019, https://www.bbc.co.uk/programmes/p0711zkr.

11. Giulia Saudelli, "Romanian Carers in Italy: 'I Miss My Family So, So Much,'" *Deutsche Welle*, March 30, 2019, https://www.dw.com/en/romanian-carers-in-italy-i-miss-my-family-so-so-much/a-48110728.

12. Lorenzo Tondo and Annie Kelly, "Raped, Beaten, Exploited: The 21st Century Slavery Propping Up Sicilian Farming," *The Guardian*, March 11, 2017, https://www.theguardian.com/global-development/2017/mar/12/slavery-sicily-farming-raped-beaten-exploited-romanian-women.

13. "The Beginning of the End of Britain's Biggest Episode of Migration," *The Economist*, September 14, 2017, https://www.economist.com/britain/2017/09/14/the-beginning-of-the-end-of-britains-biggest-episode-of-migration.

14. Alina Rzepnikowska, "Racism and Xenophobia Experienced by Polish Migrants in the UK before and after Brexit Vote," *Journal of Ethnic and Migration Studies* 45, no. 1 (2018): 61–77, doi: 10.1080/1369183X.2018.1451308.

15. Christian Davies, "Everything Changed in 2016: Poles in UK Struggle with Brexit," *The Guardian*, January 27, 2019, https://www.theguardian.com/politics/2019/jan/27/everything-changed-in-2016-poles-in-uk-struggle-with-brexit.

16. Philip Ebels, "Dutch Far-Right Open Anti-Polish Hotline," *EUobserver*, February 9, 2012, https://euobserver.com/news/115208; "Dutch Website Causes Stir in Central Europe," *Euractiv*, February 10, 2012, https://www.euractiv.com/section/justice-home-affairs/news/dutch-website-causes-stir-in-central-europe/.

17. Gilbert Kreijger, "Dutch Allow Wilders' Anti-Pole Website, EU Critical," *Reuters*, February 10, 2012, https://uk.reuters.com/article/uk-dutch-immigrants/dutch-allow-wilders-anti-pole-website-eu-critical-idUKTRE8191ML20120210.

18. Banu Nilgün Uygun, "Post-Socialist Scapes of Economy and Desire: The Case of Turkey," *Focaal: European Journal of Anthropology*, no. 43 (2004): 24.

19. Armand Clotilde, "Eastern Europe Gives More to the West Than It Gets Back," *Financial Times*, February 12, 2020, https://www.ft.com/content/39603142-4cc9-11ea-95a0-43d18ec715f5.

20. Bruce O'Neill, *The Space of Boredom: Homelessness in the Slowing Global Order* (Durham, NC: Duke University Press, 2017), 82–83.

21. Alejandro Portes, "Migration and Development: Reconciling Opposite Views," *Ethnic and Racial Studies* 32, no. 1 (2009): 5–22, doi: 10.1080/01419870802483668.

22. White et al., *The Impact of Migration on Poland*; Philipp Ther, *Europe since 1989*, trans. Charlotte Hughes-Kreutzmüller (Princeton, NJ: Princeton University Press, 2016).

23. Kristen Ghodsee, *The Red Riviera: Gender, Tourism, and Postsocialism on the Black Sea* (Durham, NC: Duke University Press, 2005).

24. Kristen Ghodsee, *Muslim Lives in Eastern Europe: Gender, Ethnicity and the Transformation of Islam in Postsocialist Bulgaria* (Princeton, NJ: Princeton University Press, 2009).

25. Ther, *Europe since 1989*, 132–136.

26. Ther, *Europe since 1989*, 132–136.

27. Ther, *Europe since 1989*, 132–136.

28. Atoyan et al., *Emigration*, 6.

29. Marta Anacka and Marek Okólski, "Direct Demographic Consequences of Post-accession Migration for Poland," in *A Continent Moving West? EU Enlargement and Labour Migration from Central and Eastern Europe*, ed. Richard Black et al. (Amsterdam: Amsterdam University Press, 2010), 141–164.

30. Pawel Kaczmarczyk, "Labour Market Impacts of Post-Accession Migration from Poland," in *Free Movement of Workers and Labour Market Adjustment: Recent Experiences from OECD Countries and the European Union* (Paris: OECD Publishing, 2012), 173–190.

31. Atoyan et al., *Emigration*, 5–6.

32. Atoyan et al., *Emigration*, 7.

33. Atoyan et al., *Emigration*, 7.

34. Atoyan et al., *Emigration*, 14.

35. Atoyan et al., *Emigration*, 17.

36. Atoyan et al., *Emigration*, 17.

37. Krastev and Holmes, *The Light that Failed*.

38. Chris Harris, "The World's Fastest Falling Population Will Be in Eastern Europe," *Euronews*, January 26th, 2018, https://www.euronews.com/2018/01/26/the-world-s-fastest-falling-populations-will-be-in-eastern-europe-.

39. Aamna Mohdin, "The Fastest Shrinking Countries on Earth Are in Eastern Europe," *Quartz*, January 24, 2018, https://qz.com/1187819/country-ranking-worlds-fastest-shrinking-countries-are-in-eastern-europe/.

40. Ivan Krastev, "Why Viktor Orbán and His Allies Won't Win the European Elections," *The Guardian*, March 20, 2019, https://www.theguardian.com/commentisfree/2019/mar/20/viktor-Orbán-eu-elections-rightwing-populists-immigration.

41. Duthé et al., "Adult Mortality Patterns," 589.

42. Brainerd and Cutler, "Autopsy," 107–130.

43. "Population, Total," World Bank, 2018, https://data.worldbank.org/indicator/SP.POP.TOTL.

CHAPTER 9

1. European Bank for Reconstruction and Development (EBRD), *Life in Transition: A Survey of People's Experiences and Attitudes* (London: EBRD, 2011), https://www.ebrd.com/documents/comms-and-bis/pdf-life-in-transition-survey-i.pdf.

2. It also included Turkey, which was considered a part of the Europe and Central Asia region for the EBRD.

3. Krastev and Holmes, *The Light that Failed.*

4. EBRD, *Life in Transition: A Survey.*

5. For some examples, see EBRD, *Transition Report 2007: People in Transition* (London: EBRD, 2007), 61.

6. EBRD, *Life in Transition: After the Crisis* (London: EBRD, 2011), 3.

7. European Commission, "Life Satisfaction," in *Eurobarometer Interactive*, European Commission, https://ec.europa.eu/commfrontoffice/publicopinion/index.cfm/Chart/index.

8. EBRD, 2006, *Life in Transition Survey I*, https://www.ebrd.com/news/publications/special-reports/life-in-transition-survey-i.html.

9. EBRD, *Life in Transition: After the Crisis*, 74–75.

10. EBRD, *Transition Report 2007.*

11. James R. Kluegal and David S. Mason, "Fairness Matters: Social Justice and Political Legitimacy in Post-Communist Europe," *Europe-Asia Studies* 56, no. 6 (2004): 816; Grigore Pop-Eleches and Joshua A. Tucker, *Communism's Shadow: Historical Legacies and Contemporary Political Attitudes* (Princeton, NJ: Princeton University Press, 2017).

12. Pop-Eleches and Tucker, *Communism's Shadow*, 190.

13. EBRD, *Transition Report 2007.*

14. Michael Mutz, "Life Satisfaction and the UEFA EURO 2016: Findings from a Nation-Wide Longitudinal Study in Germany," *Applied Research in Quality of Life* 14, no. 2 (2019): 375–391.

15. Filippos T. Filippidis and Anthony A. Laverty, "'Euphoria' or 'Only Teardrops'? Eurovision Song Contest Performance, Life Satisfaction and Suicide," *BMC Public Health* 18, no. 582 (2018): 582.

CHAPTER 10

1. Judith S. Kullberg and William Zimmerman, "Liberal Elites, Socialist Masses, and Problems of Russian Democracy," *World Politics* 51, no. 3 (1999): 324–325, doi: 10.1017/S0043887100009102.

2. Dena Ringold, Mitchell A. Orenstein, and Erika Wilkens, *Roma in an Expanding Europe: Breaking the Poverty Cycle* (Washington, DC: World Bank, 2004), http://documents.worldbank.org/curated/en/600541468771052774/Roma-in-an-Expanding-Europe-breaking-the-poverty-cycle.

3. Kullberg and Zimmerman, "Liberal Elites," 325.

4. Kullberg and Zimmerman, "Liberal Elites," 324–325.

5. Bernd Hayo, "Eastern European Public Opinion on Economic Issues: Privatization and Transformation," *American Journal of Economics and Sociology* 56, no. 1 (1997): 85–102, dx.doi: 10.1111/j.1536-7150.1997.tb03453.x.

6. Hayo, "Eastern European Public Opinion," 90.

7. Elaine Weiner, *Market Dreams: Gender, Class, and Capitalism in the Czech Republic* (Ann Arbor: University of Michigan Press, 2007).

8. Pieter Vanhuysse, *Divide and Pacify: Strategic Social Policies and Political Protests in Post-Communist Democracies* (Budapest: Central European University Press, 2006).

9. Tomasz Inglot, *Welfare States in East Central Europe, 1919–2004,* (Cambridge: Cambridge University Press, 2008).

10. Linda J. Cook, *Postcommunist Welfare States: Reform Politics in Russia and Eastern Europe* (Ithaca, NY: Cornell University Press, 2011).

11. Ghodsee, "Red Nostalgia?"

12. Joakim Ekman and Jonas Linde, "Communist Nostalgia and the Consolidation of Democracy in Central and Eastern Europe," *Journal of Communist Studies and Transition Politics* 21, no. 3 (2005), 355, doi: 10.1080/13523270500183512.

13. Ekman and Linde, "Communist Nostalgia," 359.

14. Ekman and Linde, "Communist Nostalgia," 371–372.

CHAPTER 11

1. Pew Research Center (Pew), *Two Decades after the Wall's Fall: End of Communism Cheered but Now with More Reservations* (Washington, DC: Pew Research Center, 2009), http://assets.pewresearch.org/wp-content/uploads/sites/2/2009/11/Pew-Global-Attitudes-2009-Pulse-of-Europe-Report-Nov-2-1030am-NOT-EMBARGOED.pdf.

2. Pew, *Two Decades.*

3. Pew, *Two Decades.*

4. Pew Research Center, *European Public Opinion Three Decades after the Fall of Communism* (Washington, DC: Pew Research Center, 2019), https://www.pewresearch.org/global/wp-content/uploads/sites/2/2019/10/Pew-Research-Center-Value-of-Europe-report-FINAL-UPDATED.pdf.

5. Pew, *Two Decades.*

6. EBRD, *Life in Transition: After the Crisis,* 7.

7. EBRD, *Life in Transition: After the Crisis,* 21.

8. Nazim Habibov and Elvin Afandi, "Pre- and Post-crisis Life-Satisfaction and Social Trust in Transitional Countries: An Initial Assessment," *Social Indicators Research* 121, no. 2 (2015): 503–524, find that institutional trust deteriorated after the 2008–09 crisis.

9. EBRD, *Life in Transition: After the Crisis,* 4.

10. Simeon Djankov, Elena Nikolova, and Jan Zilinsky, "The Happiness Gap in Eastern Europe," *Journal of Comparative Economics* 44, no. 1 (2016): 108–124.

11. EBRD, *Life in Transition: After the Crisis*, 3.

12. Pew Research Center, *Twenty Years Later: Confidence in Democracy Wanes in Former Soviet Union* (Washington, DC: Pew Research Center, 2011), https://www.pewresearch.org/global/2011/12/05/confidence-in-democracy-and-capitalism-wanes-in-former-soviet-union/.

13. EBRD, *Life in Transition: After the Crisis*, 3.

14. EBRD, *Life in Transition: After the Crisis*, 3.

15. EBRD, *Life in Transition: After the Crisis*, 3.

16. Dominik Batorski et al., "Social Diagnosis 2011: Objective and Subjective Quality of Life in Poland," ed. Janusz Czapiński and Tomasz Panek, *Contemporary Economics: Quarterly of Finance and Management in Warsaw* 5, no. 3 (2016): 182.

17. *Barometrul ADEVĂRUL despre ROMÂNIA* (Bucharest: Inscop Research, 2014), http://www.inscop.ro/wp-content/uploads/2014/01/INSCOP-noiembrie-ISTORIE.pdf.

18. Zach Bikus, "World-Low 9% of Ukrainians Confident in Government," Gallup, March 21, 2019, https://news.gallup.com/poll/247976/world-low-ukrainians-confident-government.aspx.

19. John Helliwell, Richard Layard, and Jeffrey Sachs, *World Happiness Report* (New York: United Nations, 2012), https://worldhappiness.report/ed/2012/.

20. Helliwell, Layard, and Sachs, *World Happiness Report*.

21. Helliwell, Layard, and Sachs, *World Happiness Report*.

22. EBRD, *Life in Transition Survey III: A Decade of Measuring Transition*, 2016, 12, https://www.ebrd.com/what-we-do/economic-research-and-data/data/lits.html.

23. Pew Research Center (Pew), *European Public Opinion Three Decades after the Fall of Communism* (Washington, DC: Pew Research Center, 2019), https://www.pewresearch.org/global/2019/10/15/european-public-opinion-three-decades-after-the-fall-of-communism/pg_10-15-19-europe-values_updated2/.

24. European Commission, *Standard Eurobaromter 91*, August 2019, https://ec.europa.eu/commfrontoffice/publicopinion/index.cfm/survey/getsurveydetail/instruments/standard/surveyky/2253.

CHAPTER 12

1. James R. Kluegel and David S. Mason, "Fairness Matters: Social Justice and Political Legitimacy in Post-Communist Europe," *Europe-Asia Studies* 56, no. 6 (2004): 816.

2. Maurizio Bussolo, Maria Eugenia Davalos, Vito Peragine, and Ramya Sundaram, *Toward a New Social Contract: Taking on Distributional Tensions in Europe and Central Asia* (Washington, DC: World Bank, 2018).

3. Krastev and Holmes, *The Light That Failed*.

4. James R. Kluegel, David S. Mason, and Bernd Wegener, "The International Social Justice Project," *Social Justice and Political Change: Public Opinion in Capitalist and Post-Communist States* (Berlin: Walter de Gruyter, 1995).

5. David Stewart Mason, James R. Kluegel, and Lîdmila Aleksandrovna Khakhulina, *Marketing Democracy: Changing Opinion about Inequality and Politics in East Central Europe* (Lanham, MD: Rowman & Littlefield, 2000), 164.

6. Mason et al., *Marketing Democracy*, 36.

7. Appel and Orenstein, *From Triumph to Crisis*.

8. British Broadcasting Corporation, "Zuzana Caputova Becomes Slovakia's First Female President," March 31, 2019, https://www.bbc.com/news/world-europe-47756368.

9. Joel S. Hellman et al., "Seize the State, Seize the Day: An Empirical Analysis of State Capture and Corruption in Transition Economies," in *Annual Congress of the ABCDE* (Washington, DC, 2000): 1–39.

10. Stephen Knack, "Measuring Corruption: A Critique of Indicators in Eastern Europe and Central Asia," *Journal of Public Policy* 27, no. 3 (2007): 255–291.

11. Daniel Treisman, "Postcommunist Corruption," in *Political Economy of Transition and Development: Institutions, Politics, and Policies*, ed. Nauro F.Campos and Jan Fidrmuc (Norwell, MA: Kluwer Academic, 2003). 201–226.

12. Anna Grzymała-Busse, "Encouraging Effective Democratic Competition," *East European Politics and Societies* 21, no. 1 (2007): 91–110; Anna Grzymala-Busse, *Rebuilding Leviathan: Party Competition and State Exploitation in Post-Communist Democracies* (Cambridge: Cambridge University Press, 2007).

13. Marc Santora, "Slovakia's First Female President, Zuzana Caputova, Takes Office in a Divided Country," *New York Times*, June 15, 2019.

14. Claire Wallace and Rossalina Latcheva, "Economic Transformation Outside the Law: Corruption, Trust in Public Institutions and the Informal Economy in Transition Countries of Central and Eastern Europe," *Europe-Asia Studies* 58, no. 1 (2006): 81–102.

15. European Bank for Reconstruction and Development, *Life in Transition: A Decade of Measuring Transition* (London: EBRD, 2017), 36.

16. European Bank for Reconstruction and Development (EBRD), *Transition for All: Equal Opportunities in an Unequal World* (London: EBRD, 2017).

17. EBRD, *Transition for All*, 23.

18. EBRD, "Country Assessments," in *Life in Transition: A Decade*, 73–136.

19. Pew Research Center, *Religious Belief and National Belonging in Central and Eastern Europe* (Washington, DC: Pew Research Center, 2017), https://www.pewforum.org/2017/05/10/religious-belief-and-national-belonging-in-central-and-eastern-europe/.

20. Pew, *Religious Belief*, 142.

21. Pew, *Religious Belief*, 143.

22. Pew, *Religious Belief*, 166.

23. Pew, *Religious Belief*, 167.

24. Pew, *Religious Belief*, 166.

25. Pew, *Religious Belief*, 170.

26. Pew Research Center, *Public Opinion in Hungary, Poland, Czech Republic and Slovakia* (Washington, DC: Center for Insights in Survey Research, 2017), https://www.iri.org/sites/default/files/four_country_full_presentation_may_24_2017.pdf.

27. Pew Research Center, *European Public Opinion Three Decades After the Fall of Communism* (Washington, DC: Pew Research Center, 2019), 5 [figure], https://www.pewresearch.org/global/2019/10/15/european-public-opinion-three-decades-after-the-fall-of-communism/.

28. Pew, *European Public Opinion Three Decades After*, 25.

29. Bussolo et al., *Toward a New Social Contract*, 3.

30. Bussolo et al., *Toward a New Social Contract*, 12.

31. Bussolo et al., *Toward a New Social Contract*, 33.

32. Pop-Eleches and Tucker, *Communism's Shadow*.

CHAPTER 13

1. Eric Wolf attributes this quote to Kroeber but with no citation. Eric Wolf, *Anthropology* (New York: Norton, 1974).

2. Eugene Raikhel, *Governing Habits: Treating Alcoholism in the Post-Soviet Clinic* (Ithaca, NY: Cornell University Press, 2016), 49.

3. Bruce O'Neill, *The Space of Boredom: Homelessness in the Slowing Global Order* (Durham, NC: Duke University Press, 2017), 103.

4. Neringa Klumbytė, "Post-Soviet Publics and Nostalgia for Soviet Times," in *Changing Economies and Changing Identities in Postsocialist Eastern Europe*, ed. Ingo W. Schröder and Asta Vonderau (Münster: LIT Verlag, 2008), 27–46.

5. Alison Smale, "In a United Germany, the Scars of the East-West Divide Have Faded," *New York Times*, October 2, 2015, http://www.nytimes.com/interactive/2015/10/02/world/europe/germany-unification-anniversary.html.

6. Some anthropologists do occasionally "study up" by choosing for their ethnographic subjects people in positions of wealth and power. See, for example, Karen Ho, *Liquidated: An Ethnography of Wall Street* (Durham, NC: Duke University Press, 2009).

7. Laura Nader, "The Phantom Factor: Impact of the Cold War on Anthropology," in *The Cold War and the University: Toward an Intellectual History of the Postwar Years* (New York: New Press, 1998), 107–148; Martha Lampland, afterword to *Altering States: Ethnographies of Transition in Eastern Europe and the Former Soviet Union*, ed. Daphne Berdahl, Matti Bunzl, and Martha Lampland (Ann

Arbor: University of Michigan Press, 2000), 209–218; David H. Price, *Cold War Anthropology: The CIA, the Pentagon, and the Growth of Dual Use Anthropology* (Durham, NC: Duke University Press, 2016); Kristen Ghodsee, "When Research Becomes Intelligence: Feminist Anthropology, Ethnographic Fieldwork and the Human Terrain System," *Feminist Formations* (formerly the *National Women's Studies Association Journal*) 23, no. 2 (Summer 2011): 160–185.

8. Katherine Verdery, *My Life as a Spy: Investigations in a Secret Police File* (Durham, NC: Duke University Press, 2018).

9. *Religious Belief and National Belonging in Central and Eastern Europe* (Washington, DC: Pew Research Center, 2017), 143, https://www.pewforum.org/2017/05/10/religious-belief-and-national-belonging-in-central-and-eastern-europe/.

10. Caroline Humphrey, *The Unmaking of Soviet Life* (Ithaca, NY: Cornell University Press, 2002), xxi and xxii.

11. Humphrey, *The Unmaking of Soviet Life*, xvii.

12. Maria Bucur and Mihaela Miroiu, *Birth of Democratic Citizenship: Women and Power in Modern Romania* (Bloomington: Indiana University Press, 2018), 98.

13. Bucur and Miroiu, *Birth of Democratic Citizenship*, 98–99.

14. Bucur and Miroiu, *Birth of Democratic Citizenship*, 108.

15. Bucur and Miroiu, *Birth of Democratic Citizenship*, 144.

16. Tommaso Trevisiani, "After the Kolkhoz: Rural Elites in Competition," *Central Asian Survey* 26, no. 1 (2007): 85–104.

17. Maria Tordova, "Daring to Remember Bulgaria, pre-1989," *The Guardian*, November 9, 2009, https://www.theguardian.com/commentisfree/2009/nov/09/1989-communism-bulgaria.

18. Daphne Berdahl, *Where the World Ended: Re-Unification and Identity in the German Borderland* (Berkeley: University of California Press, 1999), 193.

19. Berdahl, *Where the World Ended*, 193.

20. Gerald W. Creed, *Domesticating Revolution: From Socialist Reform to Ambivalent Transition in a Bulgarian Village* (University Park: Pennsylvania State University Press, 1998), 265.

21. Creed, *Domesticating Revolution*, 270.

22. Creed, *Domesticating Revolution*, 270.

23. Buroway and Verdery, eds., *Uncertain Transition*.

24. Daphne Berdahl, Matti Bunzl, and Martha Lampland, eds., *Altering States: Ethnographies of Transition in Eastern Europe and the Former Soviet Union* (Ann Arbor: University of Michigan Press, 2000).

25. "Reconstructing Environment and Memory in Postsocialist SaxonyAnhalt," in Berdahl, Bunzl, and Lampland, *Altering States*.

26. Matti Bunzl, "Gay Male Sex Tourism and the Neocolonial Invention of an Embodied Border," in Berdahl, Bunzl, and Lampland, *Altering States*.

CHAPTER 14

1. Pieter Vanhuysse, *Divide and Pacify: Strategic Social Policies and Political Protests in Post-Communist Democracies* (Budapest: Central European University Press, 2006).

2. For instance, see Kristen Ghodsee, *Lost in Transition: Ethnographies of Everyday Life after Communism* (Durham, NC: Duke University Press, 2011).

3. Serguei Abashin, "Migration from Central Asia to Russia in the New Model of World Order," *Russian Politics & Law* 52, no. 6 (2014a): 8–23.

4. Abashin, "Migration," 14, 22.

5. See, for instance, Carrie Douglass, *Barren States: The Population "Implosion" in Europe* (Berlin: Berg 2005); Anne White et al., *The Impact of Migration on Poland: EU Mobility and Social Change* (London: UCL Press, 2018).

6. Leyla J. Keough, *Worker Mothers on the Margins of Europe: Gender and Migration between Moldova and Istanbul* (Bloomington: Indiana University Press, 2016).

7. Madeleine Reeves, "Black Work, Green Money: Remittances, Ritual, and Domestic Economies in Southern Kyrgyzstan," *Slavic Review* 71, no. 1 (2012): 108–134.

8. Reeves, "Black Work," 108–134.

9. Ivan Krastev and Stephen Holmes, "Explaining Eastern Europe: Imitation and Its Discontents," *Journal of Democracy* 29, no. 3 (2018).

10. David M. Abramson, "Socialism's Bastard Children," *Political and Legal Anthropology Review* 23, no. 1 (2000): 51, doi: 10.1525/pol.2000.23.1.49.

11. Abramson, "Socialism's Bastard Children," 55.

12. Till Mostowlansky, *Azan on the Moon: Entangling Modernity along Tajikistan's Pamir Highway* (Pittsburgh: University of Pittsburgh Press, 2017).

13. Mateusz Laszczkowski, *City of the Future: Built Space, Modernity and Urban Change in Astana* (New York: Berghahn Books, 2016).

14. Philipp Schröder, *Bishkek Boys: Neighbourhood Youth and Urban Change in Kyrgyzstan's Capital* (New York: Berghahn Books, 2017).

15. Nick Megoran, *Nationalism in Central Asia: A Biography of the Uzbekistan-Kyrgyzstan Boundary* (Pittsburgh: University of Pittsburgh Press, 2017).

16. Morgan Y. Liu, *Under Solomon's Throne: Uzbek Visions of Renewal in Osh* (Pittsburgh: University of Pittsburgh Press, 2012).

17. Julie McBrien, "Mukadas' Struggle: Veils and Modernity in Kyrgyzstan," *Journal of the Royal Anthropological Institute*, 15, no. 1 (2009): 127–144; Julie McBrien *From Belong to Belief: Modern Secularisms and the Construction of Religion in Kyrgyzstan* (Pittsburgh: University of Pittsburgh Press, 2017).

18. McBrien, "Mukadas' Struggle," 128.

19. McBrien, "Mukadas' Struggle," 132–133.

CHAPTER 15

1. Neringa Klumbytė, "Post-Soviet Publics and Nostalgia for Soviet Times," in *Changing Economies and Changing Identities in Postsocialist Eastern Europe*, ed. Ingo W. Schröder and Asta Vonderau, 27–46 (Münster: LIT Verlag, 2008), 29.
2. Klumbytė, "Post-Soviet Publics," 30.
3. Kristen Ghodsee, *Muslim Lives in Eastern Europe: Gender, Ethnicity and the Transformation of Islam in Postsocialist Bulgaria* (Princeton, NJ: Princeton University Press, 2009).
4. Nancy Ries, "Potato Ontology: Surviving Postsocialism in Russia," *Cultural Anthropology* 24, no. 2 (2009), http://dx.doi.org/10.1111/j.1548-1360.2009.01129.x.
5. Doug Rogers, "Moonshine, Money, and the Politics of Liquidity in Rural Russia," *American Ethnologist* 32, no. 1 (2005), http://dx.doi.org/10.1525/ae.2005.32.1.63.
6. Gerald W. Creed and Janine Wedel, "Second Thoughts from the Second World: Interpreting Aid in Post-Communist Eastern Europe," *Human Organization* 56, no. 3 (1997), http://dx.doi.org/10.17730/humo.56.3.9rn36067p41h6jin.
7. Tova Höjdestrand, *Needed by Nobody: Homelessness and Humanness in Post-Socialist Russia* (Ithaca, NY: Cornell University Press, 2009).
8. Irina Popova, "Inside Belarus's 'Rehab Prisons' for Alcoholics—in Pictures," *The Guardian*, December 17, 2015, https://www.theguardian.com/world/gallery/2015/dec/17/belarus-soviet-jail-for-alcoholics-irina-popova.
9. David Kideckel, *Getting By in Postsocialist Bulgaria: Labor, the Body, and Working Class Culture* (Bloomington: Indiana University Press, 2008), 208.
10. O'Neill, *The Space of Boredom*, 121.
11. Kideckel, *Getting By in Postsocialist Bulgaria*, 209–210.

CHAPTER 16

1. Serguei A. Oushakine, *The Patriotism of Despair: Nation, War, and Loss in Russia* (Ithaca, NY: Cornell University Press, 2009), 20.
2. Katherine Verdery, *What Was Socialism, and What Comes Next?* (Princeton, NJ: Princeton University Press, 1996).
3. Judd Stitzel, *Fashioning Socialism: Clothing, Politics and Consumer Culture in East Germany, 1948–1971* (Berlin: Berg, 2005).
4. Kristen Ghodsee, *Muslim Lives*.
5. See the documentary film *Soviet Hippies*, directed by Terje Toomitsu (Tartu: 2017), www.soviethippies.com, and Loren Balhorn, "The Soviet Hippies," *Jacobin Magazine*, November 17, 2017, https://www.jacobinmag.com/2017/11/soviet-hippies-antiwar-film.
6. Michaela Pixová, "Alternative Culture in a Socialist City: Punkers and Long-Haired People in Prague in the 1980s," *Český Lid* 100, no. 3 (2013): 319–338, http://www.jstor.org/stable/42640574; Oskar Mulej, "We Are Drowning in Red Beet,

Patching Up the Holes in the Iron Curtain": The Punk Subculture in Ljubljana in the Late 1970s and Early 1980s," *East Central Europe* 38 (2011): 373–389, doi: 10.1163/187633011X597207.

7. Appel and Orenstein, *From Triumph to Crisis*.

CONCLUSION

1. Branko Milanovic, "For Whom the Wall Fell? A Balance Sheet of the Transition to Capitalism," globalinequality, November 3, 2014, https://glineq.blogspot.com/2014/11/for-whom-wall-fell-balance-sheet-of.html.

2. Milanovic, "For Whom the Wall Fell?"

3. David Brooks, "The Legacy of Fear," *New York Times*, November 10, 2014, https://www.nytimes.com/2014/11/11/opinion/david-brooks-the-legacy-of-fear.html.

4. See, for instance, Martin Müller, "Goodbye Postsocialism!," *Europe-Asia Studies* 71, no. 4 (March 7, 2018): 533–550, https://ssrn.com/abstract=3151362.

5. Jeffrey Sachs, "What Is to Be Done?," *The Economist*, January 13, 1990, https://www.economist.com/europe/1990/01/13/what-is-to-be-done.

6. Krastev and Holmes, *The Light That Failed*, 5.

7. Krastev and Holmes, *The Light That Failed*, 9.

8. Krastev and Holmes, *The Light That Failed*, 7.

9. Jutta Bolt, Robert Inklaar, Herman de Jong, and Jan Luiten van Zanden, "Rebasing 'Maddison': The Shape of Long-Run Economic Development," VoxEU, January 25, 2018, figure 2, https://voxeu.org/article/rebasing-maddison.

10. Mario I. Blejer and Alan H. Gelb, "The Contraction of Eastern Europe's Economies: Introduction to the Conference," in *Eastern Europe in Transition: From Recession to Growth?*, ed. Mario I. Blejer et al. (Washington DC: World Bank, 1993), 1–7.

11. Cornia, "Poverty, Inequality and Policy."

12. Werner Güth, Rolf Schmittberger, and Bernd Schwarze, "An Experimental Analysis of Ultimatum Bargaining," *Journal of Economic Behavior & Organization* 3, no. 4 (1982): 367–388, doi: 10.1016/0167-2681(82)90011-7.

13. Donna Bahry and Rick Wilson, "Confusion or Fairness in the Field? Rejections in the Ultimatum Game under the Strategy Method," *Journal of Economic Behavior & Organization* 60 (2006): 52.

14. Katherine Verdery, *What Was Socialism*.

15. Anna Grzymala-Busse, "How Populists Rule: The Consequences for Democratic Governance," *Polity* 51, no. 4 (2019): 707–717; , Milada Anna Vachudova. "From Competition to Polarization in Central Europe: How Populists Change Party Systems and the European Union," *Polity* 51, no. 4 (2019): 689–706.

16. David Ost, *The Defeat of Solidarity: Anger and Politics in Postcommunist Europe* (Ithaca, NY: Cornell University Press, 2005).

17. Vladimir Popov, "Shock Therapy versus Gradualism Reconsidered: Lessons from Transition Economies after 15 Years of Reforms," *Comparative Economic Studies* 49, no. 1 (2007): 1–31; Mathias Dewatripont and Gérard Roland, "The Virtues of Gradualism and Legitimacy in the Transition to a Market Economy," *Economic Journal* 102, no. 411 (1992): 291–300.

18. Sachs, *Poland's Jump*.

19. János Kornai, *The Socialist System: The Political Economy of Communism* (Princeton, NJ: Princeton University Press, 1992).

20. Robert M. Buckley and Sasha Tsenkova, "Urban Housing Markets in Transition: New Instruments to Assist the Poor," in *The Urban Mosaic of Post-Socialist Europe: Space, Institutions and Policy*, ed. Sasha Tsenkova and Zorica Nedović-Budić (Heidelberg: Springer, 2006), 173–194; Raymond Struyk and Anastasia Kolodeznikova, "Needs-Based Targeting without Knowing Household Incomes: How Would It Work in Russia?," *Urban Studies* 36, no. 11 (1999): 1875–1889; Raymond Struyk, Ekaterina Petrova, and Tatiana Lykova, "Targeting Housing Allowances in Russia," *European Journal of Housing Policy* 6, no. 2 (2006): 191–220.

21. Stuckler and Basu, *The Body Economic*; Lawrence King, Patrick Hamm, and David Stuckler, "Rapid Large-Scale Privatization and Death Rates in Ex-Communist Countries: An Analysis of Stress-Related and Health System Mechanisms," *International Journal of Health Services* 39, no. 3 (2009): 461–489.

22. Elaine Sciolino, "U.S. Is Abandoning 'Shock Therapy' for the Russians," *New York Times*, December 21, 1993, https://www.nytimes.com/1993/12/21/world/us-is-abandoning-shock-therapy-for-therussians.html.

23. Sciolino, "U.S. Is Abandoning 'Shock Therapy.'"

24. Sachs, "What I Did."

25. Reuters, "10.2 Billion Loan to Russia Approved," *New York Times*, March 27, 1996, https://www.nytimes.com/1996/03/27/world/10.2-billion-loan-to-russia-approved.html.

26. Michael Kramer, "Yanks to the Rescue: The Secret Story of How American Advisers Helped Yeltsin Win," *Time* (July 15, 1996), http://content.time.com/time/covers/0,16641,19960715,00.html.

27. Dorottya Szikra, "Democracy and Welfare in Hard Times: The Social Policy of the Orbán Government in Hungary between 2010 and 2014," *Journal of European Social Policy* 24, no. 5 (2014): 486–500; Noemi Lendvai and Paul Stubbs, "Europeanization, Welfare and Variegated Austerity Capitalisms—Hungary and Croatia," *Social Policy & Administration* 49, no. 4 (2015): 445–465; Stanisława Golinowska and Agnieszka Sowa-Kofta, "Combating Poverty through Family Cash Benefits: On the First Results of the Programme 'Family 500+' in Poland," *Polityka Społeczna* 44, no. 1 (2017): 7–13; Weronika Grzebalska and Andrea Pető, "The Gendered Modus Operandi of the Illiberal Transformation in Hungary and Poland," *Women's Studies International Forum* 68 (2018): 164–172.

28. Zhanna Chernova, "New Pronatalism? Family Policy in Post-Soviet Russia," *REGION: Regional Studies of Russia, Eastern Europe, and Central Asia* 1, no. 1 (2012): 75–92; Michele Rivkin-Fish, "Pronatalism, Gender Politics, and the Renewal of Family Support in Russia: Toward a Feminist Anthropology of 'Maternity Capital,'" *Slavic Review* 69, no. 3 (2010): 701–724.

29. Yana Gorokhovskaya, "Healthcare Reform, Demographic Trends, and COVID-19 in Russia: A Conversation with Professor Judyth Twigg," *Reforum*, June 17, 2020, https://reforum.io/en/2020/06/17/healthcare-reform-demographic-trends-and-covid-19-in-russia-a-conversation-with-professor-judyth-twigg/.

30. Golinowska and Sowa-Kofta, "Combating Poverty," 7–13.

31. Grzebalska and Pető, "The Gendered Modus Operandi," 164–172.

32. Rivkin-Fish, "Pronatalism," 701–724.

33. European Commission, "First Results of Poland's Family 500+ Programme Released," from *EC: Employment, Social Affairs & Inclusion* (May 16, 2018), https://ec.europa.eu/social/main.jsp?langId=en&catId=1246&newsId=9104&furtherNews=yes#:~:text=In%20April%202016%2C%20the%20Polish,the%20programme's%20progress%20and%20impact.

34. Bussolo et al., *Toward a New Social Contract*.

35. Grzegorz Kolodko, "Postcommunist Transitions and Post-Washington Consensus: Lessons for Policy Reforms," in *Transition: The First Decade*, ed. Mario I. Blejer and Marko Skreb (Cambridge, MA: MIT Press, 2001), 45–46.

Selected Bibliography

DATA SOURCES ARE LISTED IN THE APPENDIX.

Abashin, Sergei. "Migration from Central Asia to Russia in the New Model of World Order." *Russian Politics & Law* 52, no. 6 (2014): 8–23.

Abashin, Sergei. "A Prayer for Rain: Practising Being Soviet and Muslim." *Journal of Islamic Studies* 25, no. 2 (2014): 178–200.

Abramson, David M. "Socialism's Bastard Children." *Political and Legal Anthropology Review* 23, no. 1 (2000): 49–64. doi: 10.1525/pol.2000.23.1.49.

Alexievich, Svetlana. *Second Hand Time: The Last of the Soviets.* Translated by Bela Shayevich. New York: Random House, 2016.

Altshuler, David S. "Tunneling towards Capitalism in the Czech Republic." *Ethnography* 2, no. 1 (2001): 115–138.

Anacka, Marta, and Marek Okólski. "Direct Demographic Consequences of Post-accession Migration for Poland." In *A Continent Moving West? EU Enlargement and Labour Migration from Central and Eastern Europe.* Edited by Richard Black, Godfried Engbersen, Marek Okólski, and Cristina Pantîru, 141–164. Amsterdam: Amsterdam University Press, 2010.

Appel, Hilary. "Is It Putin or Is It Oil? Explaining Russia's Fiscal Recovery." *Post-Soviet Affairs* 24, no. 4 (2008): 301–323.

Appel, Hilary, and Mitchell Orenstein. *From Triumph to Crisis: Neoliberal Economic Reform in Postcommunist Countries.* Cambridge: Cambridge University Press, 2018.

Arrow, Kenneth J. "Economic Transition: Speed and Scope." *Journal of Institutional and Theoretical Economics (JITE)/Zeitschrift für die gesamte Staatswissenschaft* 156, no. 1 (2000): 9–18.

Åslund, Anders. *Building Capitalism: The Transformation of the Former Soviet Bloc.* Cambridge: Cambridge University Press, 2002.

Åslund, Anders. *How Capitalism Was Built: The Transformation of Central Europe, Russia, the Caucasus, and Central Asia.* New York: Cambridge University Press, 2013.

Åslund, Anders. *Russia's Crony Capitalism: The Path from Market Economy to Kleptocracy.* New Haven, CT: Yale University Press, 2019.

Atoyan, Ruben, Lone Christiansen, Allan Dizioli, Christian Ebeke, Nadeem Ilahi, Anna Ilyina, Gil Mehrez, Haonan Qu, Faezeh Raei, Alaina Rhee, and Daria Zakharova. *Emigration and Its Economic Impact on Eastern Europe.* Washington, DC: IMF Staff Discussion Note, 2016. https://www.imf.org/external/pubs/ft/sdn/2016/sdn1607.pdf.

Azarova, Aytalina, Darja Irdam, Alexi Gugushvili, Mihaly Fazekas, Gábor Scheiring, Pia Horvat, and Denes Stefler. "The Effect of Rapid Privatisation on Mortality in Mono-Industrial Towns in Post-Soviet Russia: A Retrospective Cohort Study." *Lancet Public Health* 2, no. 5 (2017): e231–e238. doi: 10.1016%2FS2468-2667(17)30072-5.

Bahry, Donna, and Rick Wilson. "Confusion or Fairness in the Field? Rejections in the Ultimatum Game under the Strategy Method." *Journal of Economic Behavior & Organization* 60 (2006): 37–54.

Barlow, David, and Roxana Radulescu. "The Sequencing of Reform in Transition Economies." *Journal of Comparative Economics* 33, no. 4 (2005): 835–850.

Barometrul ADEVĂRUL despre ROMÂNIA. Bucharest: Inscop Research, 2014. http://www.inscop.ro/wp-content/uploads/2014/01/INSCOP-noiembrie-ISTORIE.pdf.

Barr, Nicholas, ed. *Labor Markets and Social Policy in Central and Eastern Europe: The Accession and Beyond.* Washington, DC: World Bank Group, 2005.

Batorski, Dominik, Piotr Białowolski, Janusz Czapiński, Izabela Grabowska, Irena E. Kotowska, Tomasz Panek, and Paweł Strzelecki. "Social Diagnosis 2011: Objective and Subjective Quality of Life in Poland." Edited by Janusz Czapiński and Tomasz Panek. *Contemporary Economics: Quarterly of Finance and Management in Warsaw* 5, no. 3 (2016): 50–112.

Berdahl, Daphne. *Where the World Ended: Re-Unification and Identity in the German Borderland.* Berkeley: University of California Press, 1999.

Berdahl, Daphne, Matti Bunzl, and Martha Lampland, eds. *Altering States: Ethnographies of Transition in Eastern Europe and the Former Soviet Union.* Ann Arbor: University of Michigan Press, 2000.

Berglöf, Erik, Yevgeniya Korniyenko, Jeromin Zettelmeyer, and Alexander Plekhanov. "Understanding the Crisis in Emerging Europe." *European Bank for Reconstruction and Development Working Paper* 109 (2009).

Bhattacharya, Jay, Christina Gathmann, and Grant Miller. "The End of the Soviet Union's Anti-alcohol Campaign May Explain a Substantial Share of Russia's 'Mortality Crisis' in the 1990's." *EUROPP* (blog). London School of Economics (October 10, 2013). https://blogs.lse.ac.uk/europpblog/2013/10/10/the-end-of-the-soviet-unions-anti-alcohol-campaign-may-explain-a-substantial-share-of-russias-mortality-crisis-in-the-1990s/.

"Bhutan's Gross National Happiness Index." Oxford Poverty & Human Development Initiative (*OPHI*). https://ophi.org.uk/policy/national-policy/gross-national-happiness-index/.

Blanchard, Olivier. *The Economics of Post-Communist Transition*. New York: Oxford University Press, 1997.

Blanchard, Olivier, Rudiger Dornbusch, Paul Krugman, Richard Layard, and Lawrence Summers. *Reform in Eastern Europe*. Cambridge, MA: MIT Press, 1991.

Blejer, Mario I., and Alan H. Gelb. "The Contraction of Eastern Europe's Economies: Introduction to the Conference." In *Eastern Europe in Transition: From Recession to Growth?* Edited by Mario I. Blejer, Guillermo A. Calvo, and Fabrizio Coricelli. Washington, DC: World Bank Group, 1993.

Botoeva, Aisalkyn, Stefan B. Kirmse, Ali Igmen, Morgan Liu, and Marianne Kamp. "Under Solomon's Throne: Uzbek Visions of Renewal in Osh." *Central Asian Survey* 37, no. 1 (2018): 160–171.

Brainerd, Elizabeth, and David M. Cutler. "Autopsy on an Empire: Understanding Mortality in Russia and the Former Soviet Union." *Journal of Economic Perspectives* 19, no. 1 (2005): 107–130. doi: 10.1257/0895330053147921.

Breinbauer, Andreas. "Brain Drain-Brain Circulation or . . . What Else Happens or Should Happen to the Brains." *Der Donauraum* 47, no. 1–2 (2007): 89–124.

Buckley, Robert M., and Sasha Tsenkova. "Urban Housing Markets in Transition: New Instruments to Assist the Poor." In *The Urban Mosaic of Post-Socialist Europe: Space, Institutions and Policy*. Edited by Sasha Tsenkova and Zorica Nedović-Budić, 173–194. Heidelberg: Springer, 2006.

Bugaric, Bojan. "The Populist Backlash against Europe: Why Only Alternative Economic and Social Policies Can Stop the Rise of Populism in Europe." In *EU Law in Populist Times*. Edited by Francesca Bignami. Cambridge: Cambridge University Press, 2018.

Bugaric, Bojan. "Protecting Democracy inside the EU: On Article 7 TEU and the Hungarian Turn to Authoritarianism, in CLOSA." *CLOSA (May 8, 2016). Reinforcing Rule of Law Oversight in the European Union*. Cambridge: Cambridge University Press, 2016.

Burawoy, Michael, and Katherine Verdery, eds. *Uncertain Transition: Ethnographies of Change in the Postsocialist World*. Lanham, MD: Rowman & Littlefield, 2000.

Bussolo, Maurizio, Maria Eugenia Davalos, Vito Peragine, and Ramya Sundaram. *Toward a New Social Contract: Taking on Distributional Tensions in Europe and Central Asia*. Washington, DC: World Bank Group, 2018.

Buzar, Stefan. *Energy Poverty in Eastern Europe: Hidden Geographies of Deprivation*. Abingdon, UK: Routledge, 2016.

Case, Anne, and Angus Deaton. *Deaths of Despair and the Future of Capitalism*. Princeton, NJ: Princeton University Press, 2020.

Cassidy, John. "Always with Us? Jeffery Sachs's Plan to Eradicate World Poverty." *New Yorker*, April 3, 2005. https://www.newyorker.com/magazine/2005/04/11/always-with-us.

Cerami, Alfio, and Pieter Vanhuysse. *Post-communist Welfare Pathways: Theorizing Social Policy Rransformations in Central and Eastern Europe*. New York: Springer, 2009.

Chari, Sharad, and Katherine Verdery. "Thinking between the Posts: Postcolonialism, Postsocialism, and Ethnography after the Cold War." *Comparative Studies in Society and History* 51, no. 1 (2009): 6–34.

Chernova, Zhanna. "New Pronatalism?: Family Policy in Post-Soviet Russia." *REGION: Regional Studies of Russia, Eastern Europe, and Central Asia* 1, no. 1 (2012): 75–92.

Clotilde, Armaud. "Eastern Europe Gives More to the West than It Gets Back." *Financial Times*, February 12, 2020. https://www.ft.com/content/39603142-4cc9-11ea-95a0-43d18ec715f5.

Cockerham, William C., Brian P. Hinote, and Pamela Abbott. "Psychological Distress, Gender, and Health Lifestyles in Belarus, Kazakhstan, Russia, and Ukraine." *Social Science & Medicine* 63, no. 9 (2006): 2381–2394. doi: 10.1016/j.socscimed.2006.06.001.

Cockerham, William C., Brian P. Hinote, Pamela Abbott, and Christian Haerpfer. "Health Lifestyles in Central Asia: The Case of Kazakhstan and Kyrgyzstan." *Social Science & Medicine* 59, no. 7 (2004): 1409–1421. doi: 10.1016/j.socscimed.2004.01.023.

Conrad, Christoph, Michael Lechner, and Welf Werner. "East German Fertility after Unification: Crisis or Adaptation?" *Population and Development Review* 22, no. 2 (1996): 331–358.

Cook, Linda J. *Postcommunist Welfare States: Reform Politics in Russia and Eastern Europe*. Ithaca, NY: Cornell University Press, 2011.

Cornia, Giovanni Andrea. *Transition, Structural Divergence, and Performance: Eastern Europe and the Former Soviet Union over 2000–2007*. No. 2010/32. WIDER Working Paper, 2010.

Creed, Gerald W. "Deconstructing Socialism in Bulgaria." In *Uncertain Transition*. Edited by Michael Burawoy and Katherine Verdery, 223–244. Lanham, MD: Rowman & Littlefield, 1999.

Creed, Gerald W. *Domesticating Revolution: From Socialist Reform to Ambivalent Transition in a Bulgarian Village*. University Park: Pennsylvania State University Press, 1998.

Creed, Gerald W., and Janine Wedel. "Second Thoughts from the Second World: Interpreting Aid in Post-Communist Eastern Europe." *Human Organization* 56, no. 3 (1997): 253–264. doi: 10.17730/humo.56.3.9rn36067p41h6j1n.

Cvajner, Martina. *Soviet Signoras: Personal and Collective Transformations in Eastern European Migration*. Chicago: University of Chicago Press, 2019.

Dąbrowska, Ewa, Aron Buzogány, and Mihai Varga. "The 'Budapest–Warsaw Express': Conservatism and the Diffusion of Economic Policies in Poland and Hungary." In *New Conservatives in Russia and East Central Europe*, 178–197. New York: Routledge, 2018.

Dewatripont, Mathias, and Gérard Roland. "The Virtues of Gradualism and Legitimacy in the Transition to a Market Economy." *Economic Journal* 102, no. 411 (1992): 291–300.

Djankov, Simeon. *Hungary under Orban: Can Central Planning Revive Its Economy?* Washington, DC: Peterson Institute for International Economics, July 2015.

Djankov, Simeon. *Russia's Economy under Putin: From Crony Capitalism to State Capitalism.* No. PB15-18. Washington, DC: Peterson Institute for International Economics, 2015.

Djankov, Simeon, Elena Nikolova, and Jan Zilinsky. "The Happiness Gap in Eastern Europe." *Journal of Comparative Economics* 44, no. 1 (2016): 108–124.

Douglass, Carrie B., ed. *Barren States: The Population "Implosion" in Europe.* Oxford: Berg 2005.

Dunn, Elizabeth. "Slick Salesman and Simple People: Negotiated Capitalism in a Privatized Polish Firm." In *Uncertain Transition: Ethnographies of Change in the Postsocialist World.* Edited by Michael Burawoy and Katherine Verdery, 125–150. Lanham, MD: Rowman & Littlefield, 1999.

Duthé, Geraldine, Michel Guillot, France Meslé, Jacques Vallin, Irina Badurashvili, Mikhail Denisenko, Natalia Gavrilova, Karine Kuyumjyan, and Liudmila Torgasheva. "Adult Mortality Patterns in the Former Soviet Union's Southern Tier: Armenia and Georgia in Comparative Perspective." *Demographic Research* 36, no. 19 (2017): 589–608. doi: 10.4054/DemRes.2017.36.19.

Dyer, Owen. "US Life Expectancy Falls for Third Year in a Row." *BMJ* 363, no. k5118 (December 4, 2018). doi: 10.1136/bmj.k5118.

Earle, John S., and Scott Gehlbach. "Did Mass Privatisation Really Increase Post-Communist Mortality?" *The Lancet* 375, no. 9712 (2010): 372. doi: 10.1016/S0140-6736(10)60159-6.

Edwards, Maxim. "Ukraine's Quiet Depopulation Crisis." *The Atlantic*, March 21, 2020. https://www.theatlantic.com/international/archive/2020/03/ukraine-eastern-europe-depopulation-immigration-crisis/608464/.

Ekman, Joakim, and Jonas Linde. "Communist Nostalgia and the Consolidation of Democracy in Central and Eastern Europe." *Journal of Communist Studies and Transition Politics* 21, no. 3 (2005): 354–374. doi: 10.1080/13523270500183512.

Elster, Jon, Claus Offe, Ulrich K. Preuss, Frank Boenker, Ulrike Goetting, and Friedbert W. Rueb. *Institutional Design in Post-communist Societies: Rebuilding the Ship at Sea.* Cambridge: Cambridge University Press, 1998.

European Bank for Reconstruction and Development. *Annual Report 1996* London: EBRD, 1996.

European Bank for Reconstruction and Development. *Life in Transition: After the Crisis.* London: EBRD, 2011.

European Bank for Reconstruction and Development. *Life in Transition: A Decade of Measuring Transition.* London: EBRD, 2017.

European Bank for Reconstruction and Development. *Life in Transition: A Survey of People's Experiences and Attitudes.* London: EBRD, 2011.

European Bank for Reconstruction and Development. *Transition for All: Equal Opportunities in an Unequal World.* London: EBRD, 2017.

European Bank for Reconstruction and Development. *Transition Report 2007: People in Transition.* London: EBRD, 2007.

Favell, Adrian. "The New Face of East-West Migration in Europe." *Journal of Ethnic and Migration Studies* 35, no. 5 (2008): 701–716. doi: 10.1080/13691830802105947.

Fidrmuc, Jan. "Economic Reform, Democracy, and Growth during Post-Communist Transition." *European Journal of Political Economy* 19, no. 3 (2003): 583–604. doi: 10.1016/S0176-2680(03)00010-7.

Filippidis, Filippos T., and Anythony A. Laverty. "'Euphoria' and or 'Only Teardrops'? Eurovision Song Contest Performance, Life Satisfaction and Suicide." *BMC Public Health* 18, no. 582 (2018): 582.

Fodor, Éva. *Working Difference: Women's Working Lives in Hungary and Austria, 1945–1995.* Durham, NC: Duke University Press, 2003.

Frink, Helen. *Women after Communism: The East German Experience.* Lanham, MD: University Press of America, 2001.

Ghodsee, Kristen. *Lost in Transition: Ethnographies of Everyday Life after Communism.* Durham, NC: Duke University Press, 2011.

Ghodsee, Kristen. *Muslim Lives in Eastern Europe: Gender, Ethnicity, and the Transformation of Islam in Postsocialist Bulgaria.* Princeton, NJ: Princeton University Press, 2009.

Ghodsee, Kristen. *Red Hangover: Legacies of Twentieth Century Communism.* Durham, NC: Duke University Press, 2017.

Ghodsee, Kristen. "Red Nostalgia? Communism, Women's Emancipation, and Economic Transformation in Bulgaria." *L'Homme* 15, no. 1 (2004): 33–46. doi: 10.7767/lhomme.2004.15.1.33.

Ghodsee, Kristen. *The Red Riviera: Gender, Tourism, and Postsocialism on the Black Sea.* Durham, NC: Duke University Press, 2005.

Ghodsee, Kristen. *Why Women Have Better Sex under socialism: And Other Arguments for Economic Independence.* New York: Random House, 2018.

Golinowska, Stanisława, and Agnieszka Sowa-Kofta. "Combating Poverty Through Family Cash Benefits: On the First Results of the Programme 'Family 500+' in Poland." *Polityka Społeczna* 4, no. 1 (13), Child Benefit Programme 500+ Outcomes and Outputs (2017): 7–13. http://cejsh.icm.edu.pl/cejsh/element/bwmeta1.element.desklight-deedf65b-7228-47ee-b4c8-1468c5beb549.

Gorokhovskaya, Yana. "Healthcare Reform, Demographic Trends, and COVID-19 in Russia: A Conversation with Professor Judyth Twigg." *Reforum*. June 17, 2020. https://reforum.io/en/2020/06/17/healthcare-reform-demographic-trends-and-covid-19-in-russia-a-conversation-with-professor-judyth-twigg/.

Gowan, Peter. "Neoliberal Theory and Practice for Eastern Europe." *New Left Review* 213 (1995): 3–60.

Grootaert, Christiaan, and Jeanine Braithwaite. *Poverty Correlates and Indicator-Based Targeting in Eastern Europe and the Former Soviet Union*. Washington, DC: World Bank Group, 1999.

Grzebalska, Weronika, and Andrea Pető. "The Gendered Modus Operandi of the Illiberal Transformation in Hungary and Poland." *Women's Studies International Forum*, vol. 68, pp. 164–172. New York: Pergamon/Elsevier, 2018.

Grzymała-Busse, Anna. "Encouraging Effective Democratic Competition." *East European Politics and Societies* 21, no. 1 (2007): 91–110.

Grzymala-Busse, Anna. *Rebuilding Leviathan: Party Competition and State Exploitation in Post-Communist Democracies*. Cambridge: Cambridge University Press, 2007.

Guillot, Michel, Natalia Gavrilova, Liudmila Torgasheva, and Mikhail Denisenko. "Divergent Paths for Adult Mortality in Russia and Central Asia: Evidence from Kyrgyzstan." *PLoS ONE* 8, no. 10 (2013): e75314. doi: 10.1371/journal.pone.0075314.

Guillot, Michel, Natalia Gavrilova, and Tetyana Pudrovska. "Understanding the 'Russian Mortality Paradox' in Central Asia: Evidence from Kyrgyzstan." *Demography* 48, no. 3 (2011): 1081–1104. doi: 10.1007%2Fs13524-011-0036-1.

Guseva, Alya, and Akos Rona-Tas. *Plastic Money: Constructing Markets for Credit Cards in Eight Postcommunist Countries*. Palo Alto, CA: Stanford University Press, 2014.

Güth, Werner, Rolf Schmittberger, and Bernd Schwarze. "An Experimental Analysis of Ultimatum Bargaining." *Journal of Economic Behavior & Organization* 3, no. 4 (1982): 367–388. doi: 10.1016/0167-2681(82)90011-7.

Habibov, Nazim, and Elvin Afandi. "Pre- and Post-crisis Life-Satisfaction and Social Trust in Transitional Countries: An Initial Assessment." *Social Indicators Research* 121, no. 2 (2015): 503–524.

Haney, Lynne. *Inventing the Needy: Gender and the Politics of Welfare in Hungary*. Oakland: University of California Press, 2002.

Hanson, Phillip. "Putin and Russia's Economic Transformation." *Eurasian Geography and Economics* 45, no. 6 (2004): 421–428.

Haughton, Tim. "When Does the EU Make a Difference? Conditionality and the Accession Process in Central and Eastern Europe." *Political Studies Review* 5, no. 2 (2007): 233–246.

Havrylyshyn, Oleh. *Present at the Transition: An Inside Look at the Role of History, Politics, and Personalities in Post-communist Countries*. Cambridge: Cambridge University Press, 2020.

Havrylyshyn, Oleh. "Recovery and Growth in Transition: A Decade of Evidence." *IMF Staff Papers* 48, no. 4 (2001): 53–87.

Hayo, Bernd. "Eastern European Public Opinion on Economic Issues: Privatization and Transformation." *American Journal of Economics and Sociology* 56, no. 1 (1997): 85–102. doi: 10.1111/j.1536-7150.1997.tb03453.x.

Heathershaw, John. "The Global Performance State: A Reconsideration of the Central Asian 'Weak State.'" In *Ethnographies of the State in Central Asia: Performing Politics*. Edited by Madeleine Reeves, Johan Rasanayagam, and Judith Beyer, 29–54. Bloomington: Indiana University Press, 2014.

Hellman, Joel S., Geraint Jones, Daniel Kaufmann, and M. Schankerman. "Seize the State, Seize the Day: An Empirical Analysis of State Capture and Corruption in Transition Economies." *Annual Congress of the ABCDE*. Washington, DC, 2000, 1–39.

Hensel, Jana. *After the Wall: Confession from an East German Childhood and the Life That Came After*. Translated by Jefferson Chase. New York: Public Affairs, 2004.

Herrera, Yoshiko M. *Mirrors of the Economy: National Accounts and International Norms in Russia and Beyond*. Ithaca, NY: Cornell University Press, 2010.

Höjdestrand, Tova. *Needed by Nobody: Homelessness and Humanness in Post-Socialist Russia*. Ithaca, NY: Cornell University Press, 2009.

Holmes, Leslie. *Post Communism: An Introduction*. Durham, NC: Duke University Press, 1997.

Humphrey, Caroline. "Traders, 'Disorder,' and Citizenship Regimes in Russia." In *Uncertain Transition: Ethnographies of Change in the Postsocialist World*. Edited by Michael Burawoy and Katherine Verdery, 19–52. Lanham, MD: Rowman & Littlefield, 1999.

Humphrey, Caroline. *The Unmaking of Soviet Life: Everyday Economies after Socialism*. Ithaca, NY: Cornell University Press, 2002.

Hungarian Investment Promotion Agency. Automotive Industry in Hungary, September 2018, Budapest. https://hipa.hu/images/publications/hipa-automotive-industry-in-hungary_2018_09_20.pdf.

Inglot, Tomasz. *Welfare States in East Central Europe, 1919–2004*. Cambridge: Cambridge University Press. 2008.

Innes, Abby. "Hungary's Illiberal Democracy." *Current History* 114, no. 770 (2015): 95.

Iwasaki, Ichiro, and Keiko Suganuma. "Foreign Direct Investment and Regional Economic Development in Russia: An Econometric Assessment." *Economic Change and Restructuring* 48, no. 3–4 (2015): 209–255.

Jarvis, Christopher. "The Rise and Fall of Albania's Pyramid Schemes." *Finance & Development* 37, no. 1 (2000): 46–49.

Jasiewicz, Krzysztof. "The New Populism in Poland: The Usual Suspects?" *Problems of Post-communism* 55, no. 3 (2008): 7–25.

Jirasavetakul, La-Bhus Fah, and Jesmin Rahman. *Foreign Direct Investment in New Member States of the EU and Western Balkans: Taking Stock and Assessing Prospects.* Washington, DC: International Monetary Fund, 2018.

Johnson, Juliet, and Andrew Barnes. "Financial Nationalism and Its International Enablers: The Hungarian EXPerience." *Review of International Political Economy* 22, no. 3 (2015): 535–569.

Kaczmarczyk, Pawel. "Labour Market Impacts of Post-Accession Migration from Poland." In *Free Movement of Workers and Labour Market Adjustment: Recent Experiences from OECD Countries and the European Union*, 173–190. Paris: OECD Publishing, 2012.

Karanikolos, Marina, Philipa Mladovsky, Jonathan Cylus, Sarah Thomson, Sanjay Basu, David Stuckler, Johan P. Mackenbach, and Martin McKee. "Financial Crisis, Austerity, and Health in Europe." *The Lancet* 381, no. 9874 (2013): 1323–1331.

Keough, Leyla J. *Worker Mothers on the Margins of Europe: Gender and Migration between Moldova and Istanbul.* Bloomington: Indiana University Press, 2016.

Kideckel, David. *Getting By in Postsocialist Bulgaria: Labor, the Body, and Working Class Culture.* Bloomington: Indiana University Press, 2008.

King, Lawrence, Patrick Hamm, and David Stuckler. "Rapid Large-Scale Privatization and Death Rates in Ex-Communist Countries: An Analysis of Stress-Related and Health System Mechanisms." *International Journal of Health Services* 39, no. 3 (2009): 461–489.

Klein, Naomi. *The Shock Doctrine: The Rise of Disaster Capitalism.* New York: Picador, 2008.

Kluegel, James R., and David S. Mason. "Fairness Matters: Social Justice and Political Legitimacy in Post-Communist Europe." *Europe-Asia Studies* 56, no. 6 (2004): 813–834.

Kluegel, James R., David S. Mason, and Bernd Wegener. "The International Social Justice Project." *Social Justice and Political Change: Public Opinion in Capitalist and Post-Communist States* (Berlin: Walter de Gruyter, 1995).

Klumbytė, Neringa. "Post Socialist Sensations: Nostalgia, the Self, and Alterity in Lithuania." *Lietuvos Etnologija: Socialinės Antropologijos ir Etnologijos Studijos* 9, no. 18 (2009): 93–116. http://talpykla.istorija.lt/bitstream/handle/99999/2006/Lietuvos_etnologija_9(18)_93-116.pdf?sequence=1&isAllowed=y.

Klumbytė, Neringa. "Post-Soviet Publics and Nostalgia for Soviet Times." In *Changing Economies and Changing Identities in Postsocialist Eastern Europe.* Edited by Ingo W. Schröder and Asta Vonderau, 27–46. Münster: LIT Verlag, 2008.

Knack, Stephen. "Measuring Corruption: A Critique of Indicators in Eastern Europe and Central Asia." *Journal of Public Policy* 27, no. 3 (2007): 255–291.

Kogut, Bruce, and Andrew Spicer. "Capital Market Development and Mass Privatization Are Logical Contradictions: Lessons from Russia and the Czech Republic." *Industrial and Corporate Change* 11, no. 1 (2002): 1–37.

Kolodko, Grzegorz W. "Postcommunist Transitions and Post-Washington Consensus: Lessons for Policy Reforms." In *Transition: The First Decade*. Edited by Mario I. Blejer and Marko Skreb, 45–83. Cambridge, MA: MIT Press, 2001.

Kornai, János. "Hungary's U-turn: Retreating from Democracy." *Journal of Democracy* 26, no. 3 (2015): 34–48.

Kornai, János. *The Socialist System: The Political Economy of Communism*. Princeton, NJ: Princeton University Press, 1992.

Kovács, Kriszta, and Kim Lane Scheppele. "The Fragility of an Independent Judiciary: Lessons from Hungary and Poland—and the European Union." *Communist and Post-Communist Studies* 51, no. 3 (2018): 189–200.

Krastev, Ivan. "What's Wrong with East-Central Europe?: Liberalism's Failure to Deliver." *Journal of Democracy* 27, no. 1 (2016): 35–38.

Krastev, Ivan, and Stephen Holmes. "Explaining Eastern Europe: Imitation and Its Discontents." *Journal of Democracy* 29, no. 3 (2018): 117–128.

Krastev, Ivan, and Stephen Holmes. *The Light That Failed: A Reckoning*. London: Penguin Books, 2019.

Kullberg, Judith S., and William Zimmerman. "Liberal Elites, Socialist Masses, and Problems of Russian Democracy." *World Politics* 51, no. 3 (1999): 323–358. doi: 10.1017/S0043887100009102.

Lackó, Mária. *Do Power Consumption Data Tell the Story? Electricity Intensity and Hidden Economy in Post-Socialist Countries*. No. BWP-1999/2. Budapest Working Papers on the Labour Market, 1999. https://www.econstor.eu/handle/10419/108393.

Lane, Charles. "Eastern Europe Is Headed toward a Demographic Crisis." *Washington Post*, November 11, 2019. https://www.washingtonpost.com/opinions/global-opinions/the-incredible-shrinking-nations-of-eastern-europe/2019/11/11/fd777326-04a6-11ea-b17d-8b867891d39d_story.html.

Lane, Philip R., and Gian Maria Milesi-Ferretti. "Capital Flows to Central and Eastern Europe." *IMF Working Paper* no. 6, vol. 188 (2006).

Laszczkowski, Mateusz. *"City of the Future": Built Space, Modernity and Urban Change in Astana*. Vol. 14. New York: Berghahn Books, 2016.

Laszczkowski, Mateusz. "Scraps, Neighbors, and Committees: Material Things, Place-Making, and the State in an A stana Apartment Block." *City & Society* 27, no. 2 (2015): 136–159.

Lee, Minsoo, and MoonJoong Tcha. "The Color of Money: The Effects of Foreign Direct Investment on Economic Growth in Transition Economies." *Review of World Economics* 140, no. 2 (2004): 211–229.

Lemos, Sara, and Jonathan Portes. "New Labour? The Impact of Migration from Central and Eastern European Countries on the UK Labour Market." *B.E. Journal of Economic Analysis and Policy* 14, no. 1 (2013): 299–338. https://www.econstor.eu/bitstream/10419/35467/1/582911966.pdf.

Lendvai, Noémi, and Paul Stubbs. "Europeanization, Welfare and Variegated Austerity Capitalisms—Hungary and Croatia." *Social Policy & Administration* 49, no. 4 (2015): 445–465.

Leykin, Inna. "'Population Prescriptions': State, Morality, and Population Politics in Contemporary Russia." PhD dissertation, Brown University, 2012.

Linn, Johannes. "Ten Years of Transition in Central Europe and the Former Soviet Union; The Good News and the Not-so-Good News." In *Transition: The First Decade*. Edited by Mario I. Bléjer and Marko Skreb, 15–44. Cambridge, MA: MIT Press, 2001.

Mackenbach, Johan P. "Political Conditions of Life Expectancy in Europe." *Social Science & Medicine* 82 (2013): 134–146.

Magda, Iga, Aneta Kiełczewska, and Nicola Brandt. "The 'Family 500+' Child Allowance and Female Labour Supply in Poland." *OECD Economics Department Working Papers* no. 1481 (2018).

Marmot, Michael, and Martin Bobak. "International Comparators and Poverty and Health in Europe." *BMJ* 321, no. 1124 (2000).

Mason, David Stewart, James R. Kluegel, and Liudmila Aleksandrovna Khakhulina. *Marketing Democracy: Changing Opinion about Inequality and Politics in East Central Europe*. Lanham, MD: Rowman & Littlefield, 2000.

Maynard, Gary, Eric J. Shircliff, and Michael Restivo. "IMF Structural Adjustment, Public Health Spending, and Tuberculosis: A Longitudinal Analysis Prevalence Rates in Poor Countries." *International Journal of Sociology* 42, no. 2 (2012): 5–27. doi: 10.2753/IJS0020-7659420201.

McBrien, Julie. *From Belonging to Belief: Modern Secularisms and the Construction of Religion in Kyrgyzstan*. Pittsburgh: University of Pittsburgh Press, 2017.

McBrien, Julie. "Mukadas's Struggle: Veils and Modernity in Kyrgyzstan." *Journal of the Royal Anthropological Institute* 15 (2009): S127–S144.

McLellan, Josie. *Love in the Time of Communism: Intimacy and Sexuality in the GDR*. Cambridge: Cambridge University Press, 2011.

Merlevede, Bruno, Koen Schoors, and Bas Van Aarle. "Russia from Bust to Boom and Back: Oil Price, Dutch Disease and Stabilisation Fund." *Comparative Economic Studies* 51, no. 2 (2009): 213–241.

Meurs, Mieke, and Lisa Giddings. "Decline in Pre-School Use in Post-Socialist Societies: The Case of Bulgaria." *Journal of European Social Policy* 16, no. 2 (2006): 155–166.

Mihova, G., D. Kergoat, M. Nikolova, and D. Donev. *Working Hours, Working Conditions Demographic Behaviors*. Sofia: Economic Research Institute, Bulgarian Academy of the Sciences and Academic Publishing House Marin Drinov, 2007.

Milanovic, Branko. "For Whom the Wall Fell? A Balance Sheet of the Transition to Capitalism." globalinequality, November 3, 2014. https://glineq.blogspot.com/2014/11/for-whom-wall-fell-balance-sheet-of.html.

Milanovic, Branko. *Global Inequality: A New Approach for the Age of Globalization.* Cambridge, MA: Harvard University Press, 2016.

Mitra, Pradeep, Marcelo Selowski, and Juan Zalduendo. *Turmoil at Twenty: Recession, Recovery and Reform in Central and Eastern Europe and the Former Soviet Union.* Washington, DC: World Bank Group, 2009.

Mohdin, Aamna. "The Fastest Shrinking Countries on Earth Are in Eastern Europe." *Quartz.* January 24, 2018. https://qz.com/1187819/country-ranking-worlds-fastest-shrinking-countries-are-in-eastern-europe/.

Mostowlansky, Till. *Azan on the Moon: Entangling Modernity along Tajikistan's Pamir Highway.* Pittsburgh: University of Pittsburgh Press, 2017.

Mulej, Oskar. "'We Are Drowning in Red Beet, Patching Up the Holes in the Iron Curtain': The Punk Subculture in Ljubljana in the Late 1970s and Early 1980s." *East Central Europe* 38, no. 2–3 (2011): 373–389.

Müller, Martin. "Goodbye, Postsocialism!" *Europe-Asia Studies* 71, no. 4 (March 7, 2018): 533–550.

Murrell, Peter. "Institutions and Transition." *The New Palgrave Dictionary of Economics* 2. London: Palgrave Macmillan, 2006.

Mutz, Michael. "Life Satisfaction and the UEFA EURO 2016: Findings from a Nation-Wide Longitudinal Study in Germany." *Applied Research in Quality of Life* 14, no. 2 (2019): 375–391.

Nader, Laura. "The Phantom Factor: Impact of the Cold War on Anthropology." In *The Cold War and the University: Toward an Intellectual History of the Postwar Years.* New York: New Press, 1998.

Naudé, Wim, Aleksander Surdej, and Martin Cameron. "Ready for Industry 4.0? The Case of Central and Eastern Europe." In *Industry 4.0 and Engineering for a Sustainable Future,* edited by Mohammad Dastbaz and Peter Cochrane, 153–175. Cham: Springer, 2019.

Nolan, Brian, Max Roser, and Stefan Thewissen. *GDP Per Capita versus Median Household Income: What Gives Rise to Divergence over Time?* Luxemburg Income Study (LIS) Working Paper Series no. 672 (2016).

Nölke, Andreas, and Arjan Vliegenthart. "Enlarging the Varieties of Capitalism: The Emergence of Dependent Market Economies in East Central Europe." *World Politics* 61, no. 4 (2009): 670–702.

O'Neill, Bruce. *The Space of Boredom: Homelessness in the Slowing Global Order.* Durham, NC: Duke University Press, 2017.

Ost, David. *The Defeat of Solidarity: Anger and Politics in Postcommunist Europe.* Ithaca, NY: Cornell University Press, 2005.

Oushakine, Serguei A. *The Patriotism of Despair: Nation, War, and Loss in Russia.* Ithaca, NY: Cornell University Press, 2009.

Paprotny, Dominik. "Measuring Central and Eastern Europe's Economic Development Using Time Lags." *Social Indicators Research,* 127 no. 3 (2016): 939–957.

Pavlínek, Petr, Bolesław Domański, and Robert Guzik. "Industrial Upgrading through Foreign Direct Investment in Central European Automotive Manufacturing." *European Urban and Regional Studies* 16, no. 1 (2009): 43–63.

Pelkmans, Mathijs. "On Transition and Revolution in Kyrgyzstan." *Focaal* 2005, no. 46 (2005): 147–157.

Perelli-Harris, Brienna. "The Path to Lowest-low Fertility in Ukraine." *Population Studies* 59, no. 1 (2005): 55–70. https://www.tandfonline.com/doi/abs/10.1080/00324720 52000332700.

Pew Research Center. Religious Belief and National Belonging in Central and Eastern Europe. Washington, DC: Pew Research Center, 2017. https://www.pewforum. org/2017/05/10/religious-belief-and-national-belonging-in-central-and-eastern-europe/.

Pew Research Center. European Public Opinion Three Decades after the Fall of Communism. Figure 5. Washington, DC: Pew Research Center, 2019. https://www. pewresearch.org/global/2019/10/15/european-public-opinion-three-decades-after-the-fall-of-communism/.

Philipov, Dimiter, and Jürgen Dorbritz. *Demographic Consequences of Economic Transition in Countries of Central and Eastern Europe.* Strasbourg: Council of Europe, 2003.

Piasecki, Marcin A. "Was Viktor Orbán's Unorthodox Economic Policy the Right Answer to Hungary's Economic Misfortunes?" *International Journal of Management and Economics* 46, no. 1 (2015): 41–71.

Piatkowski, Marcin. *Europe's Growth Champion: Insights from the Economic Rise of Poland.* New York: Oxford University Press, 2018.

Piatkowski, Marcin. *Poland's New Golden Age: Shifting from Europe's Periphery to its Center.* Washington, DC: World Bank Group, 2013.

Pixová, Michaela. "Alternative Culture in a Socialist City: Punkers and Long-Haired People in Prague in the 1980s.'" *Český Lid* 100, no. 3 (2013): 319–338.

Polese, Abel, Jeremy Morris, and Borbála Kovács. "Introduction: The Failure and Future of the Welfare State in Post-Socialism." *Journal of Eurasian Studies* 6, no. 1 (2015): 1–5.

Pop-Eleches, Grigore, and Joshua A. Tucker. *Communism's Shadow: Historical Legacies and Contemporary Political Attitudes.* Princeton, NJ: Princeton University Press, 2017.

Popov, Vladimir. "Shock Therapy versus Gradualism Reconsidered: Lessons from Transition Economies after 15 Years of Reforms." *Comparative Economic Studies* 49, no. 1 (2007): 1–31.

Portes, Alejandro. "Migration and Development: Reconciling Opposite Views." *Ethnic and Racial Studies* 32, no. 1 (2009): 5–22. doi: 10.1080/01419870802483668.

Price, David H. *Cold War Anthropology: The CIA, the Pentagon, and the Growth of Dual Use Anthropology.* Durham, NC: Duke University Press, 2016.

Przeworski, Adam. *Democracy and the Market: Economic Reforms in Eastern Europe and Latin America.* Cambridge: Cambridge University Press, 1991.

Raikhel, Eugene. *Governing Habits: Treating Alcoholism in the Post-Soviet Clinic.* Ithaca, NY: Cornell University Press, 2016.

Rechel, Bernd, Erica Richardson, and Martin McKee. "Trends in Health Systems in the Former Soviet Countries." *European Journal of Public Health* 24, no. suppl. 2 (2014).

Reeves, Madeleine. "Black Work, Green Money: Remittances, Ritual, and Domestic Economies in Southern Kyrgyzstan." *Slavic Review* 71, no. 1 (2012): 108–134.

Reeves, Madeleine. *Border Work: Spatial Lives of the State in Rural Central Asia.* Ithaca, NY: Cornell University Press, 2014.

Reeves, Madeleine. "Clean Fake: Authenticating Documents and Persons in Migrant Moscow." *American Ethnologist* 40, no. 3 (2013): 508–524.

Reeves, Madeleine. "Staying Put? Towards a Relational Politics of Mobility at a Time of Migration." *Central Asian Survey* 30, no. 3–4 (2011): 555–576.

Ries, Nancy. "Potato Ontology: Surviving Postsocialism in Russia." *Cultural Anthropology* 24, no. 2 (2009): 181–212. doi: 10.1111/j.1548-1360.2009.01129.x.

Ringold, Dena, Mitchell A. Orenstein, and Erika Wilkens. *Roma in an Expanding Europe: Breaking the Poverty Cycle.* Washington, DC: World Bank Group, 2004.

Riphahn, Regina T., and Klaus F. Zimmerman. "The Mortality Crisis in East Germany." *IZA Discussion Papers* no. 6 (1998): 40. http://www.econstor.eu/dspace/bitstream/10419/20852/1/dp6.pdf.

Rivkin-Fish, Michele. "Pronatalism, Gender Politics, and the Renewal of Family Support in Russia: Toward a Feminist Anthropology of 'Maternity Capital.'" *Slavic Review* (2010): 701–724.

Roaf, James, Ruben Atoyan, Bikas Joshi, and Krzysztof Krogulski. *25 Years of Transition: Post-Communist Europe and the IMF.* Washington, DC: International Monetary Fund, 2014.

Rodrik, Dani. *The Globalization Paradox: Democracy and the Future of the World Economy.* New York: Norton, 2011.

Rogers, Doug. "Moonshine, Money, and the Politics of Liquidity in Rural Russia." *American Ethnologist* 32, no. 1 (2005): 63–81. doi: 10.1525/ae.2005.32.1.63.

Roland, Gerard. "The Political Economy of Transition." *Journal of Economic Perspectives* 16, no. 1 (2002): 29–50.

Rose, Richard. *Understanding Post-Communist Transformation: A Bottom Up Approach.* London: Routledge, 2009.

Rosser, J. Barkley Jr., Marina V. Rosser, and Ehsan Ahmed. "Income Inequality and the Informal Economy in Transition Economies." *Journal of Comparative Economics* 28, no. 1 (2000), 156–171.

Ruminska-Zimny, Ewa. *Human Poverty in Transition Economies: Regional Overview for HDR 1997.* New York: Human Development Report Office, United Nations Development Programme, 1997.

Rzepnikowska, Alina. "Racism and Xenophobia Experienced by Polish Migrants in the UK before and after Brexit Vote." *Journal of Ethnic and Migration Studies* 45, no. 1 (2018): 61–77. doi: 10.1080/1369183X.2018.1451308.

Sachs, Jeffrey D. "Achieving Universal Health Coverage in Low-Income Settings." *The Lancet* 380, no. 9845 (2012): 944–947. doi: 10.1016/S0140-6736(12)61149-0.

Sachs, Jeffrey D. *Poland's Jump to the Market Economy*. Cambridge, MA: MIT Press, 1993.

Sachs, Jeffrey D. "Shock Therapy in Poland: Perspectives of Five Years." *Tanner Lectures on Human Values* 16 (1995): 265–290.

Sachs, Jeffrey D. "The Transition at Mid Decade." *American Economic Review* 86, no. 2 (May 1996): 128–133.

Sachs, Jeffrey D. "What I Did in Russia." Jeffsachs.org. March 14, 2012. http://www.acamedia.info/politics/ukraine/jeffrey_sachs/What_I_did_in_Russia.pdf.

Sachs, Jeffrey D. "What Is to Be Done?" *The Economist*, January 13, 1990. https://www.economist.com/europe/1990/01/13/what-is-to-be-done.

Salt, John, and Jane Millar. "Foreign Labour in the United Kingdom: Current Patterns and Trends." *Labour Market Trends* 114, no. 10 (2006): 335–355.

Salt, John, and Jane Millar. "International Migration in Interesting Times: The Case of the UK." *People and Place* 14, no. 2 (2006): 14.

Sandu, Dumitru. "Modernising Romanian Society through Temporary Work Abroad." In *A Continent Moving West? EU Enlargement and Labour Migration from Central and Eastern Europe*. Edited by Richard Black, Godfried Engbersen, Marek Okólski, and Cristina Pantiru, 271–288. Amsterdam: Amsterdam University Press, 2010.

Saxonberg, Steven, and Tomas Sirovatka. "Failing Family Policy in Post-Communist Central Europe." *Journal of Comparative Policy Analysis* 8, no. 2 (2006): 185–202.

Schimmelfennig, Frank, and Ulrich Sedelmeier. "Governance by Conditionality: EU Rule Transfer to the Candidate Countries of Central and Eastern Europe." *Journal of European Public Policy* 11, no. 4 (2004): 661–679.

Schneider, Friedrich. "Shadow Economies around the World: What Do We Really Know?" *European Journal of Political Economy* 21, no. 3 (2005): 598–642.

Schröder, Philipp. *Bishkek Boys: Neighbourhood Youth and Urban Change in Kyrgyzstan's Capital*. Vol. 17. New York: Berghahn Books, 2017.

Schumpeter, Joseph A. *Capitalism, Socialism, and Democracy*. 3rd ed. New York: Harper & Row, 1950.

Shah, Alpa. "Ethnography? Participant Observation, a Potentially Revolutionary Praxis." *HAU: Journal of Ethnographic Theory* 7, no. 1 (Spring 2017): 45–59. doi: 10.14318/hau7.1.008.

Sheiman, Igor. "Rocky Road from the Semashko to a New Health Model." Interview by Fiona Fleck. *Bulletin of the World Health Organization* 91, no. 5 (2013): 320–321. doi: 10.2471/BLT.13.030513.

Shevchenko, Olga. *Crisis and the Everyday in Postsocialist Moscow*. Bloomington: Indiana University Press, 2008.

Shkolnikov, Vladimir, France Meslé, and David A. Leon. "Premature Circulatory Disease Mortality in Russia in Light of Population- and Individual-Level Disease." In *Heart Disease: Environment, Stress and Gender*. Edited by G. Weidner, S. M. Kopp, and M. Kristenson. Brussels: NATO Science Series, Series 1, Life and Behavioral Sciences, 2001.

Shleifer, Andrei, and Daniel Treisman. "Normal Countries: The East 25 Years after Communism." *Foreign Affairs*, November/December 2014. https://www.foreignaffairs.com/articles/russia-fsu/2014-10-20/normal-countries.

Smale, Alison. "In a United Germany, the Scars of the East-West Divide Have Faded." *New York Times*, October 2, 2015. http://www.nytimes.com/interactive/2015/10/02/world/europe/germany-unification-anniversary.html.

Spoor, Max. "Inequality, Poverty and Conflict in Transition Economies." In *Globalisation, Poverty and Conflict*, 47–65. Dordrecht: Springer, 2004.

Staikova-Alexandrova, Raia. "Bulgaria. The Present Situation of Women." In *The Impact of Economic and Political Reform on the Status of Women in Eastern Europe. Proceedings of a United Nations Regional Seminar*. New York, 1992.

Stiglitz, Joseph. *Globalization and Its Discontents*. New York: Norton, 2003.

Stiglitz, Joseph. *Making Globalization Work*. New York: Norton, 2007.

Stitzel, Judd. *Fashioning Socialism: Clothing, Politics and Consumer Culture in East Germany, 1948–1971*. Berlin: Berg, 2005.

Stuckler, David, and Sanjay Basu. *The Body Economic: Why Austerity Kills*. New York, Basic Books, 2013.

Stuckler, David, and Sanjay Basu. "The International Monetary Fund's Effects on Global Health: Before and After the 2008 Financial Crisis." *International Journal of Health Services* 39, no. 4 (2009): 771–781. doi: 10.2190%2FHS.39.4.j.

Stuckler, David, Lawrence P. King, and Sanjay Basu. "International Monetary Fund Programs and Tuberculosis Outcomes in Post-Communist Countries." *PLoS Medicine* 5, no. 7 (2008): e143. doi: 10.1371/journal.pmed.0050143.

Stuckler, David, Lawrence King, and Martin McKee. "Mass Privatisation and the Post-Communist Mortality Crisis: A Cross National Analysis." *The Lancet* 373, no. 9961 (2009): 399–407. doi: 10.1016/S0140-6736(09)60005-2.

Struyk, Raymond, and Anastasia Kolodeznikova. "Needs-based Targeting without Knowing Household Incomes: How Would It Work in Russia?" *Urban Studies* 36, no. 11 (1999): 1875–1889.

Struyk, Raymond J., Ekaterina Petrova, and Tatiana Lykova. "Targeting Housing Allowances in Russia." *European Journal of Housing Policy* 6, no. 2 (2006): 191–220.

Szikra, Dorottya. "Democracy and Welfare in Hard Times: The Social Policy of the Orbán Government in Hungary between 2010 and 2014." *Journal of European Social Policy* 24, no. 5 (2014): 486–500.

Ther, Philipp. *Europe since 1989.* Translated by Charlotte Hughes-Kreutzmüller. Princeton, NJ: Princeton University Press, 2016.

Tolstikova, Natasha. "MMM as a Phenomenon of the Russian Consumer Culture." *European Advances in Consumer Research* 4 (1999): 208–215.

Tondo, Lorenzo, and Annie Kelly. "Raped, Beaten, Exploited: The 21st Century Slavery Propping Up Sicilian Farming." *The Guardian,* March 11, 2017. https://www.theguardian.com/global-development/2017/mar/12/slavery-sicily-farming-raped-beaten-exploited-romanian-women.

Toomitsu, Terje, dir. *Soviet Hippies.* Tartu, 2017, www.soviethippies.com.

Travis, Alan. "80% of Britain's 1.4m Eastern European Residents Are in Work." *The Guardian,* July 10, 2017. https://www.theguardian.com/world/2017/jul/10/majority-of-britain-eastern-european-residents-are-in-work.

Treisman, Daniel. "Death and Prices: The Political Economy of Russia's Alcohol Crisis." *Economics of Transition and Institutional Change* 18, no. 2 (2010): 281–331. doi: 10.1111/j.1468-0351.2009.00382.x.

Treisman, Daniel. "Postcommunist Corruption." In *Political Economy of Transition and Development: Institutions, Politics, and Policies.* Edited by Nauro F. Campos and Jan Fidrmuc, 201–226. Norwell, MA: Kluwer Academic, 2003.

Trevisani, Tommaso. "After the Kolkhoz: Rural Elites in Competition." *Central Asian Survey* 26, no. 1 (2007): 85–104.

Trevisani, Tommaso. "The Reshaping of Cities and Citizens in Uzbekistan: The Case of Namangan's 'New Uzbeks.'" In *Ethnographies of the State in Central Asia: Performing Politics.* Edited by Madeleine Reeves, Johan Rasanayagam, and Judith Beyer, 243–260. Bloomington: Indiana University Press, 2014.

United Nations. *A Decade of Transition: Regional Monitoring Report No. 8.* Florence: United Nation Children's Fund Innocenti Research Centre, 2001. https://www.unicef-irc.org/publications/pdf/monee8/eng/3.pdf.

United Nations. *The Human Cost of Transition: Human Security in South East Europe.* United Nations Development Programme (October 2013). http://hdr.undp.org/en/content/human-cost-transition.

United Nations. *Human Development in Eastern Europe and the CIS since 1990: Human Development Report Research Paper* (July 2010), by United Nations Development Programme. http://hdr.undp.org/sites/default/files/hdrp_2010_16.pdf.

United Nations Population Fund. *Shrinking Populations in Eastern Europe.* UNFPA EECARO (October 2018). https://eeca.unfpa.org/sites/default/files/pub-pdf/Shrinking%20population_low%20fertility 20QA.pdf.

Uygun, Banu Nilgün. "Post-socialist Scapes of Economy and Desire: The Case of Turkey." *Focaal* no. 43 (2004): 27–45.

Vanhuysse, Pieter. *Divide and Pacify: Strategic Social Policies and Political Protests in Post-Communist Democracies.* Budapest: Central European University Press, 2006.

Verdery, Katherine. "Fuzzy Property: Rights, Power, and Identity in Transylvania's Decollectivization." In *Uncertain Transition: Ethnographies of Change in the Postsocialist World*. Edited by Michael Burawoy and Katherine Verdery, 53–82. Lanham, MD: Rowman & Littlefield, 1999.

Verdery, Katherine. *My Life as a Spy: Investigations in a Secret Police File*. Durham, NC: Duke University Press, 2018.

Verdery, Katherine. *The Vanishing Hectare: Property and Value in Postsocialist Transylvania*. Ithaca, NY: Cornell University Press, 2003.

Verdery, Katherine. *What Was Socialism, and What Comes Next?* Princeton, NJ: Princeton University Press, 1996.

Volkov, Vadim. *Violent Entrepreneurs: The Use of Force in the Making of Russian Capitalism*. Ithaca, NY: Cornell University Press, 2002.

"Wage Bargaining in Kecskemet (Hungary) Plant of Mercedes Benz—2 Years Wage Agreement, 2019–2020." Marmol Social Research Budapest, January 8, 2019. http://www.socialresearch.hu/2019/01/08/wage-bargaining-in-kecskemet-hungary-plant-of-mercedes-benz-2-years-wage-agreement-2019-2020/.

Wallace, Claire, and Rossalina Latcheva. "Economic Transformation Outside The Law: Corruption, Trust in Public Institutions and the Informal Economy in Transition Countries of Central and Eastern Europe." *Europe-Asia Studies* 58, no. 1 (2006): 81–102.

Wedel, Janine R. *Collision and Collusion: The Strange Case of Western Aid to Eastern Europe*. New York: St. Martin's Press, 2015.

Weiner, Elaine. *Market Dreams: Gender, Class, and Capitalism in the Czech Republic*. Ann Arbor: University of Michigan Press, 2007.

White, Anne, Izabela Grabowska, Paweł Kaczmarczyk, and Krystyna Slany. *The Impact of Migration on Poland: EU Mobility and Social Change*. London: UCL Press, 2018.

Williamson, John. "What Washington Means by Policy Reform." In *Latin America Adjustment: How Much Has Happened?*, edited by John Williamson, 90–120. Washington, DC: Peterson Institute for International Economics, 1990.

World Bank. *The Face of Poverty in Europe and Central Asia*. Washington, DC: World Bank Group, February 10, 2014.

World Bank. *From Plan to Market: World Development Report 1996*. Washington, DC: World Bank Group, 1996. https://www.worldbank.org/en/news/feature/2014/02/10/face-of-poverty-in-europe-and-central-asia.

"World Economic Forum 2009: Russia and China Blame West for Economic Crisis." *The Telegraph*, January 29, 2009. https://www.telegraph.co.uk/finance/financetopics/davos/4381464/WEF-2009-Russia-and-China-blame-West-for-economic-crisis-Davos.html.

World Health Organization. *World Health Statistics Data Visualizations Dashboard: Harmful Use of Alcohol*. 2016. https://apps.who.int/gho/data/node.sdg.3-5-viz?lang=en.

Zaridze, David, Dimitri Maximovitch, Alexander Lazarev, Vladimir Igitov, Alex Boroda, Jillian Boreham, Peter Boyle, Richard Peto, and Paolo Boffetta. "Alcohol Poisoning Is a Main Determinant of Recent Mortality Trends in Russia: Evidence from a Detailed Analysis of Mortality Statistics and Autopsies." *International Journal of Epidemiology* 38 (2009): 143–153.

Zakharov, Sergei. "Russian Federation: From the First to Second Demographic Transition." *Demographic Research* 19 (2008): 907–972.

Žufan, Pavel, and Jiří Erbes. "Key Driving Forces in the Czech Brewing industry." *Agricultural Economics* 48, no. 7 (2002): 311–314.

Index

For the benefit of digital users, indexed terms that span two pages (e.g., 52–53) may, on occasion, appear on only one of those pages.

women. *See also* fertility; safety-net measures; social solidarity
experiences as migrants in Western Europe, 95–97, 167–68
healthier behaviors than men, 82–83
increasing equality when men emigrate, 93–95
as losers in transition, 104, 172–73
minorities as losers in transition, 114–15
society's labor expectations, 88
support for free market reforms, 116–17, 168–70
World Bank. *See also* international financial institutions (IFIs); Life in Transition (LiT) surveys
BEEPS survey, 138
economic data showed most countries recovered, 108–9
"From Plan to Market," 49
2018 report on social contract, 203–4
urgent concerns expressed in 2019, 149

World Economic Forum, neoliberalism blamed for global financial crisis, 58
World Happiness Report, 131–32
World Health Organization (WHO), 80–81
World Values Survey (WVS), 145, 148

Yeltsin, Boris, 24, 29–31, 55, 199
young people. *See also* opportunities; out-migration
appeal of West, 101
cultivation of free market attitudes, 168–69
increasing income insecurity, 149, 177
optimism of urban and educated, 107–8, 110, 122, 163
pessimism regarding future for, 146–48
support for free market reforms, 115

Zelensky, Volodymyr, 127–28
Zeman, Milos, 8
Zimmerman, William, 114–16, 121, 129